NIMETZ, Michael. Humor in Galdós; a Study of the Novelas Contemporáneas. Yale, 1968. 227p bibl (Yale Romantic Studies, Second Series, 18) 68-13921. 6.50

A very valuable contribution to the study of Spain's greatest modern novelist. In this first attempt to bring together the different elements used by Galdós to create humor, Nimetz proves himself to be an authority not only on Galdós but on realism in general. In order to prove the uniqueness of Spanish realism, he smoothly passes from Galdós to Balzac, Dickens, and Zola, bringing into focus the pertinence of humor — or lack of it — in the realistic novel of the 19th century. His first chapter, a study in realism and the place humor occupies in that genre, refutes the critics who deny the coexistence of realism and humor and affirms that Spanish realism is inseparable from humor. "Humor, then, lies at the very core of the Spanish realistic tradition. It is vital to realism for it aids in the perception of truth." The book is organized on a simple plan, being divided after the first chapter according to the different elements which Galdós employs for the sake of humor: satire, irony, metaphor, caricature, type, and the humor of familiarity. The style is concise and clear without any of the wordiness

Continued

NIMETZ

which so often mars studies of this kind. It is a very readable book and will be helpful to anyone interested in a study of the modern novel. Extensive bibliography.

Yale Romanic Studies, Second Series, 18

HUMOR IN GALDÓS

A Study of the *Novelas contemporáneas*

MICHAEL NIMETZ

Yale University Press | New Haven and London

1968

Copyright © 1968 by Yale University.
Designed by John O. C. McCrillis,
set in Times Roman type,
and printed in the United States of America by
The Carl Purington Rollins Printing-Office of
the Yale University Press, New Haven, Connecticut.
Distributed in Canada by McGill University Press.
All rights reserved. This book may not be
reproduced, in whole or in part, in any form
(except by reviewers for the public press),
without written permission from the publishers.

Library of Congress catalog card number: 68–13921

To My Parents

ACKNOWLEDGMENTS

I wish to thank Mrs. Kathleen Roberts and Mr. Wayland Schmitt of Yale University Press for their help in preparing this book for publication.

Mr. John Deredita kindly read the manuscript and offered a number of suggestions for its improvement.

I am particularly indebted to Professor Gustavo Correa of the Yale Spanish Department for his gracious assistance and encouragement at every stage of my effort.

M. N.

CONTENTS

CONTENTS

HUMOR IN GALDÓS

Chapter 1: REALISM AND HUMOR

In an article of 1870, "Observaciones sobre la novela contemporánea en España," Galdós laments the failure of the modern novel to gain a foothold in Spain.[1] He blames the Spaniards' inability to *observe* and the native proclivity toward lyricism, idealism, and reverie. He adds, however, that skillful observation has not always been foreign to the Spanish temper —witness Cervantes and Velázquez. This aptitude is submerged at the present time (1870), due in part to the venality of writers for whom artistic achievement means little. But of greater importance is the public's thirst for romance, serialized fiction, and salon fiction. The popularity of French authors like Dumas and Soulié and their Spanish imitators is responsible for this corruption of public taste. Galdós contrasts their extravagant concoctions with the faithful depiction of people and events in Dickens and Cervantes.

Galdós' idea of realism here has nothing to do with a specific nineteenth-century literary movement. Indeed, it need not apply to literature at all. And if Galdós is trying to distinguish between the novel as the genre of observation and realism and the romance as the genre of imagination and idealism, his implied choice of Dickens as a realist is hardly appropriate: Dickens was the most successful writer of serialized fiction in the nineteenth century, and his realism is open to question.

The article continues as Galdós praises Fernán Caballero and Pereda for having created the "novela popular." But like the fiction of French origin, the novela popular fails to satisfy his own hopes for the modern Spanish novel. Fernán Caballero's

---

1. Benito Pérez Galdós, "Observaciones sobre la novela contemporánea en España," *Revista de España, 15* (1870), 162–72.

Andalusian sketches and Pereda's "realismo bucólico" are too narrow in scope; they ignore the urban middle class, in which pulsates "el maravilloso drama de la vida actual."[2]

Twelve years later, in his prologue to the first edition of Pereda's *El sabor de la tierruca,* Galdós once more equates realism and observation but omits the middle class.[3] Pereda is the "portaestandarte del realismo literario en España" because he assimilates colloquial speech and dialogue without debasing them and because he excels in "la pintura de lo natural." Furthermore, Pereda's realism antedates more "exotic" types (Zola) and was itself preceded by the realism of Spanish picaresque literature. This passage proves that Galdós envisaged more than one kind of realism and more than one literary genre where it might be found. Pereda's pre-"exotic" realism is undoubtedly that of his cuadros—the *Escenas montañesas* and *Tipos y paisajes*—and not that of his novels. One can only speculate about still other literary genres where, in Galdós' view, realism might thrive. There is a hint in the prologue to the illustrated edition of the *Episodios nacionales* (1885) that confessional and personal literature, such as the memoir, might qualify as such.[4] Called "esta literatura de verdad palpitante," its rarity seems to imply that Spaniards, used to artifice in their daily lives, prefer an artificial literature as well.

The phrase "verdad palpitante" should be compared to another—"castiza verdad"—in Galdós' 1897 speech to the Real Academia Española.[5] Here he proposes that contemporary novelists dwell on individuals rather than types, on the

2. Ibid., p. 167.

3. Benito Pérez Galdós, "Prólogo" to José María de Pereda, *El sabor de la tierruca* (Madrid, 1889), pp. 5–20. The prologue was written in April 1882 for the first edition.

4. William H. Shoemaker, ed., *Los prólogos de Galdós* (México, 1962), p. 57.

5. Benito Pérez Galdós, "La sociedad presente como materia novelable," *Discursos leídos ante la Real Academia Española* (Madrid, 1897), pp. 5–29.

human, rather than the social, being. Such a concentration, free of prior artistic convention, would provoke a greater truth—a "castiza verdad." Galdós' praise for Velázquez, Cervantes, Dickens, and Pereda rests on his belief that all of them portray society *truthfully*. Whether they embrace society as a whole or as a specific social class thereof, whether they paint or write, these men are observers and reflectors of the truth—that is, "realists."

The major document in this series of theoretical pronouncements is the prologue to the third edition of Leopoldo Alas' novel, *La Regenta*.[6] Galdós might almost be "summing up" here when he again says that "naturalismo" is basically of Spanish origin, that Pereda was faithfully depicting "la vida" before the French, and that nineteenth-century "naturalismo" is a disfiguration of the original Spanish brand. (Lest there be confusion about the term "naturalismo," it is synonymous here with "arte de la naturalidad" (xi) or simply "la realidad" (x)—that is, "realism" as understood by Galdós.) Spanish "naturalismo," says Galdós, marking new ground, "con su feliz concierto entre lo serio y lo cómico responde mejor que el francés a la verdad humana."[7] For the first time, he brackets truth and realism with humor. He calls the happy fusion of serious and comic elements in the picaresque novel and the Cervantine tradition "humorismo." And although "humorismo," as Galdós makes very clear, is not the same as English "humor," the "socarronería" (x), "gracia y donosura" (x), "sal" (xi), "graciosa picardía" (xii), and "gravedad socarrona" (xii) of the Spanish classics and Alas' novel suggest a fairly cosmopolitan gamut of comic technique. Despite the difference in nuance, I shall continue to use the English counterpart of "humorismo."

Humor, then, lies at the very core of the Spanish realistic tradition. It is vital to realism, for it aids in the perception of

6. Benito Pérez Galdós, "Prólogo" to Leopoldo Alas, *La Regenta* (3d ed. Madrid, 1900), pp. v–xix.
7. Ibid., p. xi.

truth. Writing in 1907, Galdós refers to "el saludable humor aristofanesco y cervantino, que nunca cierra el paso a la verdad seria en todos los órdenes de la vida."[8] Henry James, in a review of Zola's *Nana,* is similarly disposed to see an alliance between humor and truth: humor would have eased the squalor and sordidness of *Nana,* heightened its illusion of reality, and added depth to its characterizations. Nana herself has "no touch of superior verity." James asks: "Is it not . . . owing to the absence of a sense of humor that this last and most violent expression of the realistic faith is extraordinarily wanting in reality?"[9]

James insinuates that humor may be used to "deodorize" subject matter. This recalls George Meredith's devotion to the "Comic Spirit" as an antidote to French realism.[10] Galdós' *La Regenta* prologue, where Quevedo's "máscara burlesca" is said to have rendered the repugnant harmless, presents an even closer parallel.[11] If humor acts as a balm *against* reality and at the same time helps, with its weight of truth, to *achieve* a sense of reality, its functions are twofold and at variance with one another. The contradiction is further testimony that Galdós' conception of realism is more expansive than that held by many modern critics, who see it as a specific literary movement of the nineteenth century. These critics tend to divorce humor from nineteenth-century realism or play down the relationship. Before the nineteenth century, says Auerbach, the treatment of everyday reality belonged to comic, satiric, didactic, or moralistic literature; Stendhal and Balzac introduce "existential and tragic *seriousness* into realism." The works of Flaubert and the Goncourts, he adds, "are full of reality and intellect but *poor in humor* and inner poise."[12]

8. Shoemaker, p. 76.

9. Henry James, *The Future of the Novel,* ed. Leon Edel (New York, 1956), pp. 95–96.

10. E. Arthur Robinson, "Meredith's Literary Theory and Science: Realism Versus the Comic Spirit," *PMLA, 53* (1938), 857–68.

11. "Prólogo" to *La Regenta,* p. xi.

12. Erich Auerbach, *Mimesis* (Princeton, 1953), pp. 481, 506 (italics mine).

Raymond Giraud states that "a realistic novelist is one who cannot ignore the candidacy of the bourgeois for *serious,* even heroic treatment in a novel."[13] Some critics believe that a writer may disqualify himself as a realist if he avails himself of humor: Dickens' realism, according to Mario Praz, "is merely delight in the picturesque"; it is alien to true realism, which is unflinchingly observant of "wretched human details."[14] George Gissing imagines one of Dickens' female characters "in the hands of a rigorous realist, with scorn and disgust . . . taking the place of humour."[15]

The union of realism and humor, on the one hand, and their estrangement, on the other, are due, respectively, to nonhistorical and historical frames of reference. This has long been a stumbling block to any understanding of literary realism.[16] One cure for such an impasse is to quietly etherize the nonhistorical or "existential" (Wellek) concept of realism, which does not confine itself to the nineteenth century. This is easier said than done, for Galdós' concern with truth, besides affording entrée to a key problem of nineteenth-century realism, objectivity, will eventually force a confrontation with existential realism.

"Objectivity" is one of the two watchwords of realism; the other is "type."[17] Some see an exclusive club convening around the word "objectivity," with those authors who falter in the proper incantations and ceremonials being debarred from true realism forthwith. Thackeray's moralizing bent stands in the way of objectivity; hence his realism is flawed.[18] Similar charges stand against Dickens, George Eliot, Trollope,

---

13. Raymond Giraud, *The Unheroic Hero in the Novels of Stendhal, Balzac and Flaubert* (New Brunswick, N.J., 1957), p. 11 (italics mine).

14. Mario Praz, *The Hero in Eclipse in Victorian Fiction,* trans. Angus Davidson (London and New York, 1956), p. 149.

15. *Novelists on Novelists,* ed. Louis Kronenberger (New York, 1962), p. 71.

16. René Wellek, *Concepts of Criticism* (New Haven, 1963), pp. 222–25.

17. Ibid., p. 246.

18. Praz, pp. 204–07.

and Scott and could indeed be made against Balzac and Zola.
As Wellek says, Balzac continually moralizes, and Zola is
didactic in his social reforms.[19] An amusing paradox occurs
when realism is made to rely too heavily on objectivity. This
paradox is exemplified by the critic who is sure that subconscious probings are compatible with realism and yet finds them
anomalous, since any attempt to explore the subconscious
mind is "subjective, incapable of direct documentation, and
verifiable in the last analysis only in the consciousness of the
reader."[20] Such sophistry speaks for the need of a flexible
approach to objectivity, especially since subject matter, as well
as technique, is involved: Zola, the most doctrinaire of realists,
had a subjective predilection for the "low."

The second chapter of this book studies Galdós' satire
and could not have been written had the Novelas contemporáneas displayed complete authorial objectivity. Ridicule,
indignation, and bemused skepticism are all there, and a theory
of realism ample enough to encompass them is the only one in
which Galdós will fit. He states his own view of the matter
quite plainly in the prologue to El sabor de la tierruca. After
praising Pereda as the "standard-bearer of literary realism in
Spain," Galdós speaks of his biting satire: Pereda is a con-
noisseur of "los infinitos tipos de ridiculez que sabe ver y
clasificar como nadie"; his political novels are "cruelmente
sarcásticas y guerreras."[21] Partisanship, intolerance, sectari-
anism—realism does not, in Galdós' opinion, preclude any of
these. If his own satire in the Novelas contemporáneas is less
cutting than Pereda's, such is not the case in Doña Perfecta
and Gloria. Moreover, Galdós indulges in a good deal of
moralizing. To limit realism to strict objectivity would be to

19. Wellek, pp. 236–38. For a discussion of Zola's belief in the
utility of art, see Albert J. Salvan, "L'Essence du réalisme français,"
Comparative Literature, 3 (1951), 226.

20. George J. Becker, ed., Documents of Modern Literary Realism
(Princeton, 1963), p. 26.

21. "Prólogo" to El sabor de la tierruca, p. 16.

slight this important element in his novels, as well as the many costumbrista themes and types which abound there. The one is largely dependent upon the other. In Francisco Ayala's words, "a lo largo de la historia universal . . . el empleo de las costumbres como 'material' para la creación literaria ha estado ligado casi siempre a intenciones moralizadoras."[22] Galdós' efforts to expose lo cursi is an example of this link.

Any discussion of objectivity must also include the question of authorial self-effacement, alleged by some to be a standard feature of nineteenth-century realistic technique.[23] At issue here is the author's detachment, the amount of autonomous life his characters enjoy. From the brief foregoing comments about Galdós' satire, it would be absurd to say that his attitude is one of complete detachment. Undoubtedly his masterpiece, *Fortunata y Jacinta,* exhibits this quality to a very great degree, but whether detachment should serve as a criterion for judging fiction or as a norm for realism is a crucial distinction. Ricardo Gullón claims that Galdós' personages are more independent of their creator than Emma Bovary is of Flaubert.[24] One need not agree with this observation (made, perhaps, with one eye on Galdós' reluctance to talk about his fiction and another on Flaubert's profuse willingness to do so) to refute the proposition that Flaubert is less a realist than Galdós, or a poorer writer. Similarly, a narrator's intrusion does not necessarily mean that his personages are any less real or alive. Wellek mentions Becky Sharp and Sancho Panza; he might easily substitute Isidora Rufete or Torquemada, the difference being that of direct versus oblique intrusion.[25] If

22. Francisco Ayala, "Sobre el realismo en literatura," *La Torre, 7* (Abril-Junio 1959), 113.

23. Becker, ed., p. 131. For Wayne C. Booth *(The Rhetoric of Fiction* [Chicago, 1961], p. 23 and passim) self-effacement involves "showing" rather than "telling"; he questions the widespread critical acceptance of the latter standard.

24. Ricardo Gullón, *Galdós, novelista moderno* (Madrid, 1960), p. 83.

25. Wellek, p. 250.

authorial self-effacement or detachment were any test of realism, one would have to subscribe to the logical but false conclusion that a novel in dialogue is more realistic than a traditional narrative. Galdós may have aimed for greater realism by utilizing the dialogue form, but aim and achievement in this case are poles apart.

Here then is an impasse much like the one cited previously. If "objectivity" is a watchword for the nineteenth-century literary movement known as realism, one needs a more spacious and pliable interpretation of realism when dealing with Galdós. The other watchword—"type"—will come under scrutiny later, but for the moment I wish to point out the relevancy of all this to humor. In the Novelas contemporáneas, the barriers to rigid objectivity—satire, moral stance, and authorial intrusion—are basically humoristic. Galdós' satire has little in common with the mordant savagery of Quevedo or Swift; his moralization often takes the guise of mock moralization; and he intrudes upon the narrative athwart an ironic tone which rarely leaves any doubt as to his attitude vis-à-vis the subject at hand and which has been called "the only personal element to be found in his work."[26]

Throughout literary history, the encasing of satiric, moralistic, and ironic intentions within a humorous mold has been standard procedure.[27] The greatest comic novelists of eighteenth-century England, Fielding and Jane Austen, are moralists who clothe every other phrase or situation in irony or satire. Galdós has been seen as a moralist of the nineteenth century, in the company of Balzac and Dickens.[28] Certainly *La de Bringas,* from first word to last, is a morality play, the moral of which—that private and public corruption have an indestructible existence in Spain despite appearances to the contrary—is conveyed ironically. V. S. Pritchett's description

26. Gerald Brenan, *The Literature of the Spanish People* (Cambridge, 1962), p. 405.

27. Mary A. Grant, *The Ancient Rhetorical Theories of the Laughable* (Madison, 1924), p. 47.

28. Gullón, p. 47.

of Galdós as a "social moralist" is most aptly confirmed by this novel.[29]

Naturally, the amount of satire and moralization in the *Novelas contemporáneas* is in direct proportion to the author's concentration on milieu and manners, on the one hand, and individuals, on the other. *Fortunata y Jacinta* is more objective in its approach than *La de Bringas,* as is *El abuelo* in comparison to *El amigo Manso.* But even in 1897, the year of Galdós' speech to the Real Academia Española calling for greater emphasis on individual "modelos humanos," one finds in *Misericordia* at least three persons clearly borne of costumbrista satire (the study of milieu and manners): doña Paca, the spendthrift, financially inept female; Obdulia, the romantic dreamer of lugubrious bent; and Frasquito Ponte, the "protocursi." Further evidence of the longevity of Galdós' satire appears in *El caballero encantado* (1909), where the Gaitanes, Gaitines, and Gaitones are merely the rural, cacique cousins of the ubiquitous Peces.

The misalliance of humor and realism, if by the latter is understood objectivity, should now be clear. As I said before, the question of objectivity would again force a rapprochement with the nonhistorical or existential concept of realism. This involves a literary genre—the novel—and a change in stress—from objectivity to irony.

The novel is universally acknowledged to be the realistic genre without peer. However, the presentation of everyday reality predates the novel for it first appears in Greek comedy. The significance of this ancestral tie between realism and comedy has received its due from the critics.

Here we have the only points of Greek literature to which we can fasten the thread of novelistic evolution. The novel is born with a comic sting and it will preserve this nature

29. V. S. Pritchett, "Review of *The Spendthrifts* by Benito Pérez Galdós," in *The New Statesman and Nation, 42* (Dec. 5, 1951), 710. This review is published in the same author's *Books in General* (London, 1953), pp. 31–36.

forever. The criticism, the banter, is not an unessential
ornament of *Quixote,* but rather the very texture of the
genre, perhaps of all realism.[30]

The progression novel–realism–comedy–criticism underscores
the negative bias of the genre.

The tendency of the novel's realism, like that of philosophical realism, is critical. The search for real explanations
of human behavior, leads to the rejection of the more
flattering pictures of man supported by many established
ethical, social, and literary codes.[31]

The key word here is "rejection." One rejective procedure in
Galdós is satire; irony is another. The two join forces with most
telling effect precisely when Galdós rejects those "more flattering pictures of man" in favor of "real explanations of human
behavior," that is, when he pits realism against romance.

The schism between realism and romance antedates the
novel. In medieval France there was a tendency to adopt a
crude realism ("une réalité grossière") to counteract an excessively idealistic literature ("une littérature que le rêve a par
trop séparée de la vie").[32] The medieval fabliaux and satires
fix their bourgeois gaze somewhat brazenly upon the knightly
epic and the courtly romance. In fifteenth-century Spain, *La
Celestina* combines idealism and a rejection of idealism in the
same work. Later, the picaresque novel provides an alternative
to the novela de caballerías. Finally, in *Don Quixote,* the two
currents merge in a single narrative prose fiction which Levin
has called "an archetype for all novelists and future realists."[33]

Don Quixote is archetypal because Cervantes parodies
romance and goes on to probe the effect of romance on

30. José Ortega y Gasset, *Meditations on Quixote* (New York, 1961),
p. 147.

31. Ian Watt, "Realism and the Novel," *Essays in Criticism, 2* (1952),
p. 394.

32. Salvan, "L'Essence du réalisme français," p. 219.

33. Harry Levin, "What Is Realism?" *Comparative Literature, 3*
(1951), 196.

impressionable minds. The reaction against the chivalric novel is expressed satirically, whereas the revelation of truth and the simultaneous exposure of delusion belong to the domain of irony. After Cervantes, Fielding, in *Joseph Andrews,* brilliantly satirizes a specific literary model—Richardson's *Pamela*—and punctures Joseph's emulation of its chaste and unreal heroine with ironic darts. Jane Austen's first three novels, rather than satirizing any single literary prototype, record the heroines' inability to distinguish between literature and life, romance and reality.[34] The nineteenth century spurs this trend, especially with the triumph of positivism. To be sure, literature is still satirized for its own sake: Galdós' *Tormento* is a parody of the novela por entregas, and throughout the century novelists take great pains to "de-fictionalize" their novels just as Cervantes had done. For example, in the original conclusion to *La Fontana de Oro,* Galdós playfully exclaims that he had originally planned to have Lázaro and Clara live happily ever after, but that "la colaboración de un testigo presencial de los hechos . . . le obligó a desviarse de este buen propósito, dando a la historia el fin que realmente tuvo."[35] By and large, however, satire and irony no longer challenge idealistic fiction, but idealism itself; the novel debunks romance, not merely *the* romance. In the Novelas contemporáneas, the idealism against which Galdós' negative bias is directed is often called la loca de la casa—and unbridled and overheated imagination, the congenital vice of Spaniards. Likewise, the needling of romance in these novels betokens Galdós' attempted break with decadent romanticism.

Most of the Novelas contemporáneas follow the realistic norm in spurning metaphysical speculation and romantic taste in literature. A novelist, however, can react against more than one thing; Galdós' eventual disenchantment with positivism

34. Walter Allen, *The English Novel* (London, 1954), p. 107.
35. Benito Pérez Galdós, *La Fontana de Oro* (Madrid, 1871), p. 404. The ending of *La Fontana de Oro* in this 1871 edition is entirely different from that of the Aguilar edition of 1960. In the latter, Lázaro and Clara *do* live happily ever after.

marks him as a realist just as do his joshing thrusts at unhinged imaginations and romanticism. Indeed, Torquemada, the positivist anti-hero incarnate, can safely claim to be a type in the Marxist sense and to represent the apogee of Galdós' realism.

Much of Galdós' humor in the *Novelas contemporáneas* stems from his satire of romanticism and romantic taste and from his exposure, through irony, of the speculative and imaginative aberrations of his characters. As might be expected, Galdós ridicules romanticism most effectively in those novels set in the years prior to the Revolution of 1868—*El doctor Centeno, Tormento,* and *La de Bringas.* Alejandro Miquis' historical drama *El Grande Osuna,* Ido del Sagrario's literary precepts, and Bringas' cenotaph are all satirized by the author. Romanticism is a rich source of humor in other novels as well—in *Misericordia,* for example, where Frasquito Ponte is a "proto-cursi" precisely because he is a mummified romantic, the vestige of an epoch whose cultural demise took place in 1868.[36] Ponte embodies the bad taste which Galdós so invariably associated with romanticism. Bad taste, as Ponte's sobriquet suggests, is linked to yet another source of humor, lo cursi.

Lo cursi is discussed in the chapter on satire because it is best understood as a social phenomenon. Actually it is pivotal, at once a public vice and folly (an ideal target for satire) and personal self-deception (best exposed by irony). In any case, Galdós' humorous dissection of lo cursi is very much at home with the kind of realism which, with its negative bias, corrodes illusion, corrects distorted values, and unearths the truth behind appearance.

Lo cursi provides the ideal transition from satire to irony. As Enrique Tierno Galván explains in a brilliant article, the posture assumed by a spectator of lo cursi is ironical—heavily

---

36. Benito Pérez Galdós, *Obras completas,* 5 (6 vols. Madrid, Aguilar, 1951–61). Pp. 1920–22 sketch the cultural ambience in Spain before 1868. All subsequent references to Galdós' works are to this edition, except when otherwise stated.

immersed in pity *(not* commiseration) and superiority.[37] Miquis *(La desheredada),* Refugio *(La de Bringas),* and José María *(Lo prohibido)* are fiercely ironic when, as clairvoyants and outsiders, they x-ray society or certain of its members and strip the sheathing from lo cursi. Caballero *(Tormento)* and Abelarda *(Miau)* are more reflective and resigned in their analyses and allow Galdós himself to assume the ironic tone.

Irony plays a major role in the Novelas contemporáneas. It charts the discrepancy between appearance and reality. In this sense, its unites realism and humor: "Realism . . . is implicitly ironic, since it implies an odious comparison between the real and the ideal."[38] Galdós finds in this comparison a vein of humor so rich that it profits even his most forlorn characters. Federico de Onís has this in mind when, speaking of Galdós' protagonists, he sees a "desproporción . . . entre lo que son y lo que creen ser, entre lo que pueden y lo que quieren. Este desequilibrio entre su idea de la realidad y la realidad misma da a estos personajes un sentido cómico que toma a menudo caracteres patológicos que llegan a veces hasta la locura."[39] The desproporción and desequilibrio cited here are products of an unruly imagination and an excessive trust in abstract speculation.

Joaquín Casalduero was the first to identify the plot of *Marianela* as the symbolic triumph of positivism over metaphysical speculation. "En *Marianela,"* he says, "Galdós declara la superioridad del mundo de la realidad sobre el de la imaginación y el deber de abandonar éste para penetrar en aquél."[40] Pattison also accepts this interpretation, adding that "positivism taught Galdós a new concept of realism, a much greater reliance on observation and a great diminution of the impor-

37. Enrique Tierno Galván, "Aparición y desarrollo de nuevas perspectivas de valoración social en el siglo XIX: lo cursi," *Revista de Estudios Políticos, 42* (Marzo-Abril 1952), 85–106.

38. Harry Levin, *The Gates of Horn* (New York, 1963), p. 135.

39. Federico de Onís, "El humorismo de Galdós," *Revista Hispánica Moderna, 9* (1943), 293.

40. Joaquín Casalduero, *Vida y obra de Galdós* (Buenos Aires, 1943), p. 67.

tance of the speculative faculties (fantasy and imagination)."[41] Nevertheless, Galdós' "formal" espousal of positivism in *Marianela* does not represent any abrupt change in his attitude toward imagination but rather intensifies an attitude already held. The characterization of Lázaro in Galdós' earliest novel, *La Fontana de Oro* (1870), is a sign of this:

> Aquel muchacho era sumamente impresionable, nervioso, con uno de esos temperamentos propensos al idealismo, dispuestos a vivir siempre de lo imaginario. . . . Su fantasía tenía una espantosa fuerza conceptiva, y puede asegurarse que esta gran facultad era para él un enemigo implacable, un demonio atormentador que martirizaba su naturaleza toda, sujetándola a terribles trastornos.[42]

Lázaro believes that he is destined to fulfill some great mission in life, but exactly what that mission will be remains vague: "Los jóvenes como aquel no gustan de concretar las cosas porque temen la realidad: creen demasiado en la predestinación, y engañados por la brillantez del sueño, creen que los sucesos han de venir a buscarlos en vez de buscar ellos a los sucesos."[43]

Lázaro is an embryonic Isidora de Rufete or Alejandro Miquis. And doña Paulita, who admits to having led a fictitious existence as a kind of lay saint, foreshadows the deluded Angel Guerra or Halma of many years later.[44] The protagonist of *La familia de León Roch* may also be compared to one of the characters in the Novelas contemporáneas. Here the juxtaposition is especially apt, because Máximo Manso *(El amigo Manso)* is a humorous character. He is the comic counterpart of his "friend" León Roch, whom he mentions by name *(4,* 1211). The hazy line between tendentiousness and humor, and indeed between Galdós' serious and comic characters, is

41. Walter T. Pattison, *Benito Pérez Galdós and the Creative Process* (Minneapolis, 1954), p. 132.

42. *La Fontana de Oro,* p. 78.

43. Ibid., p. 79.

44. Ibid., pp. 390–97.

nowhere more obvious than in the juxtaposition of Roch and Manso: both men are cut from the same cloth; they are puritans temperamentally, rationalists who rely more upon theory than observation and who succeed only in deceiving themselves about the women they love. They both suffer a desengaño.

Desengaño, self-deception, and falsification are laid bare through irony. The Novelas contemporáneas do not inaugurate this process but instead consolidate it. A further bond between the earlier and later novels, regarding irony, centers around the "ironic reprise."[45] Seemingly irreconcilable ideas or persons are shown in a contrapuntal relationship and echo or burlesque each other. *Doña Perfecta* and *Gloria,* among the earlier novels, illustrate a dual fanaticism; in *La familia de León Roch,* Roch and his wife share a mutual intransigence. Ironic reprise is more subtle in the Novelas contemporáneas and takes the form of "internal repetitions."[46] In *La desheredada,* Isidora's pipe dreams are transmitted to and grotesquely disfigured by the brutish Mariano; the chapter entitled "Beethoven" depicts the genuine aristocrats, the Marquesa de Aransis and her musically gifted grandson, while in the following chapter, "Sigue Beethoven," the false aristocrat Isidora roams the Aransis palace to the accompaniment of Miquis' crude music-making. With this ironic reprise, Galdós makes sport of Isidora's aristocratic pretensions.

Closely related to the ironic reprise is the irony of incongruity.[47] Brightening the potential grimness of the Novelas contemporáneas, it makes tragic situations ludicrous and, by extension, humorous. A perfect example occurs in Part IV of *Fortunata y Jacinta (5,* 437–40). Suicide is one of the rites of Maxi's newly adopted "religion." At a certain point in the

45. Monroe Z. Hafter, "Ironic Reprise in Galdós' Novels," *PMLA,* *76* (1961), 233–39.

46. Ibid.

47. This is not to be confused with Northrop Frye's "incongruous" irony, in which collective guilt is transferred to a scapegoat or Christ figure. See his *The Anatomy of Criticism* (Princeton, 1957), pp. 41–42.

narrative, he shows Fortunata a knife and then a selection of
poisons and asks her advice as to which is preferable. Given
the utter incompatibility of the two spouses, Fortunata's efforts
to play along with her husband, to "humor" him, are so incongruous that the reader must laugh. Fortunata repeats some
of Maxi's phrases ("Claro, la bestia hay que matarla") and then,
to lull him to sleep, mouths others having to do with "aquello de
la liberación" and "la hermosura de la muerte," of whose mean-
ings she is totally ignorant *(5,* 440). Galdós himself admits that
her words would have been funny in less somber circumstances.
The fact is they *are* funny, and the circumstances make them
so. The scene is an anthology piece of black humor of a kind
much favored by Galdós, and in which the irony of incongruity
is an important element. Doña Lupe's somewhat over-sec-
ularized death agony in *Torquemada en la cruz* is another
prime specimen.

Purely verbal irony (as opposed to irony of plot or situation)
provides a key to a true understanding of Galdós realism. The
most crucial strain of verbal irony in the *Novelas contemporáneas* is "referential irony." It involves an outrageously
inappropriate comparison, either explicit or implicit, of one
subject with another, and its aim is to give the original subject "an air of dignity, method, reason or importance which
does not belong to it and thereby emphasize its lack of the
quality suggested."[48] On its most basic level, referential irony
may easily be confused with sarcasm, as when, in *Miau,* Galdós
describes a fight between Luisito Cadalso and a classmate:
"Trabóse una de esas luchas *homéricas,* primitivas y cuerpo a
cuerpo" *(5,* 575; italics mine). The epic ring of "homéricas"
and the outlandish use of the word in this context remind the
reader that an after-school brawl is really a very trivial thing,
despite its awesome significance for participants and younger
spectators. Here the author's voice sounds directly in the
reader's ear. A procedure more characteristic of Galdós and

48. Eleanor N. Hutchens, "Verbal Irony in *Tom Jones," PMLA,* 77
(1962), 49.

requiring greater artistry is to reproduce the words and thought processes of his characters and allow these to convey the irony of reference for him. In *La de Bringas,* Rosalía thinks the world topsy-turvy for having mated her, a woman of elegance and distinction, with the plodding Bringas. She reflects that justice would have been better served had she married the politician don Manuel Pez, in which case her collaboration would have propelled an already distinguished career to even more glorious heights: "Paquito decía ayer que Napoleón no hubiera sido nada sin Josefina" *(4,* 1601). Rosalía's exaggerated self-esteem, really a form of self-delusion, is fed to the reader, who then applies to the good lady an appropriate devaluation. Adding to the merriment is the fact that Pez's superiority is illusory and that Rosalía's adolescent son serves as an authority on matters of state. One can see how effective the irony of reference is for exposing pretense. Like all forms of irony it is a corrective device, giving the novelist a firm control over his characters. It allows Galdós, the "social moralist," to judge without pedantry or unctuousness.

The preceding comparisons have been relatively straightforward—a fistfight and a Homeric battle, Rosalía and Josephine Bonaparte. A more extreme case of referential irony, in which a subject of purely personal consequence is likened to one of universal consequence, is found in a concluding chapter of *Tormento.* Francisco Bringas' new overcoat disappears at a palace ball. For don Francisco this "siniestro, horripilante caso" prefigures a dire future for Spain, a social upheaval, a revolution; he exclaims that "los descamisados harán de Madrid un lago de sangre, y lo del 93 de Francia será una fiesta pastoril en comparación de lo que tendremos aquí" *(4,* 1563).[49] Don Francisco's hallucinatory

---

49. A strikingly similar effect may be seen in Balzac's *Le Père Goriot,* where the rapacious Madame Vauquer attributes the sudden loss of her boarders to "la fin du monde." See Honoré de Balzac, *Le Père Goriot,* in *La Comédie humaine, 2* (11 vols. Paris, Bibliothèque de la Pléiade, 1962), 1029.

vision of events is typical of an egocentric mentality. Spaniards euphemistically speak of "individualism" when they broach this psychological trait, but it is a measure of Galdós' honesty that he always shows it for what it is. Nothing withers the ego so much as comic irony, and in *Tormento* Galdós shrinks don Francisco's down to size. He does the same with Caballero's and Polo's. Both these characters, at certain moments, hope for a cataclysm as a way to avenge their personal frustrations. Polo, an ordained priest who finds celibacy one of the more elusive of professional duties, hates the false life he leads; when dejected, "se encantaba con la idea de un cataclismo que volviera las cosas al revés" *(4,* 1503).[50] This means revolution, the fall of the monarchy, religious freedom, and abolition of the official church.

Perhaps the most intriguing feature of the irony of reference is that it must first inflate in order to deflate. Polo's mammoth ego must be shown to exist before it can be circumscribed and compressed into laughter. A pendular movement is at work, swinging from hyperbole to reality, from distortion to correction. Sometimes the weight of hyperbole and distortion is such that the narrative gives an impression of things being larger than life, despite the corrective pull of irony. When this pull goes slack and irony no longer acts as a counterweight, there remains an exuberance of expression which I shall call "metaphor." It is the residue of romance in realism, sharing honors with those more destructive components of realism described previously. One must therefore study those elements in Galdós' style which denote an escape from the humdrum and the commonplace. In order to do so properly, realism itself must be examined in a new light.

Both Ortega y Gasset and Levin agree that an undercurrent of criticism and irony shifts through realism.[51] Both admit, however, that this negative bias cannot prevent realism from in-

50. Caballero's reaction to Amparo's former indiscretions is similar; see *4,* 1563.
51. See n. 30 and 38, above.

corporating the very thing to which it stands opposed, whether
it be called "illusion," "fantasy," or "romance." Ortega says:

> The fact is that what is related in the books of chivalry has
> reality in the imagination of Don Quixote, who, in his turn,
> enjoys an unquestionable existence. So that, although the
> realistic novel was born in opposition to the so-called
> novel of fantasy, it carries adventure enclosed within its
> body.[52]

The realistic novel, which in its origins looks critically at
imaginary events, ends by absorbing the very events it criticizes;
a dose of "poetic substance" enters reality; myth is simultaneously destroyed and assimilated into "the real."[53] Levin
more succinctly views realism as a synthesis: it is "the imposition of reality upon romance, the transposition of reality into
romance."[54] Other critics confine their remarks to the nineteenth century and specific points of contact between romanticism and realism. Both are said to capture the "atmospheric
uniqueness" of a historical period;[55] both reject the strictures
on subject matter imposed by neoclassicism.[56] Theoretically,
then, there is continuity rather than cleavage between romanticism and realism.[57] Balzac and Dickens are the two novelists
who best exemplify this continuity; perverse proof of this is the
difficulty one has in labeling them.

The best label is Levin's: Balzac and Dickens are "romantic
realists."[58] Both novelists give the reader a great deal of
factual information, thereby making their characters appear
less than totally fantastic. In Balzac, particularly, milieu and

52. Ortega y Gasset, *Meditations on Quixote,* p. 137.
53. Ibid., p. 139.
54. *The Gates of Horn,* p. 55.
55. Auerbach, *Mimesis,* p. 473.
56. Watt, "Realism and the Novel," p. 395.
57. This is energetically refuted by Becker. See his introduction to
Documents of Modern Literary Realism. The "nonexistential" critics of
realism, like Praz, tend to agree with Becker, but for reasons of their
own.
58. *The Gates of Horn,* p. 455.

historical data act as a frame of reference. Since one knows
these to be true, one is led to believe that what transpires
within the frame is also true or at least plausible. Galdós too
is fond of constructing a historical scaffolding about his personages, an operation I call "historical metaphor."[59] His
men and women may bear a physical resemblance to real
men and women—Thiers, Rossini, Napoleon; contemporary
events may accompany personal events, as in *La desheredada*
and *Fortunata y Jacinta;* certain personages may, as indicated,
associate personal misfortune with historical cataclysm and
revolution. But no matter how tight the factual frame of reference, its net effect is to hyperbolize commonplace events.
Historical associations, even if intentionally comic or ironic,
automatically transform a given context or character. This is
especially true when Galdós juxtaposes private and public
history. The Marxist type, which will be discussed in a moment,
is the transcendent result of historical metaphor. A factual
frame of reference, moreover, seldom restrains the hyperboliz-
ing instincts of the novelist; these find expression in a great
throng of madmen, suicides, would-be suicides, consumptives,
neurotics, dreamers, monsters, misers, prodigies, mystics,
heroes, and heroines. Galdós' most memorable creations are
not "normal," just as Balzac's are not. Recall that in *Eugénie
Grandet* a description of Grandet's progress through the suc-
cessive (and verifiable) regimes of France—Revolution, Con-
sulate, Empire—is near a passage where he is likened to a
tiger and then to a boa constrictor.[60]

History and fantasy coexist in Galdós just as they do in
Balzac, and the stress and strain of their relationship is part
of romantic realism. This friction is less pronounced in Dickens
because in his case history lives not so much in events as in institutions; the latter, tradition-bound and sacrosanct, already

59. René Wellek and Austin Warren, *Theory of Literature* (New
York, 1956), p. 210. Setting and environment in Balzac are called
"metonymic, or metaphoric, expressions of character." My use of the
term "metaphor" is an amplification of its use here.

60. Honoré de Balzac, *Eugénie Grandet,* in *La Comédie humaine, 3,*
483–84, 486.

have an aura of myth. Historical metaphor, no matter how authentic the data provided, may convey an impression of reality but need not convey one of normalcy. Innumerable critics have noted the distorted image of everyday life that Balzac and Dickens create in their novels.[61] Galdós stands somewhere between the two, sharing Balzac's meticulous attention to milieu and Dickens' taste for comic psychopathy.[62] (He is perhaps most himself when de-emphasizing distortion of any kind; this, however, belongs to a different category of realism.)

Galdós' transformation of much that is humdrum in the lives of his characters into something more intense and dramatic usually ends in comedy or tragicomedy. Only occasionally—as when the lackluster Abelarda *(Miau)* becomes a potential murderess, or when Mauricia *la dura (Fortunata y Jacinta)* cavorts diabolically before the reader, or when Maxi's intentions (in the same novel) remain unnervingly obscure—does one feel that demonic surge which Balzac so often sets in motion in *La Comédie humaine*. Nor does Galdós poetize or mythologize the tentacular intrusion of institutions upon everyday life, as does Dickens. The exception is the novel *Miau,* where the Administración is as nearly omnipresent as the Court of Chancery is in *Bleak House*. Very Spanish, however, is Galdós' use of religious metaphor and his concentration upon the plight of a single individual—Villaamil's expulsion from paradise and martyrdom. Dickens uses nature metaphor—a thick fog—and symbolizes therein the institution itself.

Galdós' transformation of reality is more often tinged with comedy than with diabolism or myth. Even in *Miau,* with its plot of martyrdom, the repetition of the letters m, i, a, and u under varying circumstances gives the novel a grotesquely comic

61. Auerbach, Lukács, Giraud, and Levin with regard to Balzac. See also E. P. Dargan, "Balzac's General Method; An Analysis of His Realism," *Studies in Balzac's Realism* (Chicago, 1932), pp. 1–32. Allen and Praz comment upon this aspect of Dickens' realism.

62. See Allen, *The English Novel,* p. 161, on the thin line between Dickens' psychopaths and his comic characters. Maxi Rubín is the best example of this in Galdós.

unity of tone. Whenever the reader comes across them, he applauds the author's ingenuity in manipulating the mote, the virtuosity of which is delightful. Furthermore, miau is an animal sound, comic in and of itself. Finally, Villaamil's substitution of miau for I.N.R.I. erupts into black, sardonic humor.

One might object that what happens in *Miau* is really more a question of the irony of reference than of religious metaphor. This objection is valid. Where overlapping occurs, as in the present instance, intuition and critical judgment come into play. In the case of *Miau,* what humor arises from referential irony depends on a prior transformation of the context by religious metaphor. Similar difficulties arise in connection with literary metaphor. Luisito Cadalso's "Homeric" fight with his school chum in *Miau* is an example of the irony of reference. In *El doctor Centeno,* however, mock-epic, mock-heroic, and mock-elegiac details abound to such an extent that the net effect is one of hyperbole. The novel has more literary allusions than any of the other Novelas contemporáneas—to Quevedo, Cervantes, Calderón, Jorge Manrique, the picaresque genre, Hugo, and the pre-romantics D'Arlincourt and Madame Cottin. Furthermore, Felipe Centeno is from the very beginning a "héroe chiquito, . . . de heroico linaje y de casta de inmortales" *(4,* 1295). Galdós himself invokes the muse Clio to aid in the telling of his tale. When Felipe joins destinies with Alejandro Miquis, Galdós says that "en vez de un héroe ya tenemos dos" *(4,* 1366). The opening chapter of Part II adds a mock-elegiac note, as the narrator evokes doña Virginia's boardinghouse. The genuine elegiac source is easily identifiable in the following: "Aquellos guapos chicos, aquellos otros señores de diversa condición, que allí vimos entrar, permanecer y salir, en un período de dos años, ¿qué se hicieron? ¿Qué fue de tanto bullicioso estudiante, qué de tan variada gente?" *(4,* 1366). Toward the end, after Miquis, lying in state, has been shorn of his coat and his verse-drama has been torn asunder, Ido del Sagrario wails in a mock-moralizing vein: "¡Tales desengaños encierran los designios de los hombres! . . . ¿De qué valen las glorias humanas? ¡Ay! humo son y polvo de los caminos" *(4,* 1450).

Every one of these quotes (and the possibilities have not been exhausted) may be taken for examples of lowly sarcasm. But as they accumulate, they enrich the literary possibilities of Felipe, Miquis, and a host of minor characters and make them worthy of the author's and the reader's attention. The context in which they appear is one of literary convention, and literary convention is romance. Again, an objection may be raised: does this kind of parody not fall under the general heading of satire? Is not Galdós, after all, mocking and denigrating convention? Again this is valid, but what is true of isolated portions of a novel may or may not be true of the novel as a whole. *El doctor Centeno* recounts certain episodes in the lives of a child (Felipe Centeno) and a childlike youth (Alejandro Miquis). Much of what happens, especially in Part I where Felipe plays the dominant role, is interesting only insofar as it makes an impression on the two young minds. The distortion of reality, more often comic than not, is central to the meaning of the novel. Support for this view comes in the final dialogue. Felipe and Ido del Sagrario are on their way to Miquis' burial. Ido has just told Felipe that he is planning to write novels, to which the latter replies:

> Pues, hombre de Dios, si quiere componer libros para entretener a la gente y hacerla reír y llorar, no tiene más que llamarme; yo le cuento todo lo que nos ha pasado a mi amo y a mí, y conforme yo se lo vaya contando, usted lo va poniendo en escritura.

> Ido.—(Con suficiencia) ¡Cómo se conoce que eres un chiquillo y no estás fuerte en letras! Las cosas comunes y que están pasando todos los días no tienen el gustoso saborete que es propio de los inventados, extraídos de la imaginación. La pluma del poeta se ha de mojar en la ambrosia de la mentira hermosa, y no en el caldo de la horrible verdad. *(4, 1552)*

If in *El doctor Centeno* Galdós had merely related "las cosas comunes y que están pasando todos los días" without transforming them, the reader's patience might have been spent

long before this final dialogue. Instead, the author clearly
implies that Felipe is right in thinking his experiences unusual
and deserving of literary treatment.

This does not mean that any novel which succeeds in
capturing the interest of the reader is an example of romantic
realism (though the idea is not as farfetched as it sounds).
However, when "the imposition of reality upon romance" and
"the transposition of reality into romance" are so enmeshed
as to become indistinguishable, a decision must be made as to
the author's intentions. In *El doctor Centeno,* reality is deliberately romanced, in keeping with the author's desire to evoke
not only the past—the novel, though written in 1883, is set
in 1863 and 1864—but his *own* past. Alejandro Miquis is a
reincarnation of the Galdós of twenty years before, with his
dreams of glory and his romantic dramas in verse. Evocations
of this kind, to which bygone literary conventions contribute,
thrive on romance.[63] *Tormento,* written immediately after *El
doctor Centeno,* again fuses literary metaphor, or romance,
and satire, but Galdós' intentions here are exactly the opposite:
he invites the reader to compare the forthcoming *true* account
of events with the distorted romance that Ido del Sagrario
would make of them. The corrosion of gilding in *Tormento*
takes precedence over the application of new paint.

Literary metaphor is more complex than animal or physiological metaphor, other methods by which Galdós transforms
the commonplace. The division of humanity into zoological
species is a leitmotif in Balzac, and Galdós probably absorbed
this facile tool of character identification from the Frenchman.
For every major character in *Miau,* except Víctor Cadalso, he
devised an animal comparison. Even the porter Mendizábal
and his wife are said to resemble, respectively, a gorilla and a
cow. Sometimes an entire genus is thus spawned, as happens
with the Peces, where comic symbolism is the author's goal.
On occasion, the basically comic device of animal comparison
may incorporate the grotesque, as in *Angel Guerra,* where one

63. Shoemaker finds traces of romanticism in Galdós' tender and
sympathetic treatment of Miquis. See Benito Pérez Galdós, *Crónica de
la quincena,* ed. William H. Shoemaker (Princeton, 1948), p. 33 and n.

of Leré's brothers is aptly called "a monster." His hideousness, incidentally, is in no way dignified by Baudelaire's definition of the grotesque as the "absolute comic."[64]

Galdós and Balzac part company in the significance they attach to physical appearance. When Balzac compares a person's physiognomy to that of an animal, he gives a direct insight into the person's character. With Galdós, physiognomy very often misrepresents character: Villaamil looks like a tiger but has a lamb's temperament. The interdependence of psychology and physiognomy in Balzac becomes in Galdós the interdependence of psychology and physiology.[65] The manias, neuroses, quirks, obsessions, fears, and cravings of his men and women go hand in hand with the appropriate tic, tremor, spasm, spell, or fit. This is what is meant by physiological metaphor. Reflecting the vogue of physiological psychology in the second half of the nineteenth century, it too is basically a comic device in the Novelas contemporáneas. *Lo prohibido,* not usually considered a comic novel, is so full of physiological metaphor as to make it seem genuinely naturalistic. But the abnormal tics and spasms which dot the novel are no more naturalistic than Mrs. Bardell's fainting fits in *The Pickwick Papers.* The incessant use of physiological metaphor in *Lo prohibido* is really the updating of farce by science.

Caricature is another means by which Galdós transforms reality. Very closely related to physiological metaphor, caricature differs in that psychology and physiology are independent of one another. Physical traits, gestures, mannerisms, and speech tags are studied for their own sake, as are obsessions and "ruling passions." Dickens, Balzac, and Gogol form the triumvirate which ruled the "Age of Caricature."[66] These writers and many of their lesser contemporaries are said to

64. Cited by Paul Ilie, "Antonio Machado and the Grotesque," *Journal of Aesthetics and Art Criticism,* 22 (1963), 211.

65. Sherman Eoff, *The Novels of Pérez Galdós* (St. Louis, 1954), p. 24.

66. Michael O'Donovan (Frank O'Connor), *The Mirror in the Roadway* (New York, 1956), p. 68.

have shared "a certain delight in extravagance, in the inflation of everyday reality that sometimes gives us the impression that it was a period in which there was no such thing as a man or woman of normal dimensions and attributes.[67]

Galdós learned a great deal from the "Age of Caricature," and not all of it had to do with the techniques of characterization. From reading Balzac and Dickens he acquired the skill to enliven even inanimate objects, either by anthropomorphizing them or by simply exaggerating them. He transforms the piggy bank in *Fortunata y Jacinta* into a sacrificial victim; doña Isabel de Godoy's balcony, in *El doctor Centeno,* brimming over with more than fifteen varieties of trees, plants, shrubs, and herbs, "traía a la memoria lo que cuentan de Babilonia" *(4,* 1348). But caricature is mainly concerned with human beings, and one of the more provocative literary debates asks whether it is a legitimate form of characterization.

E. M. Forster's *Aspects of the Novel,* originally published in 1927, with its distinction between "flat" and "round"·characters, seems to have decisively anathematized caricature in the minds of literary critics. Forster explains that flat characters (caricatures and types), humorous in origin, are predictable, unchanging, and easily remembered. Unlike round characters, they do not evolve or develop. Better suited to comedy than to tragedy, flat characters are less important than round ones, who contain something of "the incalculability of life."[68] But Forster makes a grand exception for Dickens. Thus his theory consists not so much of flat versus round characters as bad versus good literature. Dickens, with his energy and genius, attained a sense of roundness even though his characters were flat: "Part of the genius of Dickens is that he does use types and caricatures, people we recognize the instant they re-enter, and yet achieves effects that are not mechanical and a vision of humanity that is not shallow.[69] If the disparagement of caricature is thus suspended with regard to

67. Ibid.
68. E. M. Forster, *Aspects of the Novel* (New York, 1956), p. 78.
69. Ibid., p. 71.

Dickens, similar qualifications must be made for any author whose caricatures reach a high level of artistry. And artistry, in any phase of creativity, rests to a great extent on memorable impact. An English critic has said that "caricature is a perfectly legitimate form of character-creation, for the quality we call life in a character comes as much from the passion the author brings to its making as from truth to life, accuracy of observation or psychological consistency."[70]

Is caricature incompatible with "truth to life, accuracy of observation and psychological consistency"? Santayana thinks not. On the contrary, he believes that caricature isolates those moments in which we are most truly ourselves, in which our eccentricities and quirks emerge from the paneled rooms of social convention. We fear caricature because it exploits our vulnerabilities, placing us in a new context in which we contradict ourselves and look absurd.[71] Santayana is defending Dickens against charges of exaggeration, but what he says can be applied to other writers as well.

Caricature is a technique upon which Galdós relies very heavily. Moreover, many of Galdós' flat characters impress themselves upon the memory of the reader whereas his round characters do not, and the former must be considered more successful than the latter. In *Angel Guerra,* the beached seadog don Pito, whose three passions are sea, skirts, and spirits, is more vivid than the protagonist. Leré and Dulcenombre, in the same novel, are wan figures in comparison with the sharply etched doña Catalina de Alencastre. The family of indianos in *El amigo Manso* and the parasitic doña Cándida, whose muletilla—"una cosa atroz"—is thoroughly a caricature, almost eclipse the lovers Irene and Peña. These caricatures are humorous, but Galdós uses the same technique when tragicomedy is his goal. Since caricature involves obsessions and ruling passions as well as physical tics, one can see how Galdós constructed his seemingly most rounded personage, Maxi

70. Allen, *The English Novel,* p. 66.
71. George Santayana, *Essays in Literary Criticism* (New York, 1956), pp. 210–23.

Rubín. Maxi goes from one obsession to another. First he wants to win the love of an honorable woman. Then his religious mania cloaks a single-minded desire to hear Fortunata confess her adultery. Later he adopts what Galdós calls the "tic del razonamiento" *(5,* 486). Maxi does not live on many different levels at once but rather passes through a succession of psychopathic moods. As these accumulate, they enrich his characterization. Further interest is gained as Maxi's obsessions grate against those of Fortunata, doña Lupe, and others.

Caricature is partly responsible for what Ricardo Gullón has called Galdós' "realismo trascendente." Caricature exalts "lo vulgar cotidiano," effecting its transmutation into "lo maravilloso" through the selection and reproduction of detail.[72] In the works of certain painters such as Vermeer and the Flemish Primitives the humble artifacts of everyday life approach "lo maravilloso" through the magic of technique. In a novel like *Fortunata y Jacinta,* artistic selection can likewise convey "lo maravilloso" by directing the reader's attention to an area of reality which he would ordinarily ignore. In any photograph of "lo vulgar cotidiano," a camera angle, a lighting effect, or a slight blurring of the lens may make a banal scene unforgettable. All this indicates that caricature is akin to any other process involving artistic judgment and selection of detail. Indeed, this bears on a previous remark that any interesting novel might logically be taken for an example of romantic realism. As soon as anything is selected, anatomized, or set apart it is distorted, because it becomes the center of attention. For many readers, the mere fact that something is in print is sanctification enough; it becomes an object of curiosity and interest per se.

Whereas in caricature distortion is achieved by magnifying, isolating, or minifying specific elements to the exclusion of others of a more general or superfluous nature, the type distorts through the addition of symbolic or generic attributes. A handbook of literary terms would deny to a type those myriad

---

72. Gullón, *Galdós, novelista moderno,* pp. 131–35.

qualities which make literary figures unique individuals.[73] Galdós himself admits as much in his speech of 1897 to the Real Academia Española. At the present time, he says,

> se desvanecen, perdiendo vida y color, los caracteres genéricos que simbolizaban grupos capitales de la familia humana. Hasta los rostros humanos no son ya lo que eran, aunque parezca absurdo decirlo. Ya no encontraréis las fisonomías que, al modo de máscaras moldeadas por el convencionalismo de las costumbres, representan las pasiones, las ridiculeces, los vicios y virtudes.[74]

He ends by exhorting writers to study individuals instead of "caracteres genéricos."

Clearly, Galdós' concept of type is allied to costumbrismo. It has already been mentioned that, in the very year of *Misericordia* (1897), Galdós was creating characters whose ancestry was deeply rooted in costumbrista satire.[75] Moreover, his works abound in such snippet descriptions as "tipo madrileño," "tipo aristocrático," "señorito," and so on. These figures are usually indistinguishable from caricatures. Even don Pito is at once a caricature and a costumbrista type, because his physical and mental attributes tally with one's preconceived notion of a retired sea captain. He is, in short, *typical*.

A more transcendent concept of type has long been expounded by Marxist critics, whose best known spokesman is George Lukács. According to Lukács, a type not only must be memorable in and of itself but must also represent a social class at a given moment of history. A completely successful type, of the kind created by Balzac and Gorky, embodies the process by which individual personality and class personality intertwine. Class personality, in turn, is formed by "social

73. H. L. Yelland, S. C. Jones, and K. S. W. Easton, *A Handbook of Literary Terms* (New York, 1950).

74. *Discursos leídos ante la Real Academia Española* (Madrid, 1897), p. 19.

75. See above, p. 11.

determinants," which in the nineteenth century meant capital-ism.[76] A great realist like Balzac, so the argument goes, is a social historian; he is not an observer of biological determinism (Zola) or of the psychological meanderings of any single in-dividual (Joyce). By creating types, the great realist is able to depict objective reality, which is the equivalent not of accus-tomed, average, direct, or immediate reality, but of *essential, intensified* reality. In a type, "all the humanly and socially essential determinants are present on their highest level of development, in the ultimate unfolding of the possibilities latent in them, in extreme presentation of their extremes, rendering concrete the peaks and limits of man and epochs."[77]

Objective reality and romantic realism resemble each other, for the creation of types necessitates a distortion and intensi-fication of everyday life. Lukács, who maneuvers easily through many a semantic maze, attributes certain romantic elements in Balzac to the depth and concentration of his realism: he is not restrained by feasibility or normalcy and is therefore free to indulge his fancy and imagination.

Galdós' most memorable type is Torquemada. Without any loss of individuality, he symbolizes the coarse materialism of the Spanish new-rich. He is the antithesis of Rafael del Aguila, a type symbolic of the blind, impoverished, moribund old aristocracy of Spain. A literary type somewhat comparable to Torquemada is Balzac's Gobseck (Balzac's Grandet and Dickens' Scrooge qualify as two other preeminent types by Marxist definition). The differences, however, are striking: Gobseck is the tyrant, Torquemada the tyrannized; one has a grip on every situation, while the other is relatively helpless. It was a stroke of genius on Galdós' part to entrust the sym-bolic triumph of the middle class to a person more pathetic than odious. But "stroke of genius" is too vague a term for what is fundamentally a humorous approach to subject matter.

In Volumes 1 and 4 of the *Torquemada* series, humor is based on Torquemada's transactions with the Almighty, the

76. George Lukács, *Studies in European Realism* (London, 1950).
77. Ibid., pp. 8, 58, 6.

failure of these transactions, and the protagonist's feeling of having been cheated. Volumes 2 and 3 have a dual source of humor: Torquemada's helplessness before the implacable Cruz and the outward metamorphosis of the protagonist, epitomized by his attempts at verbal refinement. Cruz's superiority of will is comic by repetition, while Torquemada's linguistic gaucheries reach a peak of hilarity in a climactic *scène à faire,* after which they diminish in importance. But Torquemada is not just a buffoon; he is pathetic, a spiritual amputee. Just as illness may be caused by the malfunction of a body organ, so may ignorance be caused by a crippling of the spirit. It is not self-ignorance—Torquemada is admirable in his lack of self-delusion—but rather an ignorance of higher realities that warps him. It is here that the individual merges with the type, for the last three volumes of this series are an exposé of the positivist, profoundly disoriented society which emerged triumphant in the latter decades of the nineteenth century. In *Torquemada en la hoguera,* on the other hand, the symbolic overtones which characterize the Marxist type are much less explicit. This is perhaps the principle difference between this novel and the later ones.

Toward the beginning of this chapter I remarked that "type" and "objectivity" were traditionally the watchwords of realism.[78] Objectivity has, for the time being, been disposed of. But type, as embodied in a figure like Torquemada, combines the twin aspects of realism already examined, and one more only alluded to. In his creation Galdós has synthesized existential realism, with its corrective or negative bias, romantic realism, with its distortion of reality, and, most important, a thematic preoccupation with the middle class far larger in scope than anything he attempted before. His prior efforts in this area fall mainly under the heading of historical metaphor. Even when the author's disdain of the new-rich was allowed to express itself, it did so in a sketchy, inconclusive fashion, as in the characterization of Cristóbal Medina *(Lo prohibido).* The *Torquemada* novels, especially the last three, are unusual

78. See above, p. 7.

in that Galdós finally clarifies what had formerly been a very ambiguous attitude toward the bourgeoisie.

Until the 1890s, Galdós did not describe the effects of free enterprise and incipient capitalism upon the individual and society, at least not in any unflattering way. Balzac and the mature Dickens had done otherwise. A most interesting comparison can be made between Balzac's portrait of a self-made man and Galdós' portrait of the same. Charles Grandet (in *Eugénie Grandet*) goes to America, makes a fortune, and becomes cynical, cruel, and thoroughly corrupt. Caballero (in *Tormento*) goes to America, makes a fortune, and returns generous and good-hearted. It is true that Galdós was an optimist; it is also true that in a parasitic, apathetic, and bureaucratic Madrid he saw no need, before *Torquemada,* to criticize hard work, ambition, business acumen, and new wealth. From *La desheredada,* where José Relimpio's orthopedist son-in-law appears as a model bourgeois, to *Fortunata y Jacinta,* where the vicissitudes of the Santa Cruz dry goods establishment are lovingly recorded, Galdós extols the middle-class virtues of work and financial reward. The vices of the middle class, when set forth, are more often moral than economic, more often due to excessive idealism than to excessive materialism. (Lo cursi, it should be noted, is not the equivalent of bourgeois; as Tierno Galván explains, it is a fall from bourgeois norms of conduct and appearance on the part of vulnerable members of the middle class.)[79] The *Torquemada* series marks a departure from all this. Moreover, from the point of view of this study, there is poetic justice in the fact that Torquemada, who symbolizes the socioeconomic trends of the nineteenth century and who meets the most rigid requirements of doctrinaire realism, should be a humorous creation.

A final aspect of realism that shall be discussed is perhaps the one in which humor is most intrinsically a part. It is the realism that reflects universal experience in terms common to

---

79. Tierno Galván, "Aparición y desarrollo de nuevas perspectivas de valoración social," p. 106.

us all, with little thought to satire, irony, distortion, or class symbolism. The humor so deeply ingrained in this kind of realism is neither boisterous nor cutting; its source is a fidelity to familiar truths. It is akin to what Praz has called the "low pressure" representation of life by certain Victorian novelists, such as Trollope and George Eliot, who deliberately de-emphasized melodrama and sensationalism.[80]

This may sound very much like objectivity but in fact bears it little resemblance. Objectivity has a cold-blooded, case-history air that the "realism of familiarity," with its domestic warmth, has not. Besides, the author who delights in familiarity and intimacy will hardly subscribe to the authorial self-efface-ment that objectivity demands. Instead, he will address the reader and will even assume the reader to be acquainted with his characters. This certainly is one of the charms of the Novelas contemporáneas: the reappearance of figures already known affords the reader membership in a private club in which he can relax and feel at ease. The familiarity of milieu, which in the Novelas contemporáneas is usually the city of Madrid, also gives the reader a sense of ease and participation. One has the impression that those novels which are not set in Madrid or which fail to describe the city (the novelas dialo-gadas) are atypical.[81]

The use of colloquial speech adds to the intimacy and infor-mality of the Novelas contemporáneas. Here realism and humor are truly inseparable. A list of familiar and colloquial expressions and the frequency of their occurrence has been drawn from *Fortunata y Jacinta;* a quick glance at this list will show to what extent such expressions color Galdós' prose. In a single paragraph devoted to reproducing José Izquierdo's speech (and Izquierdo, as the compilers correctly state, is a humorous characterization), Galdós uses eight familiar expres-

---

80. Praz, *The Hero in Eclipse*, pp. 162–63.
81. As if to emphasize the importance of the city-scape in Galdós, a recent English translation of *Miau* contains a map of the neighborhood in which the action takes place. See Benito Pérez Galdós, *Miau,* trans. J. M. Cohen (London, 1963), p. 8.

sions.[82] Furthermore, the author's uncanny ear for dialogue draws the reader into his fictitious world; the banter of unguarded moments is recorded with almost embarrassing fidelity, as pairs of lovers like Tristana and Horacio and Jacinta and Juanito are overheard conversing childishly and exultantly.

The realism of familiarity might almost be called "domestic realism," for its nucleus is often the family unit. By concentrating on the day-to-day affairs of a family circle (or a group of friends), the author and the reader tend to view these people with a certain indulgence. This is particularly true of the reappearing figures, whom the author is reluctant to abandon. Polo, Bringas, Refugio, doña Cándida, and many more have faults or vices which are reduced to peccadilloes by the very familiarity of the characters themselves. The reappearing figures are not the only ones who tap the author's forbearance. Galdós rarely condemns anyone. The only examples of arbitrary evil in the Novelas contemporáneas are Víctor Cadalso (Miau) and doña Juana de Samaniego (Casandra). (Others will be found in the earlier novels and in the plays.) Even Rosalía Bringas' calculated fall, if not condoned, is at least understood.[83]

Galdós' benign tolerance is synonymous with humor. The tedious and hairsplitting attempts to distinguish humor from comedy, with byroads into nuances, substrata, and the like, are better left to philosophers. One attempt at definition, however, is reasonably successful: it sees humor as the "fórmula suprema de comprensión."[84] Galdós would have liked this definition, for it binds humor to the pulse of reality and to that verdad humana which he always esteemed. One finds in the realism of familiarity an equanimity of judgment which per-

82. Graciela Andrade Alfieri and J. J. Alfieri, "El lenguaje familiar de Pérez Galdós," Hispanófila, 8 (Septiembre 1964), 35–36.

83. Robert Ricard, in his Galdós et ses romans (Paris, 1961), pp. 70–71, speculates that Galdós' possible recollection of a rigid home atmosphere prevented him from being either "oppresseur" or "opprimé" in his works.

84. Julio Casares, El humorismo y otros ensayos (Madrid, 1961), p. 79.

vades the other types of realism—existential, romantic, and historical—found in the Novelas contemporáneas. That this equanimity is born of a humorous ("comprehensive") view of humanity is evident throughout the Novelas contemporáneas. Perhaps its best expression comes toward the end of *La desheredada*. Galdós describes José de Relimpio's despondency upon learning of Isidora's projected liaison with an unsavory chulo type and comments: "El pobre hombre olvidaba que el error tiene también sus leyes, y que en la marcha del universo cada prurito aspira a su satisfacción y la consigue, resultando la armonía total y este claroscuro en que consiste toda la gracia de la Humanidad y todo el chiste del vivir" *(4, 1152)*.

In this review of the various aspects of realism with which Galdós' humor is integrated, the omission of naturalism may be puzzling. The omission was not an oversight, for naturalism is peripheral to Galdós' world view. The vagueness of the term itself has led to its fuzzy critical application. For Casalduero, Galdós' naturalism is fundamentally a distrust of the imagination. Guillermo de Torre uses the term as a means of classifying the Novelas contemporáneas and finally concedes that it represents, in Galdós, "una reviviscencia del tradicional realismo español." More recently, Robert Ricard has declared that Galdós' naturalism is more philosophic than literary, "une vision du monde, de l'homme et de la vie qui donne la primauté à la nature sans aucune référence à un être trascendant et à un absolu."[85]

Casalduero and de Torre, echoing Galdós, do not distinguish clearly between naturalism and realism. But Ricard, who tries to define Galdós' naturalism, fails to say that philosophically naturalism is a grimly deterministic, pessimistic attitude which sees man as patient rather than agent, foredoomed to struggle in vain against his heredity and environment. The apotheoses (albeit secular) of Galdós' two most

85. Casalduero, *Vida y obra de Galdós*, p. 63; Guillermo de Torre, "Nueva estimativa de las novelas de Galdós," *Cursos y Conferencias*, Año XII, *24*, 139–40–41 (Buenos Aires, Colegio libre de estudios superiores, 1943), 30; Ricard, p. 88.

memorable heroines, Fortunata and Benina, would suffice to disqualify him as an orthodox naturalist. If many of his characters are a bit weak-kneed as protagonists, social determinism and imaginative folly, rather than scientific determinism, are the cause.

Only in *La desheredada* and *Lo prohibido* does Galdós try to place a major personage within a rigidly naturalistic frame. Mariano Rufete is a product of environmental determinism, and José María de Guzmán is supposedly a product of his mixed Spanish-English ancestry. But even here there are important departures from the norm: Mariano's degeneration is due as much to the infectious nature of Isidora's illusions as it is to environment, and José María's hereditary virtues and vices are described by himself in the first person. This last feature helps to make *Lo prohibido* a technical tour de force: the naturalistic details over which José María loiters aid in his own characterization as a member of a decadent elite. Naturalism in this novel is more indicative of the literary and intellectual fashions of upper-class Madrid than of Galdós' own philosophy.

One need not refute Ricard's idea that nature, for Galdós, "domine sa pensée et . . . est à la fois le fil conducteur de son oeuvre et un de ses principes d'unité."[86] Nevertheless, for the typical naturalist nature is a malign force; with Galdós it is the great harmonizer. With humor, it bestows upon the author's works an optimism that survives squalor, misery, and death.

86. Ricard, p. 86.

Chapter 2: SATIRE

Literature affords few delights as eagerly anticipated as that of the young provincial, newly established in town, who froths in disgust at the vices and follies he meets at every urban turn. The reader of Galdós, however, must resign himself to a spectacle less rich in outrage and invective than in wry amusement and contempt. Satire belongs to the national patrimony of Spain, and Galdós was fully conscious of his birthright before leaving the Canary Islands for Madrid in 1862. Cervantes, Quevedo, and Guevara seasoned his youth with a tart skepticism, which was reinforced by the contemporary vogue for costumbrista satire. Nor must one forget the very temperament of the man, who seems to have been born with a camera in one eye and a knowing wink in the other. In Las Palmas he was a precocious caricaturist; his first published article, for a school newspaper, ridiculed the uproar caused by infighting between two local opera claques.[1] Much of what Galdós wrote in later years should serve as reminder that he was a satirist before he was a novelist, and that satire is an expression of his native genius rather than a sudden reaction to life in Madrid and the mainland.

This continuity is best shown by the amount of satire rooted in costumbrismo which is scattered throughout the novelist's most mature works as well as his juvenilia. Although Menéndez y Pelayo has called costumbrismo "la observación y la censura *festiva* de las costumbres nacionales" (italics mine), this lighthearted genre often takes on deeper tints in the Novelas contemporáneas.[2] A fair sampling of certain costum-

---

1. José Pérez Vidal, *Galdós en Canarias (1843–1862)* (Las Palmas, El Museo Canario, 1952), p. 80.

2. Marcelino Menéndez y Pelayo, "Don Benito Pérez Galdós," *Estudios y discursos de crítica histórica y literaria* (Santander, 1942), 5, 81–103.

brista types that lay embedded in these novels includes the
señorito, the misanthropic Spaniard, the smug Spaniard, the
indiano, the nodriza, the poet, and the cesante.[3]

Of all the authors, native and foreign, for whom Galdós has
a kind word, he treats none at more generous length than
Ramón de la Cruz, the eighteenth-century creator of satiric
one-act sainetes.[4] Cruz, "el mejor pintor de las costumbres de
su siglo" *(4,* 1478), was fond of using the figure of the
petimetre in his little playlets. The petimetre is a middle-class
fop whose daily exertions include the pampering, perfuming,
preening, and glossing of his own person. He interrupts this
ritual only to attend the dressing table of his dama (usually
engaged in the same activities). The petimetre becomes a stock
figure of the nineteenth-century cuadro de costumbres, as is
proven by his inclusion in the popular collection, *Los españoles pintados por sí mismos.*[5] In the intervening years, the
petimetre has become "El elegante," and his basic traits
have been more carefully itemized: he douses himself in cosmetics, fusses over clothes, renders constant homage to the
city of Paris, peppers his conversation with Gallicisms, and
promotes himself as a great lover. In the sketch by Ramón de
Navarrete, however, something new has been added: the
decline of the elegante—his autumnal reliance on false teeth,
toupée, and rejuvenating cosmetics, and the disdain and sarcasm his appearance elicits everywhere. In old age, "se ali-
mienta con el recuerdo de sus glorias."[6]

Readers of Galdós will inevitably recall Frasquito Ponte of
Misericordia. This chapter contains several references to Ponte
because, like his beloved Gaul, he is tripartite: señorito, romántico, and cursi. For the moment, he claims attention as a seño-

3. Types in the sense in which Galdós used the term, not Marxist
types.

4. "Don Ramón de la Cruz y su época," *Obras completas, 6,*
1453–79.

5. Ramón de Navarrete, "El elegante," in *Los españoles pintados
por sí mismos* (Madrid, 1851), pp. 157–60.

6. Ibid., p. 160.

rito. But before discussing Ponte, mention should be made of an early poem in which the señorito makes his debut in the work of Galdós, and in which the link with costumbrismo is obvious. The poem, written in 1862 when Galdós was still in Las Palmas, is called "El pollo":

> ¿Ves ese erguido embeleco,
> ese elegante sin par
>   ...?
>
> ... va al teatro y pasea
> sus miradas ardorosas,
> contemplando a las hermosas
> jóvenes de la platea ...
>
>   ...
>
> Ese estirado pimpollo
> que pasea y se engalana
> de la noche a la mañana,
> es lo que se llama un pollo.[7]

The characterization of Ponte is closer to Ramón de Navarrete's sketch than to this bit of juvenilia, but "El pollo," a product of Galdós' formative years, does set a precedent for the future. When one considers Galdós' prodigious memory and the number of unifying threads which lace his work, such precedents cannot be ignored.

Ponte, regretfully, is no longer an "erguido embeleco." The "estirado pimpollo" has withered on the vine. An abundant mane of hair and tiny feet, nicely shod, are the only parts of his physique which retain their former splendor. For the rest, Ponte is much like the elegante, both before and during his decline: he dyes his beard, uses cosmetics, has a fetish about clothes, idolizes Paris, speaks of sus, correspondencias, restauranes, and the pourboire, willingly narrates some of his amorous adventures, and nourishes himself on memories of the past *(5, 1917–23)*. At one point, Galdós even calls him

---

7. H. Chonon Berkowitz, "The Youthful Writings of Pérez Galdós," *Hispanic Review, 1* (1933), 97–98.

"un elegante'' (5, 1921). There are, however, major differences between Ponte and his precursor of Los españoles pintados por sí mismos. The latter's decline is purely physical, while Ponte's is both physical and economic. Pathos is added to satire as the señorito literally starves himself in order to keep up appearances. His indigence helps to bring on the blight of cursilería: as Tierno Galván remarks, "todo cursi es un señorito de lapso."[8] To the relatively shallow stereotype of the señorito, Galdós has added new depth.

Ponte's characterization is made more complex by his cursilería and romantic allegiances. But even if Galdós had been content to portray nothing more than an impoverished señorito, he would have met the standard set by the anonymous author of Lazarillo de Tormes. The stoicism of the poor hidalgo in that classic work has its counterpart in the burden of vergüenza which the well-bred and sensitive Ponte silently bears. Both personages are satiric and yet win the reader's compassion: one, for being kind in a world devoid of kindness, the other, for being grateful in a world of ingrates.

A second major difference between Ponte and the elegante is that Galdós, at this stage of his career (1897), found it increasingly difficult to satirize those who live on pipe dreams and past glories. Ponte has "la facultad preciosa de desprenderse de la realidad," a haven later referred to as "esta divina facultad" (5, 1917). His imagination is his one source of strength, assuring his survival. By the time he wrote Misericordia, Galdós believed that survival, and not perfectibility, was heroism enough.

The final evolution of the señorito takes place in El caballero encantado (1909). Carlos de Tarsis is in some ways the reincarnation of the pollo and the elegante, but his role is allegorical rather than satirical, and for the greater part of the novel he appears as the rustic Gil.[9] Even before his transformation, he has none of the vanity, francophilia, or effemi-

8. Tierno Galván, "Aparición y desarrollo de nuevas perspectivas de valoración social," p. 96.
9. Berkowitz suggests the connection. See "Youthful Writings," pp. 96–98.

nacy of the typical señorito. His vices, two generations removed
from the restraints of costumbrismo, are absenteeism, cynicism,
inertia, and lack of social conscience. These and a basic
frivolity (the only trait he shares with his ancestors) are effaced
as Carlos embarks on a program of national reconstruction.
What little pungency and bite went into his initial portrait
disappears in a glow of missionary rose.

Larra satirizes the misanthropic Spaniard in his artículo of
1833 entitled "En este país."[10] Galdós' version of the perennial
grouch is don Manuel Moreno-Isla of *Fortunata y Jacinta*.
Like the don Periquito of Larra's sketch, Moreno-Isla is
scornful of everything Spanish. He differs from don Periquito,
however, in that his peregrinations through the world take him
beyond the Madrid suburb of Carabanchel. Larra is satirizing
a young man who is as ignorant of his own country as he is of
other countries, whereas Galdós has the more difficult task
of satirizing a mature cosmopolite. Larra, moreover, was a
satirist in the classical sense and wished to create social types,[11]
while Galdós usually aimed at plucking the individual from
the crowd. In this case he succeeded, with the result that
Moreno-Isla bears little family resemblance to his costumbrista ancestor or, for that matter, to any other character in
the Novelas contemporáneas. His misanthropy is a cloak for
loneliness—he is truly an isla—and poor health. It is akin to
that peculiar love–hate which transplanted Spaniards feel
toward their native land and is exacerbated here by an unre-
quited love for the married Jacinta. Galdós again adds pathos
and depth to a one-dimensional type.

The most striking thing about Moreno-Isla is that he would
have made the perfect "man in the know." As an outsider he
could easily have wielded a satiric whip to Spain, just as
Caballero—another displaced Spaniard—does in *Tormento*.
Instead, he himself is exposed: he complains about the beggars

10. José Mariano de Larra, *Artículos de costumbres* (Madrid,
Clásicos castellanos, 1959), pp. 124–34.
11. Alan S. Trueblood, "El *Castellano viejo* y la *Sátira III* de
Boileau," *Nueva Revista de Filología Hispánica, 15* (1961), 530–31.

of Madrid and about the maidservants who never stop singing, yet he feels the most acute nostalgia upon hearing a beggar-girl singing jotas in the Plaza Mayor *(5,* 460–61). The religious faith which he has lost and to which he makes unflattering allusions would be fully restored if Jacinta returned his love in the smallest way *(5,* 452). Galdós never succumbs to the temptation to use Moreno-Isla as a scourge. His narrative aloofness makes an object of pity out of what had been an object of ridicule in Larra.

Larra's most famous artículo is "El castellano viejo" (1832), in which Braulio, the smug superpatriot, invites the disinclined author to his home and to the most farcical repast in Spanish literature. In the Novelas contemporáneas, the basic elements of Larra's sketch are drawn and quartered: don Florencio Morales y Temprado *(El doctor Centeno)* is the smug Spaniard of whom it may be said, as Larra says of Braulio, "es tal su patriotismo, que dará todas las lindezas del extranjero por un dedo de su país."[12] Farcical meals, mentioned here as a parenthesis, are described in *El amigo Manso, La de Bringas,* and *Lo prohibido.*

Don Florencio is more chauvinistic than Braulio but is no more profound as a character study. He might be stepping out of an artículo de costumbres as he reports that "Castille is granery to the globe," "each of our sailors is worth eight of theirs," "our army is known to be the world's finest," "in generals . . . lawyers . . . actors . . . poets . . . painters" Spain has no equal, and so on *(4,* 1415–16). Little Felipe Centeno, in whose presence this homily is delivered, resolves to memorize as much of it as possible for his master's enjoyment.

The calamitous feast is a topos of satire which dates back to Horace.[13] In "El castellano viejo" Larra attacks a churl— Braulio again—who never entertains formally and is unfamiliar with polite society, but who on one occasion decides to dine

12. Larra, p. 12.
13. Trueblood, p. 529 and passim. See also Gilbert Highet, *The Anatomy of Satire* (Princeton, 1962), pp. 220–24.

in style. The meal is a travesty: many guests are invited, few come; dinner is hours getting started; the table is too small for the company; the food is execrable; host and hostess almost come to blows; their child makes projectiles of the olives; two servants collide and destroy a dozen plates and glasses. The sketch ends as the author, besmudged with grease and gravy, makes his getaway.

Galdós knew Larra's sketch. He refers to it in *Lo prohibido,* where Cristóbal Medina's gruff manners remind Eloísa of "El castellano viejo" *(4,* 1701). But whether Galdós had Larra in mind when he described "La comida en casa de Camila" *(Lo prohibido,* 1709–14) is hard to say. José María, the narrator, is invited to his cousin's house for an ostensibly elegant meal which does not quite live up to expectations. No two pieces of china or crystal are the same; the food is wretched; the service haphazard; host and hostess snap at each other; and conversation centers around the hostess' pregnancy. What makes Camila's meal different from Braulio's is that Galdós is uncritical. Whatever adverse comments are made come from the guests, not one of whom acts as spokesman for the author. No attempt is made to satirize a type of Spaniard or a typical meal. Camila, indeed, turns out to be the heroine of the novel, and her meal stands in pleasant contrast to the spiritually rancid banquets of her sister Eloísa.

Two other memorable repasts are that of the impecunious Milagros which Rosalía Bringas recounts in *La de Bringas* *(4,* 1596–97)—with its boar's head smelling of garbage and its cream puff tasting of cod liver oil—and that of José María Manso which Máximo describes in *El amigo Manso (4,* 1187–88).[14] The latter sketch is a comic gem, wherein the narrator, a prim, meditative bachelor, is obliged to sustain himself amid a disruptive family of Cubans. The satiric picture of criollo languor and petulance in this scene and throughout the book

---

14. The latter reminds Robert Russell of Larra's "Castellano viejo." See his *"El amigo Manso:* Galdós with a Mirror," *Modern Language Notes, 78* (1963), 165. Mariano Baquero Goyanes, in his *Perspectivismo y contraste* (Madrid, 1963), also relates Larra's sketch to the meal in *El amigo Manso;* see pp. 58–60.

is broad but always gentle.[15] This is not true of the paterfamilias, José María Manso—the narrator's indiano brother.

Like José María, the indiano of *Los españoles pintados por
sí mismos* (pp. 16–20) hails from Asturias, smokes cigars,
returns to Spain with a Panama hat and plenty of cash, and
would accept a seat in Parliament if offered one. Galdós
exploits this last motif—the seductive pull of public life—and
satirizes in José María the vain indiano who wants to become a
notabilidad. Properly speaking, Galdós' satire is directed not
against the indiano, but against the political aspirations of
new money and the hangers-on who sniff and court it. In the
best satiric tradition, José María's progress is never checked,
his folly never corrected. Máximo tells us at the end of the
novel that his brother "ha reunido en torno suyo un grupo de
somnámbulos que le tienen por eminencia, y lo más gracioso
es que entre el público . . . ha ganado . . . simpatías ardientes
y un prestigio que le encamina derecho al Poder" *(4,* 1291).
The indiano sheds whatever local color the costumbristas had
given him and enters the mosaic of national life.

Although the melting pot of peninsular affairs absorbs
José María Manso, the same cannot be said of Agustín
Caballero, the indiano of *Tormento* and one of Galdós' most
likable characters. Long years away from Spain prepare him
for his role as an instrument rather than an object of satire. It is
obvious why Caballero was chosen for the role, and not José
María: he has worked hard to build his fortune, which has
commercial and mercantile roots; José María, on the other
hand, has been a war profiteer and is married to an heiress. He
is an opportunist of the old school. Caballero is also aware of
his own defects, and thus one is less likely to accuse him of
malice when he criticizes the defects of others.

Criticize he does, especially in the letters he writes to his
cousin in America. Only one of these—dealing with the
inanity of the average madrileña—appears in the novel. De-

15. For a study of Galdós' portrayal of South Americans, see
Angel del Río, "Notas sobre el tema de América en Galdós," *Nueva
Revista de Filología Hispánica, 15* (1961), 283–84.

spite its brevity, the perceptive reader feels in this letter a breath of eighteenth-century satire and the pseudo-epistles of Montesquieu or Cadalso.[16] Caballero's very relationship to Madrid society, which he himself sees in terms of savagery versus civilization, is a throwback to the eighteenth century. Galdós and his readers know full well that this self-effacing indiano is far more civilized than his doltish "social superiors," who would snub him were it not for his wealth. Caballero never quite realizes this and never fights back on native soil. But he vindicates the reader's faith in him by snatching Amparo from the grip of civilization—a nunnery—and crossing the border into France. The indiano thus becomes a complete foreigner.

The nodriza, or wet nurse, is the subject of a vignette by Bretón de los Herreros in *Los españoles pintados por sí mismos*. Galdós, in *El amigo Manso,* puts his own brand on this bovine type, and the result is a farcical scene without peer *(4,* 1244–47)—"farcical," because the wet nurse in question is inaccessible to satire, her sole commerce with the human race being of a glandular nature. Moreover, her original "folly" was so casual that it left no blemish on her soul. She is "inocentísima": "no recuerda de dónde le vino la desgracia, ni sabe quién fue el Melibeo" *(4,* 1246). Satire is obviously too subtle a weapon against virtue of this kind. Máximo, who has been commissioned to fetch a wet nurse for his godson, merely expresses repugnance toward the "humana fiera" and her "rebaño," who alternately caw, bark, regurgitate, and bellow. This scene is unusual in its contrast between sordid content and flippant narrative tone. Otherwise it is a traditional cuadro de costumbres, although more succulent and grand-guignolesque than Bretón's.

The poet makes a foreseeable appearance in *Los españoles pintados por sí mismos,* where no ill wind of satire is allowed to ruffle his composure. José Zorrilla, the author of the sketch,

16. Margarita Ucelay Da Cal, '*Los españoles pintados por sí mismos (1843–1844),*' *Estudio de un género costumbrista* (México, 1951), p. 81.

would not have permitted it, for he was a poet himself and took his profession seriously. With understandable pride he says that poets no longer garret themselves in Bohemia, and that society receives them amiably and pays them a respectable wage.

Galdós held a jaundiced view of poets even as a young man. In his late teens he wrote a satiric dialogue between a poeta and "yo," in which he pricks the grandiloquence, pedantry, and stock poetic imagery of his interlocutor.[17] An essay of the same period—"El sol"—also shows him satirizing poetic convention, especially the stale similes used in landscape description.[18] These playful tirades culminate in (and on) the poet Francisco de Paula de la Costa y Sainz del Bardal, one of the ornaments of *El amigo Manso*. Zorrilla's observation that poets had been embraced by society is borne out by what is seen here. "El tífus," as Sainz del Bardal is dubbed, is a fixture of José María Manso's salon and many other prosperous hearths (Galdós refers to "su numerosa clase" in *4,* 1192). This makes him all the more eligible for satire. His acceptance by society makes the latter a partner in the crime, and Galdós is quick to poke fun at the Cuban ladies who adore Sainz del Bardal's mellifluous versifying *(4,* 1193). Galdós, however, reserves the big guns for the poet himself.

Conceited and officious, this "pariente lejano de las Musas" would have delighted Quevedo, particularly when Máximo calls him, in true conceptista style, "peste del Parnaso y sarampión de las Musas" *(4,* 1222). His rhetorical effluviums, fed by a cheap contemporary mysticism—if Núñez de Arce was a major poet of the age, what could the minor poets have been like?—are as totally unrelated to genuine poetry as Pez's oratory is to responsible politics. A deft Quevedesque touch is reserved for the end of the novel: Sainz del Bardal falls ill and is about to cross the bar, but Máximo and his disembodied companions mutiny just in time. God, in His infinite goodness,

17. Berkowitz, "Youthful Writings" pp. 113–14. See also Pérez Vidal, *Galdós en Canarias,* pp. 103–06.
18. Berkowitz, pp. 112–14.

prolongs the poet's terrestrial life *(4,* 1291). Here is another example, comparable to that of the wet nurse, where Galdós' costumbrismo surpasses prior efforts through sheer inventiveness.

In one of his Escenas matritenses Mesonero Romanos vividly describes a cesante as "el hombre público reducido a . . . muerte civil"; he is a bureaucrat who has lost his job not through incompetence, "sino por un capricho de la fortuna, o más bien de los que mandan a la fortuna."[19] Mesonero's costumbrista sketch, written half a century before *Miau,* anticipates the arbitrary and humiliating death-in-life that afflicts Villaamil. There is further premonition of Villaamil in Gil y Zárate's "El cesante" *(Los españoles pintados por sí mismos).* Of several categories recorded in this piece, the "cesante mendicante" is closest to Villaamil. Always inopportune, always begging for a job, money, or a recommendation, Gil y Zárate's cesante is a macabre sight to behold: "flaco y estenuado; rostro macilento, extirado e intenso, ojos hundidos pero perspicaces y codiciosos."[20]

Villaamil is introduced in *Fortunata y Jacinta (5,* 347–48), where he is said to resemble a "momia animada" ("muerte civil"). He waylays an acquaintance from whom he begs a recommendation ("mendicante") and shortly thereafter slithers away, to reappear as the central character in Galdós' next novel, *Miau.* Here his basic configuration is preserved. He writes supplicating letters to bureaucrats more fortunate than himself. Physically, he is skeletal, blotchy, and fearsome. As the novel progresses, there is no change for the better: Villaamil is thoroughly down and out.

Satire thrives on obstacles, and when these are replaced by helplessness and innocence—when resistance is nil—it retreats. Villaamil is immune to attack, even if he does represent, by

19. Mesonero Romanos (El Curioso Parlante), *Escenas matritenses* (Madrid, 1862), p. 77.
20. *Los españoles pintados por sí mismos,* p. 47. For the costumbrista origins of the cesante, see also Robert J. Weber, *The Miau Manuscript of Benito Pérez Galdós* (Berkeley and Los Angeles, 1964), pp. 1–6.

implication, the bureaucratic Everyman, the mass dupe.[21] This does not mean that *Miau* is free of satire: the spirit of Quevedo hovers over Pantoja ("el prototipo del integralismo administrativo") and invades the sequence in which Villaamil, accompanied by his friend Argüelles, roams the corridors of Hell (i.e. the Administración).[22] But this "mundo por de dentro" revelation chides not the cesante, but the unholy system that has discarded him. It would be helpful then to descend with Villaamil into the nether world of officialdom and examine the buttresses and foundations of the Spanish State.

The second half of the nineteenth century might be called the Age of Parliamentarianism. Nations were impressed by the strength and wealth of England, and the reason for English ascendancy was thought to rest on its system of government, which was copied throughout Europe. Regretfully, the system did not work as well elsewhere as it did at the source of Pax Britannica and was often a travesty of the original. Even in England there was frequent disillusionment with Parliament. At times the utmost patience was needed to sift the differences between one political party and another. Behind the barrage of words nothing seemed to change. Progress was imperceptible or nonexistent.

Early in the century, in *The Pickwick Papers,* Dickens lampooned the similar tactics used by rival factions in the Eatanswell election and set a pox on both parties involved in the opera-buffa struggle. Later, in the more mature *Bleak House,* he satirized Parliament itself, emphasizing the uniformity which lurked beneath its facade of contention and variety. Lords Boodle, Coodle, and Doodle and the Rights Honorable Buffy, Cuffy, and Duffy are allegorical legislators, whose nonsense names, rhyming from A to Z, spell out a conspiracy against change.

21. The "villa" is Madrid; "Villaamil"=a thousand similar or prospective cases of cesantería.

22. In the original, "los recintos infernales." Note that Pantoja, who is indispensable to the Administración and need never worry about becoming a cesante, is a legitimate object of attack.

The period of Spanish history known as the Restoration (1874–1923) offered ideal hunting to the satirist, for it consisted of the alternation in power of Boodles and Buffys—that is, of nominal Liberals and nominal Conservatives. Elections were prearranged, with one party lending the other a helping hand. In *Lo prohibido,* there is a summary view of Restoration politics: two M.P.'s, one incumbent and the other opposition, represent the same province and agree to alternate in power. "Su rivalidad política," says the narrator, speaking for Galdós, "era sólo aparente, una fácil comedia para esclavizar y tener por suya la provincia" *(4,* 1692). The cynicism of the period affected not only the Establishment but all shades of political opinion and is summed up by Galdós in *Fortunata y Jacinta:*

> Esto de que todo el mundo sea amigo particular de todo el mundo es síntoma de que las ideas van siendo tan sólo un pretexto para conquistar o defender el pan. Existe una confabulación tácita (no tan escondida que no se encuentre a poco que se rasque en los políticos), por la cual se establece el turno en el dominio. En esto consiste . . . la ayuda masónica que se prestan todos los partidos, desde el clerical al anarquista. *(5,* 295)

The intellectual and moral miasma produced by such lack of conviction drove Galdós to satire just as it had Pereda.[23] "Las desdichas nacionales," he wrote in 1911, "pierden algo de su amargura cuando en ellas ponemos unos granos de la dulcedumbre satírica, tan grata a nuestros paladares."[24]

Galdós' greatest contribution to political satire is the Pez family. All the nepotism and corruption of the era is distilled in this aquatic bureaucracy, which permeates at least ten of the Novelas contemporáneas.[25] As their name indicates, the

23. In the "Prólogo" to *El sabor de la tierruca,* Galdós says that Pereda's satire was inspired by the prevailing political system.

24. Shoemaker, ed., *Los prólogos de Galdós,* p. 105.

25. It must be kept in mind that the Peces are most prominent in those novels set in the years 1868–81, and that in 1881 Galdós was just getting started on the Novelas contemporáneas. What he did was

Peces multiply quickly, live beneath the surface, come in a
wide range of colors, shapes, and sizes, and are wonderfully
mobile and slippery. In spite of minor variations, they belong
to the same genus. They are the pisciform cousins of Dickens'
Barnacles *(Little Dorrit)*, but their superiority over the latter
is unquestionable, for they survive ten novels, a revolution
(1868), a civil war, and the ebb and flow of Restoration
politics with something like pristine piscivorousness.[26]

Immutability lies at the heart of all authentic satire. What has
been said of the satiric plot may also be applied to the Peces:
usually some agitation will appear on the surface, but otherwise
the current flows on as before.[27] According to this definition,
La de Bringas is structurally a perfect satire of Spanish bureaucracy. The novel ends with the Revolution of 1868, an event
which, it was hoped, would give the nation a fresh start.
Supposedly the Peces will be forever banished. But nothing
really changes.[28] Don Manuel Ramón José María del Pez,
the Founding Fish, has had the wisdom to join the "partido
moderado" *(4,* 1623), whose vague allegiances, abstractness,
and lack of specific ideals ensure the political resiliency of its
members. Unlike Bringas, a fervent monarchist who willingly
suffers the consequences of his beliefs, Pez calmly accepts the
fait accompli and will inevitably slip back into power:

> ¡Y qué feliz casualidad! Casi todos los individuos que
> compusieron la Junta eran amigos suyos. Algunos tenían
> con él parentesco, es decir, que eran algo Peces. En el

---

to transfer the contemporary political scene (the 1880s) back a decade.
For a useful chart giving the time span of each of the Novelas contemporáneas, see John Phillip Netherton, "The *Novelas españolas
contemporáneas* of Pérez Galdós: a study of method" (University of
Chicago, Unpublished doctoral dissertation, 1951), p. 84.

26. Compare with the Barnacles in Charles Dickens, *Little Dorrit*
(London, Chapman and Hall, 1863), *1,* 114.

27. Alvin B. Kernan, *Modern Satire* (New York, 1962), pp. 176–77.

28. In an article of 1903 entitled "Soñemos, alma, soñemos,"
Galdós says that the Revolutions of 1854 and 1868 changed only "la
superficie de las cosas." See *Obras completas, 6,* 1483.

Gobierno provisional tampoco le faltaban amistades y parentescos, y dondequiera que volvía mi amigo sus ojos, veía caras pisciformes. *(4,* 1670)

Only once does Galdós put the Pez fortunes in jeopardy. This occurs in *La desheredada (4,* 1067–68), when the Second Carlist War is over and the Restoration, with its hypocritical turnstile government, is about to begin: "Los Peces grandes y chicos se ven desterrados de las claras aguas de sus plazas y oficinas. Bien quisieran ellos aclamar también al rey nuevo; pero la disciplina del partido les impone, ¡ay!, una consecuencia altamente nociva a sus intereses." The Pájaros take over, although a few minor Peces stay in office: "son Peces alados, transición zoológica entre las dos clases, pues la triunfante tuvo en situaciones anteriores sus avecillas con escamas" *(4,* 1067–68). This setback is only temporary, however, and perhaps may be attributed to Galdós' uncertainty as to any future role for the Peces.[29] After *La desheredada* he mentions them in most of the novels written through 1890.

If the proliferation of Peces is a typical defect of bureaucracies, so too is hollow oratory, the lingua franca of politicians everywhere. Throughout his career Galdós expressed a loathing for official claptrap. He shows again and again that Spaniards prefer sounds to sense. From the demagogues of *La Fontana de Oro* to Hipérbolas in *La razón de la sinrazón,* the motif is constant and obsessive. In *El caballero encantado* "Mother Spain" warns the hero about this capital vice: "vivís exclusivamente la vida del lenguaje, y siendo esto tan hermoso, os dormís sobre el deleite del grato sonido. Habláis demasiado, prodigáis sin tasa el rico acento con que ocultáis la pobreza de vuestras acciones" *(6,* 256). Everyone associated with public life is full of bombast. Villaamil's letters, in which he begs for money, are ludicrously couched in the "official" style *(5,* 591).

29. The evolution of this extended metaphor may be traced to *La familia de León Roch.* Don Joaquín Onésimo *(4,* 763) is compared to a "fanal," and his bureaucratic family is at once a "pléyade" and an "epidemia." In *El amigo Manso* a Pez is compared to "un astro," clearly a carry-over from *León Roch (4,* 1193).

José María Manso, now the Marquis of Taramundi, cloaks
his paucity of ideas behind an emphatic delivery *(Angel
Guerra, 5,* 1245). Even youngsters are contaminated by the
grandiloquent worm: Paquito Bringas and his friend Joaquinito
Pez unleash their forensic ardor on the "Social Question,"
which they expound in language worthy of the subject
(Tormento, 4, 1472).

It is to the elder Pez that one must turn for a lesson in
parliamentary rhetoric. His normal speech pattern so resembles that of Mr. Conversation Kenge, one of the lawyers of
Bleak House, that I cannot resist quoting from the latter first.
Kenge addresses a client ruined by a law suit: "You are to
reflect . . . that this has been a great cause, that this has been a
protracted cause, that this has been a complex cause."[30] These
consoling circumlocutions may well be the origin of Pez's
speech.[31] Since Pez believes in multiplication as a cure-all for
the nation's ills ("Su ideal era montar un sistema administrativo perfecto, con ochenta o noventa direcciones generales"),
it comes as no surprise that he should say everything in duplicate or triplicate. Commenting on the revolution, he declares,
"¿Qué ha pasado? Lo que yo venía diciendo, lo que yo venía
profetizando, lo que yo venía anunciando" *(La de Bringas, 4,*
1670). Syntax such as this, a joint creation of Cortes and the
press, enshrines him as an oracle and a sage.

One critic calls Galdós' world "un mundo oral," in which
even the tópico—a trite figure of speech—transcends satire
to denote character development and a psychological give-and-
take between personages.[32] With regard to the political or
journalistic tópico, it would be more correct to speak of "dos
mundos orales." The elder Pez, José María Manso, the Mar-

30. Charles Dickens, *Bleak House* (London, Centenary Edition,
1911), *2,* 512.

31. Galdós had two copies of *Bleak House* in his library. One was
a French translation. See H. Chonon Berkowitz, *La biblioteca de
Benito Pérez Galdós* (Las Palmas, El Museo Canario, 1951), pp. 188–
89.

32. Stephen Gilman, "La palabra hablada y *Fortunata y Jacinta,*"
Nueva Revista de Filología Hispánica, 15 (1961), 542 and passim.

quis of Tellería, and others have a split verbal personality, part official, part colloquial. When discussing national affairs, especially crises, they mount a soapbox and declaim. Even Bringas, whose speech is usually straightforward, must pump his lungs with gas before launching an occasional jeremiad: "De modo, ¡Santo Cristo del Perdón!, que estamos en poder de la canalla, de los descamisados, de las *llamadas* masas" *(4, 1668).* These and other official *tópicos* scattered throughout the *Novelas contemporáneas* would fill a small catalog. My own favorite belongs to José María Manso, whose entry into politics is announced by his assimilation of its jargon: "Las cosas caen del lado a que se inclinan" *(4, 1202).*

Galdós' satire of the *tópico* reaches its high point in *Torquemada en el purgatorio,* when Torquemada speaks at a banquet held in his honor. One must be careful not to mistake Galdós' intentions here: he ridicules the *speech,* not the *speaker.* Torquemada, in a conversation with his brother-in-law, admits that what he said at the banquet was a compendium of hackneyed phrases heard in the senate or pilfered from the press: "Creo que todos los que me oían, salvo *un núcleo* de dos o tres, eran más tontos que yo" *(5, 1108).* He is right, judging from the sincere applause on his behalf. Torquemada's insight and self-awareness save him, in this instance, from personal attack. Those who applaud are the fools.

Torquemada stands for the rise to power of a new class. His verbal acquisitions, best described as cultismos, go far beyond the few dozen *tópicos* which other characters bandy about, and they are not restricted to politics. Although Galdós satirizes Torquemada's cultismos, he does so with a larger purpose in mind. His satire is a means to an end, that end being symbolic, or "typic."

Nepotism, bloated syntax, and a reliance on *tópicos* take up three quarters of all available space in the Spanish bureaucracy. The ship of state resembles a blimp. This is the entity toward which Pantoja feels such Teutonic allegiance and from which Villaamil expects a fair shake. *Miau,* Galdós' "bureaucratic" novel, deals with a lower echelon of government employee and thus avoids the stratospheric rhetoric of the

Peces, Mansos, and Torquemadas. Portions of the novel revive a kind of satire which Galdós had written in his youth under the tutelage of Quevedo and Guevara. In what amounts to a vision or a fantastic journey in miniature, the reader tours the Administración and is told a few of its secrets. Foremost among these is a sine qua non for bureaucratic success—the patronage of an influential female. Villaamil, of course, has no such connections. He cannot even get a job, no less a promotion. His contact with the fair sex is unprofitable. Wife, daughter, and sister-in-law, the three Miaus, do not have a dime's worth of influence and, if they did, would spend it on a new button or ribbon. Villaamil's long monologue at the end of the novel, in which he heaps scorn upon the Miaus, is inspired by their failure to help his career as well as by their general ineptitude.

Villaamil had long been aware of the utility of faldas (skirts). Therefore he is amused, but not incredulous, when he learns how old and worn are his hated son-in-law's: the suave and handsome Víctor, a prototype of Byronic seductiveness, has been wooed by, and has wooed in turn, a dowager whom "no paint job can salvage nor patching mend" ("no hay pintura que la salve ni remiendo que la enderece," 5, 658). This is very castizo satire, reminiscent of Quevedo's Sueños. It becomes even more so when one understands that Víctor and his crone have a special nook for their assignations. One is reminded of Goya's famous Capricho, "¿Qué tal?" which shows a toothless hag admiring herself in the mirror while a young gallant and a few snickering girls stand by.

The exchange of bureaucratic favors for amorous ones would be of dubious legality without the participation of some member of the Pez family. It is thus a balm for the conscience to discover that one of Villaamil's co-workers, who has come up in the ranks rather quickly, has his momia in the widow of Pez y Pizarro, a cousin of don Manuel Pez and former director of Havana lotteries (5, 659).[33] Villaamil's hopes for justice

33. Previously, Villaamil had denied the efficacy of Pez's backing, saying that he and his school were on the way out (see 5, 630).

are futile because his physique is not of the sort that arouses such matronly philanthropies. Furthermore, one of his bywords is "morality."

A tour of the Administración would be incomplete without a look at Pantoja, the model bureaucrat. Here, finally, is a person who serves his country with complete dedication. Unstained by graft or intrigue and free of pisciform ties, Pantoja lights the surrounding darkness with exemplary rays. He is tenacious, thorough, and inflexible in his duties. As tax auditor for the Treasury he hunts down every renegade contributor. He assumes that every claim against the state is fraudulent and that all money in private hands is "hot." "A certain Communism" welds his interests to those of the Treasury, whose stocks he defends against businessmen, politicians, and would-be exploiters. Pantoja's ant-like anonymity and fierce, misguided altruism strike a modern note, but his origins are really Quevedesque (the satire of professions). His personal amiability and common sense blunt the effect of Galdós' satire, adding roundness to his characterization. Readers acquainted with George Orwell's acid satires of mechanical men and with the criminal toadyism of recent history will be taken aback by Galdós' humanization of the model bureaucrat.

Pantoja is a genial premonition of things to come, but he has no past or progeny in the Novelas contemporáneas. Galdós is more concerned with the long-winded, ambitious, only too visible notabilidad than with the anonymous drudge.

A prerequisite of satire is that it be topical, that it deal with the here and now. Why then should Galdós have spent so much time satirizing romanticism in the Novelas contemporáneas? He wrote these novels between 1881 and 1915, when the worst excesses of romanticism had been sloughed off years before. Surely he felt no impulse to satirize Pereda, Alarcón, or "Clarín," his major contemporaries, for romantic crimes against literature, nor was there any need to avenge his own or their lack of popularity with the reading public.

Some generalizations may be made in answer to the question posed above. During Galdós' formative years, the romantic

fever was still very much in the air. The costumbristas would
not have satirized romanticism with such relish if this had not
been the case. Mesonero Romanos, whose "El romanticismo
y los románticos" explores the sepulchral side of the movement, was a personal friend of Galdós. Mesonero's sketch
describes a young man who informs his sweetheart (in verse)
about the advantages of suicide, strewn petals, and a single
gravestone.[34] It prefigures the episode in *Misericordia* where
Obdulia, smitten with "cosas de muertos, cipreses y cemente-
rios," elopes with an undertaker's son *(5,* 1897). This cor-
roborates prior evidence, to the effect that costumbrista elements abound in the Novelas contemporáneas.

Another reason for Galdós' satire along these lines is more
strictly chronological: three of the novels—*El doctor Centeno,
Tormento,* and *La de Bringas*—are set in 1863–68, and these
years are evoked by depicting concurrent artistic fashion.
Four other novels—*La desheredada* (time span 1872–76), *El
amigo Manso* (time span 1878–81), *Fortunata y Jacinta* (time
span 1869–76), and *Miau* (time span 1878)—although set in
the recent past, portray a society whose tastes had been formed
by romanticism.[35] Galdós also often uses romantic literature
in much the same way that Cervantes used the novelas de
caballerías—to denote romance.

Finally, Galdós' satire of romanticism may be attributed
to self-discipline. He wanted to avoid the bogs of sentiment
which occasionally marred his earlier novels. For example, his
treatment of romantic love in *La Fontana de Oro, Doña Perfecta,* and *Gloria* is almost mawkish by comparison with his
ironic treatment of the same phenomenon in the Novelas
contemporáneas. Youthful passion constitutes a childish phase,
a silly urgency in the later novels. A comparison of Rosario
(Doña Perfecta) with Luisa Villaamil *(Miau),* both of whom
are driven mad by exalted passion, shows a change of tone from
quasi-tragic to tragicomic. Nor can one imagine Gloria confid-
ing the ups and downs of her infatuation "to the moon, the stars,

34. *Escenas matritenses,* pp. 115–33.
35. See n. 25, above.

the cat, the goldfinch, God and the Virgin" as does Luisa, who is a victim of Galdós' caustic attitude toward inflammatory passion *(5,* 589).[36]

The most successful marriage in the Novelas contemporáneas, between Barbarita Arnáiz and Baldomero Santa Cruz *(Fortunata y Jacinta),* was not originally a love match. It was arranged by the parents of both spouses. This does not mean that Galdós slights romantic love entirely in the Novelas contemporáneas. Latent sentimentality, however, often defers to the illicit liaison, which caters to the reader's taste for spice rather than syrup. Caballero and Amparo *(Tormento),* Isidora and Martín *(Torquemada en la hoguera),* Santa Cruz and Fortunata *(Fortunata y Jacinta),* and Tristana and Horacio *(Tristana)* have bittersweet, "irregular" love affairs in defiance of the moral code. Ironically, in his anxiety to suppress the emotional zeal of his post-1881 heroes and heroines, Galdós merely substitutes one form of romanticism for another. What Ricard calls a pursuit of "les exigences du coeur" is as romantic a guide to behavior as any other.[37]

Galdós also tries to rid himself of any tendency to romanticize the appearance of his personages. He does this in one of three ways: by poking fun at the "romantic" physique, by reporting a flaw in an otherwise attractive physique, or by offsetting outward beauty with some inner defect. The following description of Olimpia Samaniego *(Fortunata y Jacinta)* is satirical:

> hubiera causado gran admiración en la época en que era moda ser tísico, o al menos parecerlo. Delgada, espiritual, ojerosa, con un corte de cara fino y de expresión romántica, la niña aquella habría sido perfecta beldad cincuenta años ha, en tiempo de los tirabuzones y de los talles de sílfide. *(5,* 423)[38]

36. This tempestuous affair erupts precisely in the year 1868, the year which Galdós saw as the dividing line between romanticism and sanity. A costumbrista satire on romantic love affairs is found in Larra's "El casarse pronto y mal."

37. Robert Ricard, *Aspects de Galdós* (Paris, 1963), p. 103.

38. See also the description of Obdulia in *Misericordia (5,* 1896–97).

Amparo and Refugio Emperador escape the cloying charm of
the "romantic orphan" in *Tormento,* because the novel is a
parody of the serialized romantic novel. Refugio is very pi-
quant but is missing a tooth, has too much down on her upper
lip, and is curvilinear to the point of lopsidedness; her sister
Amparo, a true romantic beauty, is blemished morally (not
that Galdós ever holds this against her).[39] Amparo and Refugio are certainly more contemporary than Clara, the wist-
ful orphan of *La Fontana de Oro.* They may almost be a
parody of her.

Galdós as an unconscious parodist of his own work is a
subject which deserves critical attention. It is not outlandish
to see in Maxi Rubín a physical and ideological disfiguration
of Daniel Morton, the darkly romantic Jew who dies insane
looking for a new religion. And Máximo Manso is a satirical
reincarnation of his "friend," León Roch. Manso is a philoso-
pher-pedagogue whose professional skills—observation, method, dispassionateness—smother all knowledge based on instinct or intuition. His pragmatism is just another form of
idealism and allows him to make false assumptions about
people. He learns finally that human beings must be experienced, not only observed, if their capricious ways are to be
understood at all.

Manso would like Manuel Peña to be his disciple. His
initial approach to Peña's education is liberal enough and is
related to the krausista goal of a well-rounded character,
harmoniously integrated and highly moral. He is deeply cha-
grined, therefore, when Peña tells him that he has been reading
Machiavelli (an author whose principles hardly correspond
to those of the Institución Libre de Enseñanza). Manso's
reaction is dogmatic and pedantic: "Mala, perversa lectura
si no va precedida de la preparación conveniente. Es mi tema,
querido Manuel: si no haces caso de mí, tu inteligencia se
llenará de vicios. Dedícate al estudio de los principios generales" *(4,* 1214). This is precisely what Peña refuses to do. He

39. Netherton is very good on Galdós' descriptive techniques. See
his "The *Novelas españolas contemporáneas* of Pérez Galdós," pp. 171–
80.

is more interested in life than philosophy, more fond of
Machiavelli than Hegel. Galdós is of the same opinion. His
satirical portrait of Manso is in perfect accord with a remark of
Northrop Frye's: "Insofar as the satirist has a 'position' of his
own, it is the preference of practice to theory, experience to
metaphysics. . . . Thus philosophical pedantry becomes, as
every target of satire eventually does, a form of romanticism or
the imposing of over-simplified ideals on experience."[40]

Satire enters the Novelas contemporáneas wherever an
attempt is made, as in *El amigo Manso,* to ignore the contin-
gencies of life. Experience should teach one to take no human
being for granted. To trust in any sort of philosophy, whether
metaphysical or pragmatic, for explanations of human behavior
is a sign of naïve idealism. The pitfalls of such idealism are
rigidity and self-deception. In Manso's case, these failings are
as predictable as the periphrastic sermons of don Manuel
Pez. The only difference is that Manso evolves while Pez
is static. Manso, for all his reliance on reason and method,
must help straighten out the unreasonable and disorderly
dilemmas which befall several characters of the book. He
dirties his hands with great success (the only dilemma he fails to
resolve is his own). So complete is his thawing out that he
tires of being a satiric butt and becomes an ironist. In fact he
has been Galdós' personal agent all along, and it is through
his eyes that one sees the poet, the indiano, the wet nurse, the
Pez, and other satiric figures that flit about. For a "dead" man,
Manso has a keen sense of humor.

Manso is "dead" because he failed to take into account the
more recondite spurs to behavior—"Yo no existo." One cannot
live in a blueprint. An artistic style may also stagnate if clois-
tered in pattern or precedent. To maintain a certain vigor, art
must renew itself. Hand-me-down canons—canons which once
might have gauged experience or reality faithfully—become
lifeless anachronisms in the long run. This is what happened
to Spanish romanticism in the second half of the nineteenth
century. It is little wonder, then, that Galdós so often links
romanticism with death or disease. Moreover, romanticism

40. Frye, *Anatomy of Criticism,* pp. 230–31.

always abounded in graveyard elements. Mesonero Romanos was a satiric forerunner of Galdós in this respect, but Galdós went further than any of the costumbristas in holding an almost deterministic view of the *effects* of romanticism. Most of the characters in the Novelas contemporáneas who have romantic tastes in art or literature are doomed to one or more of the following: death (Alejandro Miquis), figurative death (Isidora), physical deterioration (Bringas, Ponte), or mental deterioration (Ido del Sagrario).[41]

Predetermined gloom does not prevent Galdós from satirizing these people. Bringas works long and hard on a hair-picture. Both picture—which represents a cenotaph—and medium—which once graced the head of an infant Pez, now deceased—meet only the most relaxed aesthetic standards. V. S. Pritchett calls this opening description of *La de Bringas* a satire on the Spanish cult of death.[42] The cult wore all the trappings of romanticism in 1868, the year in which the novel takes place. A weeping willow looms above a score of animal, floral, and angelic mourners to become the dominant motif in the cenotaph: "El tal sauce era irreemplazable en una época en que aún no se hacía leña de los árboles del romanticismo" *(4, 1573)*. The background comes from an illustrated "Lamartinesque" volume that is all treacle *(4, 1576)*.

Apparently there was a European market for similar collages. The ladies in Mrs. Gaskell's *Cranford* (1853) count among their personal effects brooches "like small picture-frames with mausoleums and weeping-willows neatly executed in hair inside."[43] Whether the Cranford ladies urged that only family hair (pelo de la familia) be used in these treasures, as Carolina Pez demands of Bringas, can never be known. It is certain, however, that Mrs. Gaskell had no ulterior design upon society when she described the tastes of past years. Galdós, on the contrary, wanted Bringas' hair-picture (and the Royal Palace where he lives) to symbolize Spain on the eve of Queen

41. The high-strung Obdulia escapes this drastic fate, as does the poet Sainz del Bardal *(El amigo Manso)*.

42. Pritchett, "Review of *The Spendthrifts*," p. 710.

43. Mrs. Gaskell, *Cranford* (London, 1894), p. 135.

Isabel's forced abdication in 1868. Like the Royal Palace, the cenotaph is grandiose in conception. Bringas copied his willow tree from Napoleon's tomb and his angel from some funereal pageant in the Escorial. But Bringas fills in the monumental outline with microscopic wisps of hair of the utmost fragility, and the total sum which he can afford to spend on its execution is a paltry twenty-eight to thirty reales. This corresponds exactly to the apparent strength and real weakness, the outward pomp and inner poverty, of the royal household.

Bringas' outmoded romanticism betrays his political affiliations. He is a monarchist, or, as Galdós would have it, an obscurantist ("era partidario frenético del oscurantismo en todas sus manifestaciones," *4,* 1628). This too is symbolized by the hair-picture. Snug in his palatial niche, patiently gluing bits of hair together, Bringas substitutes myopia for vision, sight for insight. He soon goes blind. The revolution erupts, the hair-picture eventually becomes a dust-catcher, and the romantic era is (or should be) dead. Unlike the shattered Bringas, for whom the cenotaph has become a personal memento mori, Rosalía and don Manuel Pez survive the catastrophe in good shape. They can face up to promiscuous times, having had all the training necessary. They are not bound by old allegiances— sentimental, political, or artistic—and neither is very enthusiastic about Bringas' romantic offering; Pez goes so far as to consider it a "mamarrachada" and an "esperpento" *(4,* 1602).

Frasquito Ponte *(Misericordia),* like Bringas, cannot adjust to new circumstances. Nurtured by romanticism, his growth is stunted by its demise. Physically and intellectually, he is "dead" to the present: "así como su cuerpo se momificaba, su pensamiento iba quedando fósil" *(5,* 1920). Once again, 1868 or thereabouts marks the fatal hurdle: "En su manera de pensar no había rebasado las líneas del 68 y 70" *(5,* 1920). In his conversations with Obdulia, Ponte reminisces about the romantic age—its scandals, personalities, fashions, and entertainments. He recalls the names of certain theatrical works of the era— ridiculous titles like *Flor de un día* and *La trenza de sus cabellos* —and hums arias by Bellini and Donizetti. But most of all, he likes to evoke the Paris of the Second Empire—the Empress

Eugénie, Lamartine, Hugo, Thiers, Paul de Kock, Octave Feuillet, and Sue. These authors comprise the romantic repertoire of the Novelas contemporáneas. Bringas is said to bear a physical resemblance to Thiers *(Tormento, 4, 1461)*, Juan Bou gives Isidora a volume of Lamartine *(La desheredada, 4, 1129)*, and *Les Misérables* takes the reading public by storm in *El doctor Centeno (4, 1409)*. Ironically, Feuillet's *Histoire de Sibylle,* which Ponte names specifically, once made enough of an impression on Galdós himself to influence the genesis of *Gloria.*[44]

A previous remark about the señorito origins of Ponte brought Galdós' poem of 1862, "El pollo," to mind. Another early piece—"Un tribunal literario" (1872)—prefigures Ponte's romantic sensibilities and cursilería. In this satirical sketch, Galdós presents the Duque de Cantarranas—impoverished nobleman, renovator of a single wardrobe, and lover of romantic literature. The curious thing about the sketch is that Galdós chose a different roster of authors to indicate the duke's outmoded romantic tastes: Mme. de Genlis, Mme. de Staël, Rousseau, and Young.[45] Mme. de Genlis, the last surviving member of this group, died in 1830. Therefore, Galdós' perspective on romanticism changed considerably between 1872 and 1897, the date of *Misericordia.* It might even be proposed that Galdós was unaware that *La Fontana de Oro* and *Gloria,* at the time of their composition, were as romantic in their way as the novels written by Mme. de Staël and others.

Ponte's six-week sojourn in Paris reflects Galdós' own experience. He made his first trip in 1866, and it is not without nostalgia that he consigns to the "mummy" a reconstruction of his own past. Fortunately, Galdós happened upon a volume of Balzac during his stay in the French capital; he did not linger long over Sue and Feuillet. Ponte, on the other hand, must have devoured the worst examples of romantic pulp fiction, for

44. Pattison, *Galdós and the Creative Process,* p. 81 and passim.

45. Another character in the sketch has a preference for the humanitarian novel of proletarian sympathies—Hugo. This is the only connection with the authors mentioned by Ponte. "Un tribunal literario" may be found in *6,* 455–70.

after his fateful concussion his speech takes on the baroque-ro-
mantic-operatic coloring of the novela por entregas: "Todo
Madrid lo repite. . . . De aquí, de estos salones salió la indigna
especie. Me acusan de un infame delito: de haber puesto mis
ojos en un ángel, de blancas alas célicas, de pureza inmaculada"
(5, 1989). Ponte's delirium, appropriately clothed in deepest
purple, announces his death.

Alejandro Miquis *(El doctor Centeno)* also comes to a sad
end, a victim of tuberculosis, the Romantic Disease. His physical ailment, however, is symbolic of something else—a chronic
idealism, typified by his phrase, "Yo voy siempre tras de lo
absoluto" *(4,* 1432). For Alejandro, this means wealth, fame,
love, and beauty, all just around the corner, just beyond his
grasp. He stakes his claim to glory on a play, *El Grande Osuna,*
which he believes will ignite the Spanish stage. Never performed and never published, the play is torn asunder at the
novel's end, just as the playwright, lying in state, is irreverently
shorn of his coat.

Parts of *El Grande Osuna* are inspired by Hugo's *Ruy
Blas.*[46] The verses quoted from it, however, are by Calderón
(4, 1399 and n.). It is therefore a pastiche, representative of the
favor which Spanish baroque drama enjoyed among European
dramatists of the romantic period. Alejandro had read Scribe,
Hugo, and Schiller, as well as Calderón *(4,* 1374, 1377). Like
the dramas of Scribe and others, *El Grande Osuna* would make
an ideal opera libretto: "Habrá *Il Magno Ossuna,* como hay
Il Trovatore y *Simone Bocanegra" (4,* 1430).[47] This alone
dates the play: Galdós, from his 1883 vantage point, remarks
that its dramatic structure "Ya interesa poco y ha pasado a las
óperas" *(4,* 1429). Nevertheless, in context there is nothing
preposterous about *El Grande Osuna.* It belongs to its era and
could easily have been written, performed, and admired in the
1860s, when the events of *El doctor Centeno* take place.

46. Galdós, *Crónica de la quincena,* ed. Shoemaker, p. 33.
47. Both of Verdi's operas are based on works by García Gutiérrez,
a Spanish contemporary of Hugo. Alejandro's idol, however, is not
García Gutiérrez but Ayala (see *4,* 1394).

Alejandro is not the anachronism that Ponte is, and his play, unlike Bringas' cenotaph, betokens youth and fire rather than senility and decay.

The real object of Galdós' satire in *El doctor Centeno* is quixotism, not romanticism. Alejandro is an inveterate dreamer ("soñador de empuje"), given to a very dangerous use of the imagination ("consagrado al peligrosísimo ejercicio de la imaginación," *4,* 1366, 1377). He comes from La Mancha, the seat of Don Quixote. His aunt, doña Isabel de Godoy, is also from La Mancha and is as mad as can be. Alejandro's "illness," then, is hereditary. A similar shadow falls on Isidora Rufete, Alejandro's counterpart in *La desheredada*.

For Alejandro as for Don Quixote, literature is more vivid than life. Fiction encroaches upon reality and effaces the line between the two. In *Don Quixote,* Cervantes charts this process from the very outset; in *El doctor Centeno,* Galdós reveals it gradually, beginning with Part II. Whether or not he is aware of it, Quixote always acts to restore the past—a quality of life itself, the chivalric ideal; Alejandro *dreams* of restoring the past—the glories of Spanish drama—and is concerned mainly with the quality of art. His idealism, by comparison with Quixote's, is a form of egotism, not in the narrow sense, but as the single pole of the romantic psyche. As a visionary his influence is fleeting: Felipe Centeno, his escudero, eventually abandons the pursuit of absolutes to study medicine.

Isidora Rufete *(La desheredada)* tries to impose her idea of reality upon reality itself and fails in the attempt. Having been told repeatedly, from earliest youth, that she is the illegitimate daughter of a noblewoman, she builds a splendid house of cards upon a shaky foundation. Hearsay, coincidence, false documents, and family tradition convince her that her noble pretensions are just. But the law proves otherwise. The cards collapse, and Isidora's entire life is exposed as a fiction. Rather than begin afresh with more modest goals, Isidora, unable to face cold fact, rejects her very name and plunges into the anonymous world of prostitution.

Like Alejandro Miquis, Isidora comes from La Mancha. Her delusions are also contagious. Her brother and stepfather are infected by her pipe dreams, just as Felipe Centeno is dazzled by his master's literary "genius." But Felipe straightens himself out in the long run, whereas Mariano Rufete and José Relimpio succumb to rage, anarchy, insanity, and death. Isidora's quixotism degrades without ennobling.

The difference between Isidora and Alejandro is explained in part by their reading habits. Alejandro reads the popular authors of his day, many of whom still command respect. In some cases, Galdós thought their works outdated, but he never questioned the reputations of the great romantics. Isidora quite simply reads bad literature. It is bad by comparison not only with the classics, but also with the works of a second-rate romantic author like Scribe. Her life shaped by deceit from birth, Isidora strengthens the pattern of self-deception by acting the role of heroine. She foresees the same rags-to-riches, waif-to-marquise destiny that Horatio Alger and "Our Gal Sunday" have oozed off on the gullible in the United States. Isidora reads *novelas por entregas,* and *La desheredada* makes sense only as a parody of this particular genre. All the raw materials, except the quasi-historical setting, are the same: chaste and lovely young girl, seducer, suitor, recognition scene, evil grand-mother, and knight-protector. But everything is then gro-tesquely misshapen: Isidora deflowered, the truth about her mysterious birth revealed, the seducer a Pez, the suitor an ugly lithographer, the recognition scene a debacle, the grand-mother no relation at all, the knight-protector a senile illumi-nato.

Two quotes from *La desheredada* will show how profoundly Isidora was influenced by *novelas por entregas.* The first is from Part I. Isidora has recently come to Madrid to press her claims and reflects upon her prospects:

No es caso nuevo ni mucho menos—decía—. Los libros están llenos de casos semejantes. ¡Yo he leído mi propia historia tantas veces . . . ! Y ¿qué cosa hay, más linda que cuando nos pintan una joven pobrecita, muy pobrecita, que vive en una guardilla y trabaja para mante-nerse; y esa joven, que es bonita como los ángeles, llora

mucho y padece porque unos pícaros la quieren infamar;
y luego, en cierto día, se para una gran carretela en la
puerta y sube una señora marquesa muy guapa, y va a
la joven, y hablan y se explican, y lloran mucho las dos,
viniendo a resultar que la muchacha es hija de la marquesa, que la tuvo de un cierto conde calavera? Por lo
cual, de repente cambia de posición la niña, y habita
palacios, y se casa con un joven que ya, en los tiempos de
su pobreza, la pretendía y ella le amaba. *(4,* 1011)

Three years pass. It is now 1875, and Isidora's position has
indeed changed. She has borne Joaquín Pez a son, her suit is
at a standstill, and she is obliged to find work. But work does
not frighten her:

se le representaron en la imaginación figuras y tipos inte-
resantísimos que en novelas había leído. ¿Qué cosa más
bonita, más ideal, que aquella joven olvidada, hija de una
duquesa, que en su pobreza fue modista de fino, hasta que,
reconocida por sus padres, pasó de la humildad de la guardilla al esplandor de un palacio y se casó con Alfredo,
Eduardo, Arturo o cosa tal? Bien se acordaba también de
otra que había pasado algunos años haciendo flores, y de
otra cuyos finos dedos labraban deslumbradores encajes.
¿Por qué no había de ser ella lo mismo? El trabajo no la
degradaba. ¡La honrada pobreza y la lucha con la adver-
sidad cuán bellas son! Pensó, pues, que la costura, la fabr-
icación de flores o encajes le cuadraban bien, y no pensó
en ninguna otra clase de industrias, pues no se acordaba
de haber leído que ninguna de aquellas heroínas se
ocupara de menesteres bajos, de cosas malolientes o poco
finas. *(4,* 1074)

Isidora's mind is set adrift by *novelas por entregas* in much
the same way that Don Quixote's is by *novelas de caballerías.*
There is no doubt that *La desheredada* has the greatest amount
of Cervantine satire of any of the *Novelas contemporáneas.*[48]

48. Isidora's "uncle," Santiago Quijano-Quijada, is said to dedicate
himself to hunting, gastronomy, and the reading of novels *(4,* 1060).
One can imagine what kind of novels.

Both Cervantes and Galdós, in their respective novels, satirize the same thing—romance—and this explains the difference between Isidora and Alejandro Miquis: Alejandro reads romantic literature whereas Isidora reads the literature of romance. The distinction is an important one, for it separates what is genuine from what is false.

Galdós always despised false literature, as much for its harmful effect on the reader as for its negation of all artistic standards. Among the condemned in his early Quevedesque satire, "Un Viaje Redondo" (1861), are novelists who "propagate ridiculous theories, rose-tinted absurdities, very agreeable at first sight, but which produce the same effect as a dose of poison covered by a thin coat of sugar."[49] The novels Galdós has in mind are a subgenre of the nineteenth-century historical novel. Their most notorious Spanish progenitor was Fernández y González, an admirer of Dumas *père*. Every kind of melodramatic contrivance went into the manufacture of these volumes, which are usually set in the Middle Ages and consist of a series of unlikely adventures. With the increase in literacy among women the adventure tale took on a more pronounced sentimentality, although its melodramatic baggage remained intact. In *Misericordia* Obdulia mentions a characteristic title: *María o La hija de un jornalero*.

These novels were generally published in installments, hence the name novelas por entregas. The novelas por entregas have also been called novelas folletín or novelas popular. Each installment was constructed to end on a note of suspense, thereby whetting the reader's appetite for the next one.[50] No wonder Isidora, until practically the last minute, is sure that her affairs will somehow resolve themselves—the tribulations of pulp heroines disappear in the last installment with a wave of a magic wand.

49. Pérez Vidal, *Galdós en Canarias,* p. 119.
50. Apparently Galdós was not above using this theatrical device in the first and second series of Episodios nacionales: "El autor . . . alcanza aquí efectos que nada tienen que envidiar a los de sus modelos." See Hans Hinterhäuser, *Los 'Episodios nacionales' de Benito Pérez Galdós* (Madrid, 1963), p. 345.

Galdós satirizes the authors of novelas por entregas in the person of José Ido del Sagrario. Don José first appears in the Novelas contemporáneas in *El doctor Centeno,* where he is a schoolmaster's assistant. He tires of his thankless job, which earns him neither respect nor money, and at the end of the novel makes known his plan to write novelas por entregas. His precepts are exactly opposed to those of Galdós. His language will be select and elegant, and his style "literary"; he will praise virtue and condemn vice; above all, he will avoid showing life as it is really lived. "Shun the Quotidian" might serve as his motto.

Galdós championed the realistic novel against the novela por entregas and set out to ridicule the latter in *Tormento,* which follows on the heels of *El doctor Centeno.* By parodying the techniques of serialized fiction he achieves a double aim— he satirizes romance and, at the same time, hits upon a format which evokes to perfection the literary fashions of the 1860s *(Tormento* takes place in 1867–68). [51]

The novel begins at night. Two cloaked figures collide on a dark street corner and start to insult each other. One of them threatens reprisals. The reader is thrust immediately into an atmosphere of romance and adventure. However, the mood is dissipated just as quickly when the two mysterious figures turn out to be Felipe Centeno and Ido del Sagrario. Ido tells his young friend that he is writing a novela por entregas. It is about two orphans who lead a virtuous life in spite of inducements to the contrary. An evil marquis tries to corrupt them and an evil duchess is jealous of their beauty, but the orphaned sisters imperturbably putter about their spotless little room watering their flowers or making artificial ones. Ido has been inspired by events of real life—the Emperador sisters are his neighbors—but for reasons of propriety he feels obliged to change the facts. He whispers the ugly truth about his neighbors to Felipe, who agrees that such a thing ought not to be said. "Ni se debe escribir," says Ido—"¡Qué vil prosa!" *(4,* 1458).

---

51. Hinterhäuser states that the novela por entregas maintained its popularity into the 1870s (p. 349).

Ido believes that art must improve upon nature—the un-
seemly must be banished. Galdós believes that nature imposes
itself inevitably, whether for good or ill. *Tormento* depicts the
substance of Ido's confidence to Felipe.[52] Note that Galdós
begins his novel by incorporating a favorite trick of the novela
por entregas, the device to build tension and mystery. What is
Ido's secret? What is the truth about the Emperadoras? Later
on, when Amparo hides from Marcelina Polo and the latter
assumes the role of amateur sleuth, suspense builds up again:
will Amparo be discovered? And when at the end of Chapter
34 Amparo swallows "poison," the reader dashes on to Chapter 35 to find out what will happen next.

Structurally, then, *Tormento* parodies the novela por entregas, and the parody is most deftly used in characterization and
theme. Refugio and Amparo are orphans but have long since
been deflowered; the lover, far from being a handsome young
nobleman, is an aging, gauche, somewhat uncouth indiano who
wants only to lead a sedentary and conservative life; the seducer
is no roué, but a sanguine, strapping priest; Rosalía, the "evil
stepmother," and Marcelina, the depository of compromising
letters, are comic variants of stock melodramatic types. Galdós
wittily transforms thematic elements: Caballero and Amparo
live happily ever after not as husband and wife, but as man and
concubine; Amparo's "poison" is toothache medicine; her
"suicide" is accompanied by the chirping of mechanical birds
(the romantic fallacy?); and implicit throughout the novel is
a burlesque commentary on that time-honored coup, the
robbing of a nunnery.

Ido del Sagrario reenters the novel in its concluding pages.
He has been in Caballero's employ and therefore is even better
acquainted with the facts than he was before. From the beginning, of course—and this is what he whispered to Felipe—he
knows that Amparo had an affair with the priest Polo. After
her abortive suicide attempt, Ido can think of only two alterna-

---

52. For a discussion of Ido's role in *Tormento* see Frank Durand,
"Two Problems in Galdós' *Tormento,*" *Modern Language Notes, 79*
(1964), 513–25.

tives for her: either she become a Sister of Charity and thereby
expiate her sins or expire in the arms of her would-have-been
husband with sighs of repentance. He chooses both alternatives
for their poetic value. The first particularly would help Ido with
a projected novela por entregas entitled *From the Brothel to the
Cloister (Del lupanar al claustro)*. Galdós, heedless of Ido's
poetic sensibilities, ends his novel with a prosaic trip to France,
where Caballero takes his blemished sweetheart to live without
benefit of sacrament.

Ido's fate is eventually similar to Isidora Rufete's. By the
time he appears in *Fortunata y Jacinta* Ido has ceased to write
novelas por entregas, but the aftereffects of so much romance
prove how dangerous the disease has been. He cannot digest
meat (i.e. anything substantial), and when he tries to, his
physical malaise brings on a peculiar kind of dementia. He
imagines that his wife, the long-suffering and prematurely aged
Nicanora, is having an adulterous affair with a grandee. She is
a "dama infiel" whose transgressions can be washed out only
with blood. Ido, when the fit is upon him, is disposed to redeem
his stained honor in true Golden Age, novela por entregas
fashion.

Anyone unacquainted with Ido's background might call
such extravagant means of revenge cursi, for there are close
ties between theatricality and cursilería. Pose, pretense, and
inauthenticity are inherent in the term, which unfortunately has
no English equivalent. Much of Galdós' satire is directed
against cursilería. The phenomenon itself is implicit in some of
the topics discussed in this chapter. It is present, for example,
in Galdós' description of Spanish politics.

Statecraft is a comedy, and the state, bloated with Peces and
hollow rhetoric, is a vast theater. Time and again Galdós uses
theatrical imagery to satirize the false public life of Spain.
Máximo Manso, an astute observer of the national scene, calls
it "this decorative and theatrical apparatus" and later, "this
vain catafalque of painted canvas" *(4,* 1189). Galdós knew how
false the Restoration was, with its prearranged entrances and

exits and its shabby parliamentarianism. A sound parliamentary system (and for Galdós this meant England's) made the Spanish system look cursi—inadequate to its task, pretentious, poorly imitative, and all gesture and empty ritual.[53]

If official Spain is all pose and puff, so too are the ceremonies and personalities that lend it luster. In *La de Bringas* Galdós describes a lavatorio in the Royal Palace of Madrid. Twenty-four beggars from the streets of the city are bathed, scented, dressed, and brought before the queen and her consort. The monarchs then serve them a sumptuous feast. The beggars, nonplussed at all this splendor, suffer a complete loss of appetite. Half the court takes part in what Galdós calls "the farce of that theatrical scene" *(4,* 1585). It is farcical because it bears no relation to religion, and it is cursi as well. The reader sees a queen and her consort, the heads of state of a country whose treasury is depleted, going through all the motions of pomp and circumstance for a court full of parasites. Both the ceremony and the personalities involved are monumentally threadbare. Isabel, by comparison with Victoria, was a cursi queen.

All kinds of public and private functions take place onstage. Eloísa's dinner parties in *Lo prohibido* are "a comedy; . . . [an] aristocratic *sainete."* This too is cursi, for Eloísa does not have the means to entertain so lavishly. She displays "un lujo prestado y mentiroso" *(4,* 1729). When she tries to imitate the etiquette of wealth her inexperience is obvious. The Duchess of San Salomó is "una cursi por todo lo alto" because she wants to play great roles with a middling fortune *(5,* 1832). Rosalía Bringas makes an appearance at a tertulia with such elegant airs and patronizing demeanor that anyone but a Madrilenian might be fooled into thinking her a notable's wife. But, says Galdós, "en la eterna mascarada hispanomatritense no hay engaño, y hasta la careta se ha hecho casi innecesaria" *(4,*

---

53. The very word is derived from "cursiva," a bastard imitation of English cursive script. See Tierno Galván, "Aparición y desarrollo de nuevas perspectivas de valoración social," pp. 92–93.

1507). The continual acting ends where it has to end—in a masquerade.[54]

Although everyone expects everyone else to act out a role, it is a cardinal sin to overact. When Isidora rejects Joaquín Pez's advances, runs to a window, and threatens to yell for help, the would-be seducer ridicules her melodramatic behavior— "¿Escenita? . . . ¿Gritar en la calle?"—and hurls a scornful "¡Cursilona!" at her *(4, 1041)*. Amparo Emperador intends to give her fiancé a piece of unsavory information but finds the preamble "Yo he sido víctima" too cursi *(4, 1519)*, excessively theatrical and melodramatic. She almost shelves the idea of committing suicide for the same reason: it strikes her as being affected, more appropriate to a play or novel than to real life *(4, 1555)*. Augusta *(Realidad)* also believes that suicide, for any reason whatsoever, is cursi—extravagant and too blatantly emotional *(5, 794)*. Thus, bad taste or bad form become a part of lo cursi.

Galdós and his characters often use the word to denote what is vulgar, common, or passé. This is amusingly shown by a passage in *Lo prohibido* describing the plight of fashionable clothiers who have a number of unpaid accounts on hand. These tradesmen must welcome even their most dilatory clients with open arms, fawning over them and extending them unlimited credit. If they do not, the word will spread that such-and-such a shop stocks nothing but cursilería. The results would be ruinous *(4, 1811)*.

Vulgarity and bad taste are very apt to accompany new money. Senén *(El abuelo)* is called "un cursi tremendo" because his speech and personal habits betray a clumsy attempt at refinement. He succeeds only in being ostentatious *(6, 17)*. Like the waves of cologne he splashes upon himself, everything he does is transparently overdone.

Senén, however, is rich, and cursilería is usually rampant among people who are less abundantly endowed than they would like to appear. It might be likened to social climbing on

54. As early as 1865, Galdós called Madrid a year-round carnival. Life in the city is "todo un año de farsa." See his "Crónica de Madrid," *6,* 1505.

a very precarious ladder, which, in addition to its flimsy support, does not reach quite high enough. Galdós defines cursilería as "un modo social propio de todas las clases, y que nace del prurito de competencia con la clase inmediatamente superior" *(4,* 1035). In *La desheredada* Augusto Miquis enlightens Isidora as to the never-ending flow of cursilería which makes its way along Madrid's Castellana:

> El caso es subir al escalón inmediato. Verás muchas familias elegantes que no tienen qué comer. Verás gente dominguera que es la fina crema de la cursilería, reventando por parecer otra cosa. . . . Como cada cual tiene ganas rabiosas de alcanzar una posición superior, principia por aparentarla. Las improvisaciones estimulan el apetito. *(4,* 995)

Social climbing is all right as long as one does not lose one's footing and stumble. The great fear of all climbers is that their economic liabilities (and this includes insufficient assets) will be discovered by some member of the class to which they long to associate themselves. When this happens, the luckless aspirant is nakedly exposed to the epithet "cursi." In *La de Bringas* Rosalía is told that Milagros—a marquise who stands a notch higher on the social ladder than she—has branded her "una cursi." This is like being stabbed; retaliation is impossible. However, if someone a step higher than Milagros were to catch her short of funds—and the danger is always imminent—then she in turn could be labeled "cursi." So it is all the way up, but not down, the line. Rosalía is not terribly upset that Refugio, a distant relation, knows that she is walking a financial tightrope; Refugio is *beneath* Rosalía and belongs to a social class which the latter has no wish to enter.

Fear of exposure before one's real or prospective peers is basic to the idea of cursilería. Juan Valera put it nicely: "the essence of what we now call *cursi* lies in the exaggerated fear of so appearing."[55] By this definition Rosalía Bringas is a model of her kind. She dreads having to stay in Madrid during the

55. Quoted by Tierno Galván, p. 93 n.

summer, for to do so is a confession of cursilería. People of any means go off to a spa during the dog days, and her not going is a tacit admission of defeat, of having "come down."

To be vulnerable is to be cursi. This is well illustrated by the Miaus. Having once enjoyed a certain affluence, they do everything possible to hide their miserable, makeshift existence in the present. Their clothes undergo a perpetual metamorphosis, with the Miaus affixing a new feather here and a new ribbon there with an eye to prosperity and the latest mode. But they dissimulate in vain—the world has found them out.

Like the shabby genteel Miaus, Ponte, the "proto-cursi" of *Misericordia,* values appearance more than anything else. Furthermore, he knows what it is to be taunted and humiliated because of a decline in one's fortunes. Always on guard, he avoids the downtown area of Madrid lest some old acquaintance remark his caída.

Evasion and disguise are normally associated with insecurity. From the very first, the Spanish middle class was beset with a lack of security and an instinctive urge toward self-protection. It emerged in the nineteenth century with few historical roots and, if one is to believe Tierno Galván, a guilt complex apropos of its manner of enrichment.[56] The nation's bureaucracy was also always at the mercy of political whimsy, and bureaucrats, along with rentiers, formed the backbone of the middle class. This was especially the case in Madrid.

Nothing so fortifies a weak person as the contemplation of greater weakness in someone else; therefore, whoever makes an accusation of cursi or cursilería against someone or something else is artificially bolstering his own security. Lo cursi involves a descent from bourgeois norms of conduct and appearance on the part of weak and vulnerable members of the middle class,[57] but the accusation itself—and this is the supreme irony—is made from a position of weakness, not of strength. The vicious cycle ends, in Tierno Galván's words, in "la irreducible convivencia de casi todos en la misma latente

56. Ibid., pp. 92–93.
57. Ibid., pp. 97–99, 106.

flaqueza."[58] This "latente flaqueza" was an almost universal poverty. As one of Galdós' characters says, "aquí, salvo media docena, todos son pobres" *(4,* 1662). The entire Spanish middle class, with few exceptions until later in the century, was cursi by comparison with that of other western European nations. Since the Restoration was the refuge and the tool of this class, one can understand why Spain's "great power" pretensions in the latter decades of the nineteenth century were so tragicomic. The defeat suffered in the Spanish-American War was a revelation of national cursilería.

Ortega y Gasset sees in the word "cursi" the embodiment of nineteenth-century Spanish history:

> La cursilería como endemia sólo puede producirse en un pueblo anormalmente pobre que se ve obligado a vivir en la atmósfera del siglo XIX europeo, en plena democracia y capitalismo. La cursilería es una misma cosa con la carencia de una fuerte burguesía, fuerte moral y económicamente. Ahora bien, esa ausencia es el factor decisivo de la Historia de España en la última centuria.[59]

In the Novelas contemporáneas, Galdós treats the theme of cursilería more extensively than any other author in any body of fiction. This is one reason why these novels have become invaluable historical documents.

Galdós satirizes lo cursi either by direct narrative commentary or—and this is more often the case—by proxy. He will choose a personage immune to the vice and will have him or her unmask it. This process, in which the discrepancy between appearance and reality is set before the reader, involves the use of irony.

58. Ibid., p. 106.
59. José Ortega y Gasset, *El Espectador* (Madrid, 1943), p. 933.

Chapter 3: IRONY

Any novelist who captures life in the round is an ironist, whether he sets out to be one or not. Life, with its unforeseen twists and turns and its traps for the unwary, is itself ironic. The *grande route* to which Stendhal refers in his famous definition has many rough stretches and may even present a thorny appearance throughout its entire length. Irony, even the lightest kind, is a way of reacting to these impediments. It may be gentle, good-natured, mocking, scornful, or sublimely indifferent. Irony also denotes an attitude toward that part of life not of one's own making, beyond the pale of knowledge or reason. Hence its concern with coincidence and fate.

Although irony is a part of life, the ironic attitude is one of detachment from it. One stands back, and his emotions become disengaged. He is no longer at the mercy of people or events but feels superior to them. In literature, as in life, irony is an anesthetic which checks the emotions while permitting the cerebral faculties to continue operating.

This, of course, is the position of the spectator—author, reader, or ironic outsider. The great mass of men and women, who are too wrapped up in themselves to stand back and who comprise the main subject matter of the novelist, are full of illusions regarding themselves and others. Possessed of high hopes, ambitions, ideals, and passions, they generally lack the ironic perspective. This is superimposed by the author. As an observer of human nature, he knows that reality makes inroads on illusion and often destroys it completely.

The novelist, whose primary task is to create the illusion of life, often exposes and punctures the illusions which regulate his characters' lives. Some novelists have gone so far as to expose their own novels as fiction, that is, as just one more illusion. This is a frequent device of Thackeray and is called the "romantic-ironic" mode of narration. But usually the novelist is satisfied to contrast what people expect from life with what they get out of it. The trajectory is likely to end in disappointment. When a character in Balzac's *Père Goriot* exclaims, "J'ai perdu toutes mes illusions," she unwittingly summarizes one chapter in the history of prose fiction, a chapter that begins with *Don Quixote*.[1]

Sometimes disappointment and disillusionment give to the fictional character a renewed strength and a healthy dose of self-knowledge. This is what happens, rather comically, in Galdós' *La de Bringas*. Rosalía, who discovers that Pez is really not the chivalrous nabob she thought he was, learns from her disillusionment and resolves not to make the same mistake twice. There are bigger fish in the sea, and she goes after them. Máximo Manso also survives an initial self-deception, learns from his experience, and is so completely undeceived that he becomes a full-fledged ironist. When seen for the last time, he is contemplating the world from afar—the ironic perspective—and finds the view both trivial and amusing. Manso resides in thin air; his irony is appropriately a variation of cosmic irony, whereby the fret and toil of mankind occupy an infinitesimal dot in the universal scheme of things.

Cosmic irony is the most extreme form of ironic detachment and plays a vital role in two of Galdós' finest characterizations —Maxi Rubín *(Fortunata y Jacinta)* and Benina *(Misericordia)*. Maxi voluntarily retires from the world. Purged of all earthly passion, he stands before Fortunata's grave and says to Ballester, "Miremos las cosas desde lo alto" *(5,* 546). These words are an invocation to cosmic irony. By the time he arrives at the mental institution of Leganés, Maxi has divested himself of all material ties: "Resido en las estrellas. Pongan al llamado Maximiliano Rubín en un palacio o en un muladar . . . . Lo mismo da" *(5,* 548). His grief, which arose from an ill-fated involvement in life, is neutralized as soon as he withdraws into himself. In the future, his view of the world will be that of the cosmic ironist.

Maxi's end is doubly ironic. Apart from his own detachment,

---

1. Balzac even called one of his novels *Illusions perdues*.

he has been placed by his creator in that ironic enclave which acts as a buffer between comedy and tragedy. "In comedy," one critic has said, "reconcilement with life comes at the point when to the tragic sense only an inalienable difference or dissension with life appears."[2] Maxi stands midway between comedy and tragedy, for he reconciles himself to nonlife and is happy to leave the world.[3]

Benina, the heroine of *Misericordia,* has also had a disillusioning bout with the world. As a human symbol of providence, she assumes that everyone is as good as she and consequently suffers a bitter lesson of ingratitude. *Misericordia* could have ended on this note of bitterness, but Galdós wanted to show how Benina triumphs over an emotion unworthy of her. Her victory is expressed in terms of cosmic irony:

> miró la vida desde la altura en que su desprecio de la humana vanidad la ponía; vió en ridícula pequeñez a los seres que la rodeaban, y su espíritu se hizo fuerte y grande. Había alcanzado glorioso triunfo; sentíase victoriosa, después de haber perdido la batalla en el terreno material. *(5,* 1986)

On this same plane of ironic detachment, Benina invites Almudena to share in her victory over ingratitude and, more important, over her own human reaction to it: "debemos hacer lo que nos manda la conciencia y dejar que se peleen aquéllos por un hueso, como los perros; los otros por un juguete, como los niños, o éstos por mangonear, como los mayores, y no reñir con nadie, y tomar lo que Dios nos ponga delante, como los pájaros" *(5,* 1988). Benina is Galdós' greatest heroine and one of his most striking characters. Her triumph rests on a profoundly ironic attitude toward mankind.

The confrontation scene between Rosalía Bringas and Refugio Emperador (Chapters 45-48 of *La de Bringas)* is a fine example of how irony may be used to pulverize a cursi's self-

2. Constance Rourke, *American Humor* (New York, 1953), p. 202.

3. There is a strange parallel in this respect between Maxi Rubín and Máximo Manso.

esteem. Refugio's lacerating sarcasm, which grinds Rosalía to a pulp, makes this episode one of the most powerful that Galdós ever wrote.

Sarcasm is a cruel form of irony, taunting, spiteful, and bitter—a form of verbal revenge. Refugio's revenge is wholly warranted. At one time she and her sister Amparo depended on the Bringas family for support. In return for the crumbs they received from the Bringas' none-too-abundant table and a monthly pittance, the sisters had to endure Rosalía's "humos de marquesa" *(Tormento, 4,* 1482). This was especially galling for Refugio, who escaped the bondage of a contemptuous and condescending charity by striking out on her own.

In her emancipated (or "loose") state, Refugio gets a back-stage peek at Madrid society. Men relax in her company; she learns their secrets; they pay for the privilege; she learns how much they can afford to pay. Her education is complete when she tries to sell boutique wares to the fashionable women of the city. This experience teaches her that nearly everyone shares a common bond of poverty. Most of her customers cannot pay their bills, and some even try to borrow money from her. When Rosalía Bringas comes to her door hoping to borrow five thousand reales, Refugio answers the request with the accumulated venom and malice of an untouchable who suddenly shuffles the caste system to her own advantage.

It must be remembered that, for Rosalía, Refugio is almost a "nonperson." She stands completely apart from the treadmill of cursilería. Her scale of values—she is honest and frank—is entirely different from that of her former protectress.

Refugio begins by sympathizing with Rosalía. Her first comment is "Qué más quisiera yo . . . . Bastante siento que se vaya usted con las manos vacías" *(4,* 1661). Rosalía is humiliated by this patronizing tone, and its net effect puts her more tightly within her adversary's grasp. The reader, of course, is aware that Refugio feels only a sadistic pleasure, hence the sarcasm of her expression of sympathy.[4] There is greater

4. For the role of pity in irony, see Tierno Galván, "Aparición y desarrollo de nuevas perspectivas de valaración social," p. 99, and

sarcasm still in Refugio's observation, "Francamente, yo creí que usted daba a rédito, y no que tomaba" *(4,* 1661). She thinks nothing of the kind. A backward glance at *Tormento* reveals that Refugio has long since drawn a balance sheet of the Bringas' finances: "en aquella casa no hay más que miseria, una miseria mal charolada . . . . Parecen gente, ¿y qué son? Unos pobretones como nosotras. Quítales aquel barniz, quítales las relaciones, ¿y qué les queda? Hambre, cursilería" *(4,* 1482).

Refugio now pours salt on the wound. When Rosalía offers to pay interest on the loan of five thousand reales, she is told that among members of the family such an offer is unnecessary. By feigning intimacy with the family who once treated her as maid, ward, and charity case, Refugio pulls them down to her level. She knows how much they disapprove of her conduct and how painful it is for a cursi like Rosalía to descend to the same level as a churchmouse orphan whose social standing is nil.

After making some remarks about the so-called cream of Madrid—their poverty and scorn of the honest poor who do not cheat on appearance (remarks pertinent enough to make Rosalía squirm)—Refugio takes deadly aim and hits home with the following: "Bien podía el señor de Pez librarla a usted de estas crujías . . . . Pero no siempre se le coge con dinero. Tronadillo anda el pobre ahora" *(4,* 1664). Rosalía, who on the previous day had given herself to Pez thinking—errone-ously—that he would pay for services rendered, is mortified at these words. They imply, first, that Refugio is aware of what has happened. Second, the diminutive "tronadillo," the expres-sion "el pobre," and the very exact appraisal of Pez's unreliable affluence mean that Refugio has been on the most familiar terms with him. She too has sold herself to Pez, and what is more, she has been paid—if not always, at least some of the time. The logical conclusion is that she is worth more than

---

Haakon M. Chevalier, *The Ironic Temper* (New York, 1932), pp. 5–10. In this book about Anatole France, the author does not distinguish between pity and commiseration, nor does he say that pity need be an inherent part of the ironist's attitude. He says merely that pity makes France's brand of irony more gentle.

Rosalía. In spite of the latter's "humos de marquesa," she too is revealed as a prostitute and—the culminating horror—an unsuccessful one at that. Then there is the additional shame of knowing that Pez's adulation—he was supposedly captivated by Rosalía's beauty, elegance, and distinction—was only a ruse. He wanted to get gratis what he usually had to purchase, and quality was of no concern. The scene ends as Refugio informs Rosalía that a friend has branded her "una cursi." To be thus portrayed is punishment enough, but for the information to be transmitted by a prostitute is unbearable.[5]

I cannot leave this scene without drawing attention to Galdós' use of ironic symbolism. Just as the Royal Palace and the cenotaph in other parts of the novel anticipate ruin and disintegration, so too does Refugio's apartment anticipate the coming revolution. It is a chaotic jumble of good and bad objects. Everything is strewn about, "como si *una mano revolucionaria* se hubiera empeñado en evitar allí hasta las probabilidades de arreglo" *(4,* 1659; italics mine). Refugio and her maid Celestina are on such democratic terms with each other that one would think class distinctions had already been abolished. This equality of prostitute and procuress foresees a period of anarchy and easy morals, a period well under way by the time the novel ends.

Finally, there is an element of farce here which may be related to ironic reprise.[6] Rosalía, once the master, is now the servant. She helps Refugio to dress and arranges her hair for her. "Vaya una doncella que me he echado," exclaims Refugio sardonically *(4,* 1665).[7] The psychological switching of roles is thus expressed physically.

Refugio shocks Rosalía into facing the truth about herself: if she wants to cease being a cursi, she must throw morality to

5. Had Refugio called her "una cursi" instead of attributing the remark to a marquise, the insult would have been much less effective. See Chap. 2, p. 75, above.

6. See Chap. 1, p. 17, above.

7. The master-turned-servant motif dates back to Plautus and classical farce. See William H. Shoemaker, "Galdós' Classical Scene in *La de Bringas," Hispanic Review, 27* (1959), 423–34.

the wind. Rosalía learns the lesson. The woman at the end of
La de Bringas is at once corrupt and strangely chaste. She is
less hypocritical than before and with ever greater daring
begins to wear the contraband gowns which she kept in hiding
for so long. She foregoes excuses and apologies: "Ya estaba
resuelta a explicar sus irregularidades con la incontrovertible
lógica del *porque sí" (4,* 1666). She conducts the adulterous
affairs in which she gets involved just as openly: no moral
qualms, no hesitancy, no need for self-justification hold her
back. Perhaps the greatest irony in *La de Bringas*—and again
it is a form of ironic reprise—is Rosalía's final assimilation of
Refugio's standards. As her career progresses and her novice-
like inexperience is transformed into sophisticated routine,
Rosalía might proudly proclaim with Refugio, "vivo de mi
trabajo, y nadie tiene que ver con mis acciones, y lo primero que
digo es que no engaño a nadie, que el que no me quiera así,
que me deje, ¿está usted?, porque de lo mío como" *(4,* 1663).

Refugio's is the voice of insight and experience. The Novelas
contemporáneas are full of such voices, piercing the vanity,
self-deception, and delusion to which so many of Galdós'
characters are prone. Miquis and La Sanguijelera *(La desheredada),* the narrator of *Lo prohibido,* Feijoo *(Fortunata y Jacinta),* Víctor *(Miau),* Mancebo *(Angel Guerra),* and don Lope
(Tristana) are, in varying degrees, clairvoyants who "know the
score." Although susceptible to error, on most occasions they
take an incisive, less nearsighted view of reality than their
companions.

Miquis and La Sanguijelera are ironic whenever they twit
Isidora and her noble pretensions. Miquis' weapon is sarcasm,
and he makes no effort to hide it. He addresses Isidora as
"archiduquesa" and "marquesa" in a futile effort to bring her
down to earth *(4,* 1046). La Sanguijelera is somewhat more
forceful. Although she too uses sarcasm—"vuecencia," "sere-
nísima majestad," "duquesa," " marquesa"—she quite literally
brings Isidora to her knees with a good thrashing *(4,* 984–85).
La Sanguijelera's reaction to Isidora's romantic vagaries is
very socarrón, an ironic quality which will be discussed shortly.

José María de Guzmán, the narrator of *Lo prohibido,* is

ironic when he ridicules the society to which he belongs. As both insider and outsider he is well qualified to point up the truth behind appearance, especially with regard to wealth. Appropriately, he uses theatrical terms ("comedia," "aristo-crático sainete") to describe his cousin's cursi banquets *(4, 1729)*. The whole tone of his narration is disabused and detached, as if he were describing a play that he has seen many times.

Don Evaristo Feijoo is one of Galdós' finest minor characters and could well be a self-portrait of the author. He is a moralist and is most tolerant of human frailty: "sé que decir *humanidad* es lo mismo que decir *debilidad" 5, 334)*. Feijoo's tolerance is particularly active where weakness of the heart is concerned; it is little wonder therefore that he and Fortunata get on so well together. He becomes her mentor, training her how to behave with her husband and with doña Lupe. The latter, a problem for most people, is an open book for Feijoo: "Leo en ella como leo en ti," he tells Fortunata *(5, 347)*. His worldly wisdom makes him a supreme ironist. Life no longer holds any sur-prises for him; he manipulates it at will: "Toda la ciencia del mundo la poseía al dedillo, y la naturaleza humana, *el aquel de la vida,* que para otros es tan difícil de conocer, para él era como un catecismo que se sabe de memoria" *(5, 343)*.

If Feijoo is wise to the ways of the world, Víctor Cadalso (a watered-down, almost comic version of Balzac's Vautrin) has an intimate knowledge of the underworld, the Administra-ción. The preceding chapter described how Cadalso latched on to some skirts and how his career began to flourish thereafter. He appears here among Galdós' ironic characters because he is so evidently "in the know." If the state is amoral, he reasons, its employees must also be amoral for self-protection. They cannot afford to be honest like Villaamil: "¿No hemos de ponernos a cubierto de la ingratitud del Estado agradeciéndo-nos nosotros mismos nuestros leales servicios?" *(5, 584)*.

Don Lope, who describes himself very accurately as a "perro viejo" and a "lince," is as penetrating a student of human nature as Feijoo. From what he knows of the world and of the female psyche in particular, he realizes that Tris-

tana's love affair with Horacio is doomed. Tristana, he perceives, is in love with a product of her imagination, and
Horacio, for his part, will cease to love a maimed girl. Lope is
right; things turn out as he thought they would. As a positivist
among idealists, he sees right through el bello ideal.

The priest Mancebo deserves a more thorough analysis than
any of the foregoing, because of all the clairvoyants he is the
most obviously humoristic. Mancebo's salient trait is his
socarronería, a quality that is the opposite of naïveté, ingenuousness, or gullibility. Its possessor must have an earthy
temperament, a knowledge of the human mechanism, and an
astuteness which can hold its own against any attempted
swindle or trick.

Angel Guerra believes that by sharing Leré's spiritual vocation he will sublimate, or at least compensate for, his erotic
frustrations. Mancebo, with "socarrona perspicacia" *(5,* 1419),
is the first to realize that Guerra's love is not sacred but profane.
In a monologue he ponders Guerra's religious zeal: "todo ese
furor católico que le ha entrado no es más que los movimientos
desordenados y el pataleo de la amorosa bestia que lleva en el
cuerpo" *(5,* 1416–17). Mancebo's perception of what is going
on inside Guerra is comparable to Refugio's insight into
Rosalía's character. In both cases, the observer is better
acquainted with the facts than the participant. Here is precisely
where socarronería becomes a part of irony: it reveals the
superiority of the spectator over some defect, dupery, or
foolishness which he observes and from which he feels exempt.
It also has that tinge of pity which denotes the ironic attitude.[8]

Socarronería differs from other forms of irony in its uniquely
Spanish flavor. *El caballero encantado,* stylistically the most
castizo of the Novelas contemporáneas, has more socarrón
humor than any of the others. In this novel, socarronería is the
homegrown wisdom of commonfolk, a wisdom often conveyed
by the refrán, or proverb.[9] It takes a good deal of talent and

8. Tierno Galván, p. 99.
9. See, for example, *6,* 299: a character who uses refranes incessantly speaks "con su habitual socarronería refranesca." This kind of

perspicacity to choose just the right refrán to fit a specific situation. These are of no avail, however, without a solid, almost flat-footed immersion in reality. Sancho Panza, in spite of his frequent lapses into simplicity, is still the archetypal socarrón, and Cervantes' novel remains the foremost treatise on socarronería.[10]

Sancho is never more himself than when he displays an out-and-out skepticism with regard to his master's grasp of reality. Returning to Mancebo, one feels a certain resemblance between him and Sancho. He too is a skeptic, although not in the philosophic sense. His incredulity concerning Guerra's spiritual conversion is justified. Here, socarronería and earthy realism hold him in good stead, but a priest's heavy reliance on these qualities is bound to result in mirth. They automatically dignify the temporal at the expense of the spiritual. The result in Mancebo is ludicrous: his secular and religious interests, forced to coexist, cannot always do so harmoniously. Only in a dream can he work out his conflict of interests: supremely happy, Mancebo sees himself the finance minister of England while at the same time "presbyter and beneficiary of the Cathedral of Toledo" *(5,* 1417). It would be difficult to say whether this ideal represents materialistic religion or religious materialism. Perhaps it would be more charitable to align Mancebo with Sancho Panza once more and say that he combines native shrewdness with faith.

The latter half of the nineteenth century, that Age of Parliamentarianism, may also be called the Age of Materialism.[11] However, one would not ordinarily expect a priest to be

---

humor is also called "humor sentencioso y castizo" (p. 249) and "nativo ingenio picaresco" (p. 252). On the question of Spanish humor, Galdós' prologue to *La Regenta* should be consulted.

10. Torquemada, after reading *Don Quixote,* uses many "ejemplos y dichos" from the novel with "castellana socarronería" *(5,* 1065). I might add that Mancebo is not much given to mouthing refranes. His speech is socarrón because it is colloquial and droll. It is very much like the speech of Guillermina Pacheco in *Fortunata y Jacinta.*

11. See the book by Carlton Hayes, *A Generation of Materialism* (New York, 1941).

in the vanguard of such an age or to accept its demands with such expediency and dispatch. "Ahora hay que aplicarse a defender el materialismo de la existencia," says Mancebo, "porque los demás a eso van, y no es cosa de quedarse uno en medio del arroyo mirando a las estrellas" *(5*, 1325). He is true to his word. As the breadwinner of a large family, Mancebo is intent on finding some relief for his expenditures. His hopes rest on his niece Leré. If she consents to marry Angel Guerra the whole family will be rich. The only drawback is that Leré is bent on becoming a nun; her vocation is sincere and nothing in the world will deter her. "¡Vaya con la muñeca mística . . . , qué ventolera le ha dado! Olvidarse así del interés de la familia" *(5*, 1331). Thus Leré is belittled by the very person— a priest—who should encourage her spiritual ambitions. Mancebo's worldly preoccupations—"esa otra teología del vivir material" *(5*, 1396)—are simply anachronistic within the context of his profession. In a prelate, this would be unsavory as well as anachronistic. Mancebo, however, is not the kind of religious to inspire anticlerical feelings. He seeks not so much wealth as a rest from care, and his worldliness has none of that drawing room bonhomie associated with the "society" priest.[12]

Two kinds of irony, then, make up the characterization of Mancebo. One is the socarronería of the personage himself; the other is Galdós' ironic presentation of him, whereby his incongruousness is set before the reader. Mancebo is incongruous because he refutes a preconceived norm: the average layman thinks priests otherworldly rather than positivistic. Even a hypocritical or lustful priest is more easily reconciled to literary stereotypes or personal prejudice than one who openly, and with polemic zest, defends "the materialism of existence."

Mancebo's ideology seems to be at odds with the nature of priesthood. The irony of incongruity always entails some clash with nature, convention, or the social norm (does human nature consist of anything more than consecrated norms of behavior?). For example, the marriage of Maxi Rubín to

12. Compare Mancebo, for example, with don Manuel Flórez in *Halma*.

Fortunata *(Fortunata y Jacinta)* runs counter to the nature of matrimony. Society expects, first, that a marriage be consummated and, second, that husband and wife enjoy some degree of compatibility, however slight. This is not the case with Maxi and Fortunata. Thus their union lacks integrity; it is incongruous. The same is true of Torquemada's relationship to God *(Torquemada en la hoguera).* Belief in God must rest on faith. The nature of religion itself is contingent on faith. But Torquemada's one and only thought with regard to divine favor is "money talks." He deals with God. It is a concrete business arrangement. When God fails to comply with His part of the bargain, He becomes a disreputable businessman in Torquemada's eyes. *Torquemada en la hoguera* owes much of its compactness to its having been organized around a single nucleus: Torquemada's practical attitude toward extraterrestrial affairs, an incongruous attitude.

Much of the humor and tragedy of the Novelas contemporáneas is derived from the irony of incongruity which shows life forever contradicting itself. The sadly neglected *Tristana* (1892) illustrates its presence in these novels. *Tristana* is only incidentally about la mujer nueva. Critics who have confined themselves to the social implications of its theme—superficially that of female emancipation—have been led astray. They have not given this subtle novel its proper due.

There are three main characters in the novel: don Lope, the aging guardian and seducer of Tristana, a beautiful young girl who falls in love with Horacio, a young painter. From this bare outline the reader probably expects to find something on the order of *The Barber of Seville:* don Lope, the senex of the classical triangle, will get his comeuppance, and the young lovers will exult triumphantly in each other's arms.[13] This would be the socially desirable ending; it would satisfy convention. But life is not so simple. At the novel's end, don Lope, the viejo verde, the decrepit Don Juan, the wicked guardian, the despoiler of Tristana (note the suggestion of incest) has married his ward. The lecherous stepfather (antisocial norm)

13. See Frye, *Anatomy of Criticism,* p. 180.

has become the platonic husband (antisocial norm). Horacio has fallen out of love with Tristana and has married someone else (antisocial norm). Instead of fulminating about this unexpected and undesirable turn of events, Galdós merely shrugs his shoulders. Observing don Lope, the "pacífico burgués," contentedly feeding his hens and Tristana fussing over pastries in her kitchen, Galdós asks, "Were they happy, both of them?" His answer, "Perhaps" *(5,* 1612).

As in *Fortunata y Jacinta, Tristana* shows the disparity between two marriage partners, a disparity so extreme as to give rise to the irony of incongruity. Here the resemblance ends. Nature reasserts itself in *Fortunata y Jacinta,* and a union which, from the reader's point of view, is a travesty of the institution of marriage is finally dissolved. Fortunata dies, and Maxi is brought to an asylum. The novel ends as it *must* end, and the reader is satisfied with the denouement. It is a tragic solution, but a solution nevertheless. Everything adds to the impression of consonance: Jacinta has her child; Santa Cruz, unable to retain the love and respect of his wife, is sufficiently punished; Maxi finds a haven from the humiliating and bitter world of practical reality; and Fortunata has been granted her "idea" as a reward for her final magnanimous gesture.

No such resolution of discord takes place in *Tristana.* Having asked in the beginning, "How is don Lope going to be outfoxed; how is this incongruous situation to be resolved?" the reader is forced to make a violent readjustment. The anticipated fairy-tale ending never comes. Nature does not correct the mistakes of men. The incongruous relationship between Tristana and don Lope not only continues but is legalized. The ironies are compounded as Tristana—whom the reader expects to be thrown into despair—casually and complacently goes about her domestic chores. She has married *willingly.* She might even ("perhaps") be happy, for the novel ends on a note of problematic felicity.

Galdós handles brilliantly the progression from comedy to tragicomedy and from one kind of incongruous irony to another. Both Tristana and don Lope gradually lose their ideals, their independence, and, above all, their delightful eccentricities. They compromise themselves by accepting what they scorn the most—marriage. Thereafter they corrode. What makes the novel so poignant is that the characters are seemingly unaware of their descent into vulgarity. The wonderful old rake and the unique girl cease to be interesting. When the reader perceives this, he confronts the culminating irony of the novel: Tristana and don Lope are oblivious to their fate.[14]

The plot of *Tristana* is a variation on a well-worn comic theme. Traditional elements of comedy have been turned inside out to produce a startling new effect. In another of the Novelas contemporáneas—*Lo prohibido*—these elements are kept intact but are so thoroughly smothered in naturalistic decor that they discourage any convincing interpretation of the novel. Such an interpretation would have to take into account the following: at the heart of the novel lies the triangle of José María de Guzmán (Don Juan), Camila (virtuous wife), and Constantino Miquis (trusting husband). This is the central donnée. As is typical of comic plots, the "hero" (husband) is a relative nonentity. Most of the interest is centered on the anti-hero, who in *Lo prohibido* happens to be the narrator. At the end of the novel the anti-hero, or heavy, is punished. He is figuratively castrated (recall his soprano voice) and loses all desire and capacity to possess Camila sexually. After a brief

14. The so-called flaws in the novel are nothing of the kind. Netherton speaks of its "arbitrary ending" and the "surgeon *ex-machina*" who amputates Tristana's leg (see his "The *Novelas españolas contemporáneas* of Pérez Galdós: a study of method," pp. 64–65, 200). Tristana's diseased imagination makes the ending inevitable, and her physical crippling is symbolic of her crippled spirit (compare Alejandro Miquis in *El doctor Centeno*). After the amputation ("aquel simulacro de muerte"), she begins "su nueva vida" (5, 1598). This new life is a life without will. It is no accident that Tristana's operation marks the definitive end to her love affair with Horacio, as the lynx-like don Lope realizes all too well: "Para mí, es cosa terminada . . . terminada . . . ; sí, señor . . . , cosa muerta, caída, enterrada . . . como la pierna" (5, 1604). The love affair, of course, gave Tristana a chance to be independent. She loses this independence when she substitutes abstract idealization for flesh-and-blood reality. Her loss of limb and lover become equally indifferent to her.

period of ostracism he regains the good graces of Camila and her husband.[15]

This superstructure has a fretwork that is also basically comic: feminine ineptitude in financial matters (Eloísa); the hypocritical bluestocking (María Juana); the cuckolded husband (Carrillo); the satire of cursilería, new money, financiers, and so on; physiological humor; the picardía of the heroine Camila and her amazon strength (her easily won battle with the narrator is pure farce and is similar to an episode in Alarcón's *El sombrero de tres picos);* the gratuitous moralizing of the narrator after he has become impotent; and, finally, the reference to José Ido del Sagrario as the scribe to whom the narrator has entrusted his memoirs.

When the narrator mentions the name of Ido del Sagrario, the experienced reader of Galdós is suddenly assailed by the thought that he has been "taken in." Immediately afterward, he is forced to admire the ironic twist which reinforces the book's comic design in its final pages. Who is the real narrator of *Lo prohibido,* José María de Guzmán or Ido del Sagrario? Despite José María's protestations to the contrary ("puedo asegurar que nada hay aquí que no sea escrupuloso traslado de la verdad," *5,* 1888), one has the nagging sensation that these so-called "prosáicas aventuras" are in some way a product of Ido del Sagrario's fecund imagination. Galdós, of course, assumes that the reader of *Lo prohibido* has also read *El doctor Centeno* and *Tormento,* where Ido's literary precepts are clearly set forth. We have already seen how these precepts are directly opposed to any "escrupuloso traslado de la verdad."[16] Ido believes that vice should always be punished and virtue rewarded. *Lo prohibido* is the only one of the Novelas contemporáneas in which this pat formula is carried out to the letter.

The incorporation of Ido del Sagrario in these final pages— and he could easily have been dispensed with—serves only one purpose: to invest the novel with an extra dimension of

15. Frye mentions "the tendency of the comic society to include rather than exclude" and also discusses the importance of "grace" in Shakespearean comedy (p. 166).

16. See Chap. 2, p. 70, above.

irony. In truth, this dimension has been present in the general tone of *Lo prohibido*—world-weary, sophisticated, risqué, facetious, and, above all, detached. Ido del Sagrario's curtain call at the end accentuates this last quality. The reader is warned not to accept the preceding narration on faith, but to eye it askance—ironically. The reader's attitude toward the book as a whole thus coincides with the narrator's attitude toward the people and events he describes therein. The reader becomes the "clairvoyant" and the outsider.

As soon as Ido del Sagrario's shadow is evoked by the narrator, Galdós and his readers become accomplices. It is as if they had joined forces to commit the same felony, succeeded, and returned home unapprehended. The irony of *Lo prohibido* is based on complicity between author and reader. It is a private joke. This is not the irony of incongruity, but something I shall call "structural irony."

Structural irony is wholly dependent upon narrative technique. In the *Novelas contemporáneas* it is usually derived from the equivocal role of the narrator. This is the case in *La de Bringas, Nazarín, El amigo Manso,* and *Lo prohibido.* Is one to trust José María de Guzmán (who "dies" before his memoirs are published and is unable therefore to offer positive assurance that Ido has not tampered with the facts), or is one to trust oneself as an experienced reader of Galdós? The very ambiguity of the problem, which is essentially that of appearance versus reality, is ironic. *Apparently,* José María's document is true; *in reality,* it might well be romanced. Who will believe that these events, in their grotesque accumulation, are "sucesos que en nada se diferencian de los que llenan y constituyen la vida de otros hombres" *(4,* 1888)?

In his excellent *The Rhetoric of Fiction,* Wayne Booth distinguishes between narrators who are "mere observers" and "narrator-agents, who produce some measurable effect on the course of events."[17] The structural irony in *Lo prohibido* stems from the sudden realization on the reader's part that not one

17. *Rhetoric of Fiction,* pp. 153–54.

but possibly two narrator-agents have had a hand in the events described. A similar case of structural irony occurs in *La de Bringas*. At the beginning of Chapter 6 of that novel, the narrator serves notice that he is removing himself from its pages: "quiero quitar de esta relación el estorbo de mi personalidad" *(4,* 1581). In fact, the reader soon forgets all about him. Except for a few seemingly insignificant "yo's," *La de Bringas* reads like a third-person narrative. But the reader is deceived into thinking the narrator a mere observer. Actually, he is a narrator-agent. It is on the basis of his testimony in the concluding paragraph of the book that one is made to feel the irreproachable truth of everything related previously. As a bigwig in the new revolutionary government, the narrator had attracted Rosalía's attention. She had been his mistress for a while and, only recently, had tried to renew their understanding: "Quiso repetir las pruebas de su ruinosa amistad, mas yo me apresuré a ponerles punto, pues si parecía natural que ella fuese el sostén de la cesante familia, no me creía yo en el caso de serlo, contra todos los fueros de la moral y de la economía doméstica" *(4,* 1671). The narrator turned narrator-agent thus proves beyond question that Rosalía has settled into a profligate and promiscuous existence. He is the eyewitness turned guinea pig.[18] The structural irony of *La de Bringas* substantiates the truth of the narration. That of *Lo prohibido* puts the truth in doubt. In both cases, Galdós adds a rich new dimension to conventional storytelling technique.

Another device of structural irony which Galdós uses (and abuses) throughout the Novelas contemporáneas is the "chronicle" device, whereby the author pretends to have gleaned his data from some venerable and unimpeachable source. In the midst of *El caballero encantado,* he speaks of "estos verídicos

18. Ricard, in *Aspects de Galdós,* pp. 59–60, points out the equivocal effect of the narrator's "francamente, naturalmente" *(4,* 1670). This, of course, is Ido del Sagrario's muletilla. If Galdós wanted the reader to think that Ido was narrating *La de Bringas,* he failed completely. The reader's knowledge of the personage rules out the possibility of his having taken part in the revolution or of his having enough money to tempt Rosalía.

anales" *(6,* 302); he then states that he obtained his material from a "precioso códice de Osma" and from several "historias conservadas en el archivo de los Franciscanos Descalzos de Ocaña" *(6,* 333). This amount of documentation is rare. Galdós is usually content with a simple "esta verdadera historia," "esta real historia," "esta verídica narración," or the like. It is amusing to note that in *La razón de la sinrazón* he resorts to the chronicle device even though the work is avowedly a "fábula teatral absolutamente inverosímil": "No se relata la muchedumbre de platos servidos ni el sazonado condimento de ellos, porque las crónicas de que se ha extraído esta fábula teatral mencionan muy a la ligera los manjares" *(6,* 391).

The utilization of documents of which the author acts as custodian may either intensify or dilute narrative objectivity. Camilo José Cela intensifies the photographic realism of his *La familia de Pascual Duarte* because he handles his "factual" material with the utmost gravity and assumes a dry, reportorial tone which approximates nonfiction. In the Novelas contemporáneas, however, the chronicle device emphasizes the fictitious nature of the narrative. By detaching himself from the narrative—he claims to be no more than a middleman—Galdós actually blazons his authorship. This occurs because, for one thing, the device is used too often and merely becomes idiosyncratic of Galdós' style. For another, it is used tongue in cheek. A case in point is *Nazarín.* When Nazarín and his companions approach a town, the author pleads ignorance as to its name: "las referencias *nazarinistas* son algo oscuras en la designación de esta localidad" *(5,* 1736); later "las crónicas nazaristas" are just as vague about the name of another town *(5,* 1764). These protestations of ignorance are in keeping with the narrator's comments at the end of Part I of the novel. Here the reader is warned that the forthcoming account of Nazarín's adventures, though true, is of doubtful authorship. The situation is further confused by a play of words designed to blur the boundaries between fiction and nonfiction: "yo mismo me vería muy confuso si tratara de determinar quién ha escrito lo que escribo" *(5,* 1691). This Unamunoesque paradox and the chronicle device with which it is associated play havoc with the narrative structure of *Nazarín*. One cannot become totally immersed in the hero's adventures because the illusion of life is subordinate to the concrete reality of literature.

The reader is forcibly detached from Nazarín and his companions. He is aloof and never shares their tribulations. He is implicitly superior, tending to view their comings and goings ironically. "Irony increases his sense of being a spectator, so that his sensibilities are not overwhelmed by the vicissitudes of the dramatic action."[19] This ironical attitude, which Galdós bequeaths to the reader, does not seem in keeping with the subject matter of *Nazarín*. The subject matter is of a lofty and spiritual nature—the evangelical ideal—and wants a more impassioned treatment, one less apt to elicit impartiality or indifference. The chronicle device is an invitation to levity; the emphasis on literature per se is a plug to urgency. Proof that Galdós knew what he was doing in *Nazarín* is available in *Halma,* where several characters discuss the former novel. Nazarín himself takes part in the discussion *(5,* 1812–13; see also p. 1797).

A special label governs the narrative technique which reminds the reader to read a work of fiction *as literature*. It is called the "romantic-ironic" mode of narration.[20] In this, as in so much else, the evolution of fiction owes a debt to Cervantes. Galdós, in *Nazarín* and *Halma,* follows Cervantes' lead very closely. He never admits that Nazarín is a fictitious character, just as Cervantes staunchly defends Quixote's real existence, although in both cases the reader is party to the joke. Cervantes' use of the chronicle device and literary trompe-l'oeil had the advantage of novelty, however. With the passage of time the novelty has worn off, unless, as in Cela's case, an author succeeds in pouring new life into the old mold. The narrative structure of *Nazarín* and *Halma* (considered now as Parts I and II of the same novel) is so obviously shopworn and

19. David Worcester, *The Art of Satire* (Cambridge, Mass., 1940), p. 141.
20. Wellek and Warren, *Theory of Literature,* pp. 212–13.

derivative that it seems to be either a homage to Cervantes or an exercise in playful tongue in cheek.[21]

Galdós adopts a romantic-ironic narrative to greater advantage in *El amigo Manso*. Here structure and content fit like hand in glove. This delightful jeu d'esprit has none of the transcendent symbolism of *Nazarín*. Manso's autobiography begins with a confession of nonexistence: "Yo no existo." The reader's suspension of belief is immediate; he has no time to extricate himself from the premises with a wry scoff of superiority. The mood of the piece is established right away and is framed in fantasy. Even Manso's reference to "este verdadero relato" *(4,* 1166) is part of the fun. One has no choice but to enter into the spirit of the novel. In *El amigo Manso* the romantic-ironic device enters on its own terms, in the guise of a self-conscious narrator; in *Nazarín,* it comes through the back door and subverts respect for the latter-day Christ who is the hero of the novel.

Manso not only acknowledges his fictitious status but gallivants it. The whole of Chapter 1 is taken up with his birth. He relates how a "friend"—the author of some thirty volumes—enticed him from the limbo of ideas; how he, Manso, accepted corporeality in exchange for a few literary trinkets; and how he came into the world with the usual birthpangs. Chapters 2 through 49 make very discreet use of the romantic-ironic technique. The reader is drawn into the intrigue as he would be by any well-constructed novel, only to be jolted now and then by a reminder that all is mirage.

These reminders are an object lesson in authorial tact. They come not from Galdós but from several characters in the novel itself. What is more, these characters ignore the full import of their words. Since they have no inkling that Manso is an invention, the significance of some of their remarks can be caught only by the reader. This is a comic variation on Sophoclean or dramatic irony. For example, Manuel Peña,

21. It goes without saying that Galdós tried to strengthen, rather than destroy, the fictitious world of *Nazarín*. He was not consciously a romantic ironist. We, however, are concerned with the end result.

Manso's disciple, points an accusing finger at his mentor and exclaims:

> Usted no vive en el mundo, maestro . . . . Su sombra de
> usted se pasea por el salón de Manso; pero usted perma-
> nece en la grandiosa Babia del pensamiento, donde todo es
> ontológico, donde el hombre es un ser incorpóreo, sin
> sangre ni nervios, más hijo de la idea que de la Historia
> y de la Naturaleza; un ser que no tiene edad, ni patria,
> ni padres, ni novia. *(4,* 1215)

Since Manso is a professor of philosophy, this may be taken at face value. What Peña does not realize is how apt it is in the context of Manso's "Yo no existo." Another reminder, like-wise expressed by Sophoclean irony, is the pejorative "meta-físico" which José María Manso flings at his brother *(4,* 1189).[22]

In Chapter 50, Manso decides that he has outlived his usefulness on earth. With little fuss and with the aid of his creator, he dies. Serene once more, he watches with pity and amusement the consternation of those who mourn for him.[23] From his aerial Elysium, they look like pathetic little figures, the toys of childhood as seen by the mature man *(4,* 1291).

"Come, children, let us shut up the box and the puppets, for our play is played out." So Thackeray ends *Vanity Fair. El amigo Manso* is more of one piece: it is not Galdós, but his fictitious "idea," who meditates on vanitas vanitatum. Although a mirage, Manso never quite disappears.

The romantic-ironic structure gives to this novel an aesthet-ic interest which the "inner novel" would not have achieved on its own. Even the casual reader may find himself drawn to certain problems never heeded before: literature as magic, the author as conjurer, the autonomy of fictional characters, and the autonomy of a work of art. *El amigo Manso,* with *Lo pro-*

22. For a discussion of Sophoclean irony, see below.
23. See Worcester's comments on Chaucer's Troilus (p. 137). How different Galdós' cosmic irony is from that of his contemporary Thomas Hardy!

hibido and *La de Bringas,* is enhanced by its ironic narrative
structure. If *Nazarín* is not, the fault lies in its separation of
form and content.

Sophoclean irony is the investing of words or actions with
a dual meaning, one harmless and one ominous. In Greek
tragedy, where it was extensively used, it thrilled a public already acquainted with the outcome of a given plot. A tremor
of superiority would unite members of the audience as Fate
appeared onstage, unbeknown to the very character who
evoked it and who was most likely to suffer at its hands. This
portent, clothed in innocence, was a bond between individual
members of the audience and between the audience en masse
and the playwright. Again one can see how irony thrives on
complicity.

Although Sophoclean irony is not restricted to tragedy, it is
still mainly a theatrical device, comparatively rare in prose
fiction. A play is of short duration. The spectator, even if
unacquainted with the plot and unmindful of Sophoclean
irony at the moment it occurs, can easily backtrack mentally
and make the necessary adjustment. It is much harder for the
reader of a novel to recall a verbal omen which he skimmed in
some early chapter. And how many readers can be expected
to reread a novel with an eye to the fine points of structure?
The novelist, if he wishes to make effective use of Sophoclean
irony, usually substitutes a dream or vision for the bit of
dialogue employed by the dramatist. He may also help the
reader along by suggesting the outcome of his plot beforehand.

Galdós occasionally used Sophoclean irony to reinforce the
humor of his novels. Two examples from *El amigo Manso*
have just been cited, and several more appear in *La de Bringas*.
Galdós was able to use Sophoclean irony here because the
events announced ironically—Bringas' blindness and the Revolution of 1868—are easily foreseen by the reader. As soon as
Galdós describes Bringas' microscopic genius and uncanny
"seguridad de vista" *(4,* 1574) it becomes clear that his sight
cannot last. And when a little girl admires the cenotaph, saying,
"¡Alabaaado Dios . . . , qué dedos de ángel! Don Francisco,

se va usted a quedar ciego . . ." *(4,* 1584), the reader is more or less "in the know." The suspension points, which are in the original, are especially ominous. As for the revolution, it is historical fact. Bringas might pooh-pooh the idea, but a revolution did occur in 1868, the year the novel takes places. One must also remember that contemporary readers of Galdós would have been far more sensitive to Sophoclean hints at the revolution than readers of today. The events of 1868 for many of them were personal experience, not merely historical fact.

When Bringas says, "Cuando vea, ¡Dios mío!, voy a encontrar la casa hecha una lástima" *(4,* 1621), his words are at once harmless and portentous. He does not realize how well they apply to the national household as well as to his own domestic nook. When the oculist Golfín tells Bringas "Usted verá lo que nunca ha visto" *(4,* 1630), an augury is couched in the innocent remark. The irony of Golfín's words, in a literal sense meant to cheer and comfort the patient—i.e. "You'll see better than ever"—can be understood only by the reader. Isabelita's dreams are equally prophetic. In one, she envisions the entire palace population shouting "Ya es la hora" *(4,* 1586), and in another, Rosalía and Pez are engulfed in a river of blood *(4,* 1638). Alfonsito's passion for moving vans *(4,* 1649–50) seems innocent enough but is rewarded more handsomely than either he or his parents could ever have imagined.[24]

Galdós uses Sophoclean irony not only to forecast Bringas' blindness and the impending revolution but also to show how the revolution failed to rid Spain of its entrenched bureaucracy. In Chapter 6 of *La de Bringas* the reader learns that countless pigeons inhabit the outer embrasures of the Royal Palace:

> En los infinitos huecos de aquella fabricada montaña habita la salvaje república de las palomas, ocupándola con regio y no disputado señorío. Son los parásitos que viven entre las arrugas de la epidermis del coloso. Es fama que no les importan las revoluciones; ni en aquel

24. Recall also Luisito's final vision in *Miau.*

libre aire, ni en aquella secular roca hay nada que turbe
el augusto dominio de estas reinas indiscutidas e indis-
cutibles. *(4,* 1579)

Much later, in the penultimate chapter of the novel, the Royal
Palace is taken by the revolutionaries and rebaptized "Palace
of the Nation." Doña Cándida rushes in to give Bringas the
news and praises the exemplary behavior of the descamisados:
"¿Robar? Ni una hebra. ¿Matar? Si acaso, alguna paloma. Dos
o tres de ellos se han entretenido en cazar a nuestras inocentes
vecinas; pero con muy mala fortuna. Los revolucionarios
tienen mala puntería" *(4,* 1669). Without realizing it, Cándida
(a "paloma" herself) announces the survival of the bureaucratic swarms who live off the state. The "palomas" are really
Peces.

Ironic characters, thematic irony, and structural irony alone
do not account for the distinctive tone of the Novelas contemporáneas. This special tone is a result of verbal irony, which
may be compared to a glaze whose sheen keeps the reader at a
distance from surface details so as to give him an unobstruct-
ed view of the entire panorama. It may be found in dialogues
and monologues, as well as in the sarcasm of Refugio Emperador and the socarronería of Mancebo. More often, though, it
is the peculiar nuance which the narrator gives to the people
and events he describes. The reader, on receiving the narrator's
information, is led by verbal irony to interpret it dispassionately
and with due regard for its relative lack of importance. Irony's
negative bias is nowhere more obvious than it is here.

Galdós' narrative style has not been known to inspire any
great enthusiasm among literary critics. They agree that he
was never at a loss for words, that he had a wonderful ear for
dialogue and a prodigious memory for colloquialisms, but they
accuse him at the same time of being coarse, diffuse, and
heavy-handed. It is said that he lacks finesse. The more indulgent critics brush these defects aside in light of Galdós' huge
output. They imply that so prolific an author cannot be
expected to write fine prose.

It is true that Galdós' style is hardly crisp and often coarse (although this is more appropriate to his subject matter than a cameo classicism would be). However, much of the criticism that has been leveled against Galdós in this respect is a carry-over from the Generation of 1898. The writers who are collectively known as the Generation of 1898—Azorín, Baroja, Valle-Inclán, Unamuno, and others—rebelled against the excess verbiage and artistic tawdriness of their immediate predecessors. They also rebelled against subject matter dealing with the urban bourgeoisie, the class which epitomized Restoration braggadocio before and during the Spanish-American War. Galdós was too much a product of his times to escape the unfavorable judgment of these "angry young men." The very fact that he wrote voluminously about the Madrilenian middle class was enough to stigmatize him; the fact that his outlook was basically lenient made things worse.

It was easier to lump Galdós' work in a single heap than to examine his novels one by one, judging each on its own merits. Had this been done fifty years ago, the generalizations heard today regarding his use of frases hechas, his windy digressions and lapses of taste, would be balanced by an appreciation of his stylistic amenities. It is one thing to get a bird's-eye view of a novelist's production and quite another to pretend that variations in quality do not exist. Scott, Balzac, Trollope, and Galdós wrote an enormous amount, their works may look the same from far off, but up close they may be vivid, dull, flat, textured, uneven, or excellent. This is true of the Novelas contemporáneas.

Many of these novels are as well written as anyone could wish. Others—for the most part those in dialogue—are deadly. The main reason for this difference in quality is structural rather than thematic: the novelas dialogadas leave little room for verbal irony, which flourishes best in a narrative setting. Much of Galdós' theater is virtually unreadable because the genre is nonnarrative. The special ironic tone—that wedge between sentimentality and declamation—is missing.

I shall illustrate four kinds of verbal irony here: denotative, connotative, irony of tone, and irony of reference.[25] Denotative irony is very close to sarcasm and occurs when the author uses a word to denote its exact opposite. When Galdós calls Bringas' cenotaph "esta bella obra de arte" *(4,* 1574), the reader substitutes "fea" for "bella" and that's that. A lengthy description has made it quite clear that the cenotaph is a morbid monstrosity. This uncomplicated form of verbal irony can easily be overworked. Galdós uses it sparingly.

Connotative irony is more subtle. The literal meaning of a word is maintained but is qualified by contextual overtones. Here the reader must be aware of the tone of the work as a whole in order to catch the ambiguity of a specific word in a specific context. In *Torquemada en la hoguera* Galdós refers to the "santa y laboriosa paz" in which Torquemada and his wife lived for forty years *(5,* 907). This is indeed admirable, until one stops to consider that Torquemada is a usurer and that doña Silvia is no less ruthless than her husband in all matters pertaining to business—hence the connotative irony of the word "laboriosa." Another example from the same novel is information to the effect that don José Bailón "vivía . . . muy a lo bíblico, amancebado con una viuda rica que tenía rebaño de cabras y además un establecimiento de burras de leche" *(5,* 912). Though in keeping with the pastoral subsistence of Bailón and the widow, "bíblico" has overtones very awkwardly suited to this display of domestic rusticity.

Connotative irony can produce the most delicate shadings. Of the various reactions to doña Lupe's death, Galdós writes: "Los parientes lo habían tomado con calma, y la criada y la portera mostraban una tendencia al consuelo que había de acentuarse más, cuando se llevasen el cadáver" *(Torquemada en la cruz,* 5, 940). The phrase "tendencia al consuelo" gives a pointed edge to this remark. If one *tends* to do something, one is *impelled* or *driven* to do it by temperamental inclination. To tend not to be overly affected by a person's death, therefore,

25. For these categories, as well as for much of the following, I am indebted to Miss Hutchens' article, "Verbal Irony in *Tom Jones.*"

implies indifference or perhaps satisfaction. Here is a picture of doña Lupe as her attendants see her. The reader is already aware that her treatment of servants is painfully maternal (recall Papitos in *Fortunata y Jacinta);* the grief alluded to above can be only a sacrifice to decorum. It will end as soon as the relatives and corpse clear out.

Irony of tone, the most common form of verbal irony in the Novelas contemporáneas, speaks to the "inner ear" of the reader. Its effectiveness rests on phraseology, punctuation, and word order. In *Tristana,* don Lope seduces his young ward just two months after having been made her guardian. This is an especially callous act, because Tristana's mother entrusted her daughter to Lope from her deathbed. Such a legacy ought to be sacred and inviolate. This one is not: "Total: . . . que Tristana se fué a vivir con don Lope, y que éste . . . (hay que decirlo, por duro y lastimoso que sea), a los dos meses de llevársela aumentó con ella la lista ya larguísima de sus batallas ganadas a la inocencia" *(5,* 1546–47). Here the parenthetical remark stifles all feelings of disgust or anger because it trickles in as an afterthought. The reader is not agile enough to leap from an offhand confidence to a disclosure of infamy. The remark, then, clothes the entire sentence in triviality. The euphemism "batallas ganadas" also hides whatever is scabrous in Lope's behavior.

A similar effect is achieved as Galdós protests against don Lope's doctrine of free love: "Inútil parece advertir que cuantos conocían a Garrido, incluso el que esto escribe, abominaban y abominan de tales ideas, deplorando con todo el alma que la conducta del insensato caballero fuese una fiel aplicación de sus perversas doctrinas" *(5,* 1547). This tirade is too emphatic to be taken seriously. The words "abominaban," "abominan," "deplorando," "insensato," and "perversas," all hellfire and brimstone, are not typical of Galdós' vocabulary. The subordinate clause "incluso el que esto escribe" sounds like a parenthetical statement when read aloud. And from what is known about Galdós' own love life, which was very nomadic, one may discount his condemnation of

Lope's. Galdós was always more indulgent with libertine behavior than with the lip service paid to accepted standards of
morality.

Irony of reference was defined in Chapter 1 as a comparison
between two subjects—one ordinary and one extraordinary—
a comparison so outrageous as to emphasize the banality of
the original subject. There is no need to repeat the examples
given there, but I do wish to reiterate how thin a line separates
referential irony from metaphor, a cornerstone of romantic
realism. This can best be done by citing a passage which par-
takes of both referential irony and metaphor in equal degree.

When introduced to the reader for the first time in *Tormento,*
don Francisco Bringas and his wife are installing themselves in
a new apartment. For the reader there is nothing momentous
in a chore like this, but for Bringas and Rosalía it is a heroic
action, requiring a vast expenditure of energy and valor. In
order to point up the difference between things as they are
and things as they are thought to be, Galdós uses the irony of
reference. Bringas, on all fours, disfigured by the dust and
ridiculously attired, is called a "dignísimo personaje," whose
"persona respetabilísima" is engaged in "funciones augustas"
(4, 1460). This high-flown language immediately takes him
down a peg. Galdós then says that Bringas is an exact physical
replica of the French historian Thiers. Again there is a devaluation: Bringas looks like Thiers, but spiritually and intellectually he is an "hombre común," born to fix a lock and nail a
rug *(4,* 1461). As he goes from room to room, summoned here
and beckoned there, Bringas exclaims, as Napoleon exclaimed
when he learned of Trafalgar, "Yo no puedo estar en todas
partes" *(4,* 1462). The absurd comparison with Napoleon in
this context underlines the unheroic, mediocre nature of
Bringas and his activities. At the same time, the contextual
association of Bringas with Thiers and Napoleon, an association which I call "metaphor," gives this entire passage a
boisterous intensity it would not otherwise have.

Rosalía, meanwhile, has been scouring, sweeping, and dust-
ing. Aided by Amparo and the maid, she makes some headway

against the forces of grime. Observe the battle imagery in which Galdós envelops the scene:

> La nube [of dust] las envolvía y cegaba como el humo de la pólvora envuelve a los héroes de una batalla; mas ellas, con indomable bravura, despreciando al enemigo que se les introducía en los pulmones, se proponían no desmayar hasta expulsarlo de la casa. Funcionaba después lo que un aficionado a las frases podría llamar la artillería del aseo, el agua, y contra esto no tenía defensa el sofocador enemigo. *(4,* 1461)

This is still irony of reference, but memories of the original subject—a trifling household task—are slowly giving way before extended metaphor. The process continues as Galdós hurls his combatants onto an epic plane, where Infection and Purification and Matter and Spirit are locked in eternal combat: "esta alternación de infección y purificación es emblema del combate humano contra el mal y de los avances invasores de la materia sobre el hombre, eterna y elemental batalla en que el espíritu sucumbe sin morir o triunfa sin rematar a su enemigo" *(4,* 1461). One cannot imagine an "objective realist" describing a housecleaning in these terms.

Where, then, does referential irony end and metaphor begin? They are almost indistinguishable here. An ironic devaluation of subject matter has become an exuberant piece of romantic-realist prose, and the transition has been imperceptible. Metaphor is the link between irony and hyperbole.

Chapter 4: METAPHOR

Satire and irony whittle away at the world and pare it down to its proper size. Metaphor does just the opposite: it distorts, inflates, dramatizes, and frequently poetizes reality. Like the irony of reference (which it often accompanies), metaphor is a contextual association between a subject and a correlative. The original subject is usually trivial and dull; its correlative redeems this triviality and dullness. The correlative may be historical, literary, or religious or may involve an animal comparison, a physiological tic, or nature imagery. There is frequent overlapping among these.

Galdós makes his novels more readable through the use of metaphor. The very subject matter of the Novelas contemporáneas—life during the Restoration—demands a shot in the arm, and metaphor, along with caricature and the creation of types, meets this need.

One example of metaphor is already familiar from a different context. Don Francisco Bringas exclaims, amid the bustle of his household duties, "Yo no puedo estar en todas partes," Napoleon's words upon hearing of the French defeat at Trafalgar. Napoleon is, at this moment, Bringas' correlative. The two men are placed back to back on the same coin, and the coin is metaphor. Here it is a historical metaphor, because Napoleon, the correlative, is a historical figure. True, the juxtaposition of hero and mock-hero ends with an ironic devaluation of the latter; the "romantic monster" and "raton-cito Pérez" are absurd companions.[1] But, for the time being, this is irrelevant. What matters is that Galdós has relieved the potential drabness of his context through a "mechanism of

---

1. Hinterhäuser (Los 'Episodios nacionales' de Benito Pérez Galdós, p. 271) remarks that in the Episodios nacionales, Napoleon is the incarnation of the "monstruo romántico"; Rosalía thinks her husband is a "ratoncito Pérez" in La de Bringas (4, 1657).

compensation," which in this case produces laughter.[2] Such compensation is necessary because of the basic subject matter of the Novelas contemporáneas.

The Generation of 1898 saw Galdós as a chronicler of gray lives in a monochrome era. For Baroja, his novels reproduce "la vida un poco mediocre y trivial" of Restoration society.[3] Unamuno, in a series of newspaper articles written on the occasion of Galdós' death in 1920, is more trenchant: "Apenas hay en la obra novelesca y dramática de Galdós una robusta y poderosa personalidad individual, uno de esos héroes que luchan contra el trágico Destino y se crean un mundo para sí, para sí mismos." And he adds: "La obra novelesca de Galdós es la pintura de una época y una gente profundamente anti-heroicas."[4] Unamuno was willing to concede that Galdós portrayed his society faithfully. He might also have said that Galdós had the intellectual capacity to see *through* this society, for Galdós was quite aware that his world was stagnant and, collectively at any rate, unheroic.

Beginning with *La desheredada,* where he refers to "la índole de los tiempos, que repugnan la epopeya" and to the "siglo prosaico" *(4,* 1038), Galdós makes frequent allusions to the mediocrity of his age. Generally his characters speak for him. Máximo Manso complains that Irene is of a common mold, "formada según el modelo de mediocridad en el gusto y hasta en la honradez, que constituye el relleno de la sociedad actual" *(4,* 1274). Leré, accused of conduct unbecoming a novice, rejoices in the slander because it provides an "ocasión de martirio, que rara vez se presenta en estos tiempos de vida tonta, dentro de la cual no hay drama humano ni divino, ni proporción alguna de hacer grandes méritos" *(5,* 1420). Halma describes her brother and his circle as nonentities: "No son

2. Gullón uses the term in reference to dreams in Galdós, but the phrase is applicable to many aspects of romantic-realistic technique. See *Galdós, novelista moderno,* p. 177.

3. Pío Baroja, *La caverna del humorismo* (Madrid, 1919), pp. 146–47.

4. Miguel de Unamuno, *Autodiálogos* (Madrid, 1959), pp. 99, 106.

malos, pero tampoco son buenos; viven en ese nivel medio moral a que se debe toda la vulgaridad y toda la insulsez de la sociedad presente" *(5,* 1862). Gamborena's words to Cruz del Aguila and her sister imply that great deeds are anachronistic at the present time: "La voluntad humana degenera visible-mente, como árbol que se hace arbusto, y de arbusto, planta de tiesto; no se le pueden pedir acciones grandes . . . . No, hijas mías. No os diré nunca que seáis heroínas, porque os reiríais de mí y con razón" *(Torquemada y San Pedro, 5,* 1136).

In the Novelas contemporáneas there are few personages heroic enough to dispel these impressions of lethargy and mediocrity. Galdós does isolate, from time to time, men and women worthy of emulation, but these are more estimable than heroic. The traditional accouterments of heroism—epic stature, daring exploits, great achievements, fame, acclaim, and the like—are missing. One exception is Gamborena, who claims to have conquered, in the name of God and the Faith, "porciones de tierra y de humanidad tan grandes como España" *(5,* 1119). Trailing behind Gamborena are other activists like Guillermina Pacheco and Nazarín. For the most part, however, Galdós' characters are passive. Their greatest triumph is to be at peace with themselves after undergoing hardship or despair, an attainment which the author calls "conformidad." At one point he says that conformidad is "perhaps the supreme ideal of man" *(5,* 1340). By this standard, Benina *(Misericordia)* is Galdós' most heroic figure. But even her victory is passive: by the time *Misericordia* draws to a close, she is willing to accept "lo que Dios . . . ponga delante, como los pájaros" *(5,* 1988).

Individual conformidad is replaced by collective pluck and the will to survive in *El caballero encantado.* Here, for the first time, a bit of the epic sweep of the early Episodios enters the Novelas contemporáneas; heroism is one with national survival. In this novel Galdós sets forth a program of national regeneration which La Madre articulates. But the program is more allegorical than concrete, and the heroic effort it requires is more hopeful than real. Furthermore, the very need to instill in Spaniards a spirit of heroic dedication means that such a spirit is dead or at best quiescent in them.

Galdós wrote the Novelas contemporáneas at a time when heroism, or its traditional concept, was very much a thing of the past.[5] His heroes reflect this. For most of them, heroism or any kind of personal distinction is a question of wishful thinking and nostalgic contemplation.[6] Nostalgia fires their imaginations. Contrary to what Unamuno said, Galdós' characters are unheroic but rarely anti-heroic. Many have their dreams of glory like everyone else. Galdós weaves these dreams of glory into the fabric of his novels, and in so doing, he follows the standard path of realism, which ends in the exposure of illusion. However, exposure is concurrent with disclosure, and the latter—the setting up of illusion in order to knock it down—is part of the element of romance in realism. Recall Levin's definition of realism: "the imposition of reality upon romance, the transposition of reality into romance."[7] Romance is as much a part of realism as dreams are a part of life. If few of Galdós' characters stand out from the crowd on the basis of inherent superiority, epic stature, or "tragic destiny" (Unamuno's words), their own imaginations help to make them unique.

Metaphor is a technique used in narration and characterization. Whether Galdós constructs a subject–correlative himself, or whether his characters, out of impotence or frustration, construct their own in their imaginations, the results are much the same: in both cases, a mechanism of compensation transforms the miasma of Restoration life.

5. One should remember, however, that Galdós balanced contemporary banality with an account of national heroism in the first series of Episodios nacionales. In the last paragraph of Trafalgar, Gabriel Aranceli boasts that he was witness to several heroic episodes of Spanish history: "Mi destino, que ya me había llevado a Trafalgar, llevóme después a otros escenarios gloriosos o menguados, pero todos dignos de memoria" (Benito Pérez Galdós, Trafalgar [Buenos Aires, 1956], p. 158). Through Gabriel, Galdós relived the saga of the War of Independence, Spain's greatest moment since the Golden Age. Although forced to search the past for heroic exploits (and in this backward glance he resembles certain characters in the Novelas contemporáneas), Galdós did have a vicarious "Lepanto" to look back on.

6. Gullón, p. 146.

7. The Gates of Horn, p. 55.

Metaphor stands at the convergence of two streams, one narrative and the other delusional. The two are of equal importance in Galdós, although one critic has recently denied this equality:

> El proceso de transformación artística . . . mediante el cual la materia es 'elevada' en las novelas de Galdós, probablemente depende del estilo y de la técnica en grado comparativamente pequeño. Pero el proceso de elevación siempre está activo en el terreno del retrato de caracteres.[8]

This is an artificial division. Style and technique cannot be separated from characterization.[9] Both are interlocked, both are mechanisms of compensation, and both tend to offer the reader something other than commonplace, humdrum reality. These two subdivisions—Galdós' narrative technique and his technique of characterization—can be related to the single pole of metaphor. Whenever possible, I shall choose examples of metaphor which involve a humorous transformation of context. *La desheredada* affords two examples of metaphor which illustrate the subdivisions described above. Thirty-four months elapse between the events in Part I of the novel and those in Part II. In order to fill the reader in on what has happened in the intervening period, Galdós provides a brief chronicle of Isidora's history from March 1873 through December 1875 *(4,* 1065–68). As usual, he feels obliged to document his account; in this instance José de Relimpio is the source of information. More important is the juxtaposition of private and public history, whereby Galdós automatically elevates the former to a new level of interest. Here is the résumé of news corresponding to December 1873:

> Castelar reorganiza el Ejército. La patria da un suspiro de esperanza. Se convence de que tiene siete vidas, como

---

8. Sherman Eoff, "Galdós y los impedimentos del realismo," *Hispanófila,* No. 24 (May 1965), p. 31.

9. A caricature, for example, is a *retrato* dependent on a very special technique.

vulgarmente se dice de los gatos. La marea revolucionaria
principia a bajar. Se ve que son más de lo que se creía los
cimientos de la unidad nacional. El 24, Nochebuena,
Isidora da a luz un niño, a quien ponen por nombre
Joaquín. Háblase ya de la sima de Igusquiza y se cuentan
horrores del feroz Samaniego. *(4,* 1066)

The juxtaposition of Isidora's private life and the national
affairs of her country is appropriate because both are going
through a period of anarchy. The Second Carlist War is raging
in the north. On the home front Isidora is having an affair with
Joaquín Pez, squabbling with him continually. Isidora's domestic crisis, then, is a symbolic reflection of the Spanish political
crisis. One need not know anything about the Carlist War or
its symbolic reverberations in Isidora's own life to see how
Galdós has transformed his context through metaphor. Had he
merely summarized Isidora's life during these thirty-four
months, the result might have been dry, orthodox narration—
"filler"—designed to bridge a chronological gap. By joining
Isidora's life to a historical correlative, Galdós heightens its
interest for the reader. The account of her ups and downs is
newsworthy, gossipy, and amusing.

The humor in this passage is a direct consequence of Galdós'
use of metaphor, for although history upgrades Isidora, she
degrades history. In the quotation above, the parenthetical
reference to her delivery in the midst of what might be called
"headline news" makes the latter seem trivial. Metaphor, in
this instance, devaluates public history while elevating private
history. Here one can see the intimate bond between metaphor
and the irony of reference.[10]

Galdós was by no means the first to use contemporary history as a correlative to workaday events or, in so doing, to
memorialize the commonplace. Balzac was his immediate
forerunner. A phrase from the "Avant-propos" to *La Comédie*

---

10. Galdós wrote *La desheredada* in 1881, six years after the
Carlist War. The relative stability of the Restoration allowed him to
look back on the events of that conflict ironically.

humaine shows to what extent Balzac, as the novelist-historian of everyday life, saw the importance of his task.

> En saisissant bien le sens de cette composition, on reconnaîtra que j'accorde aux faits constants, quotidiens, secrets ou patents, aux actes de la vie individuelle, à leurs causes et à leurs principes, autant d'importance que jusqu'alors les historiens en ont attaché aux événements de la vie publique des nations.[11]

By putting everyday life on a par with history in the traditional sense, Balzac paved the way toward that commemoration of the one and devaluation of the other which appears in *La desheredada*. In the nineteenth century, "la vie publique des nations" lost forever its sacred armor and became the butt of humor as never before. One has only to think of Daumier's political cartoons to realize how comic abuse of "la vie publique" (or contemporary history) became a fine art in the nineteenth century.

The escape from prosaicism often involves a flight into the past. History fascinates those who yearn for a change of identity or locale. For many of Galdós' characters, history and romance are practically synonymous. (This of course is in direct contrast to Galdós' own belief that history and realism go hand in hand.)

The contextual association of Isidora Rufete and the Second Carlist War is a historical metaphor which helps Galdós avoid monotony in his narrative. The metaphor below, which Isidora constructs in her own imagination, is a mechanism of compensation, and again the metaphor counteracts monotony. This time it originates from within the character, not from without.

Isidora eventually goes to prison on a charge of falsification of documents. The only way she can quell her shame is to search out a historical precedent. She considers herself a

---

11. Honoré de Balzac, *La Comédie humaine, 1,* 12–13. Antonio Regalado García, in *Benito Pérez Galdós y la novela histórica española: 1868–1912* (Madrid, 1966), pp. 150–51, credits Sir Walter Scott with having been the first major writer to combine historical events and private fictitious events within the same narrative.

persecuted aristocrat; it is therefore quite natural that by a
process of mental legerdemain she should compare her experience to Marie Antoinette's in the Conciergerie. Isidora believes
that she is being harassed not by the masses, the descamisados,
but by her jealous fellow aristocrats. She takes pleasure in
visualizing an ideal society in which "un populacho fino o
. . . . una plebe elegante y bien vestida" replaces the nobility
(4, 1134). What Galdós slyly calls "a daring excursion into the
future" happily preserves the Second Estate and is about as
revolutionary as a promenade from Versailles to La Petite
Trianon.

Isidora's correlative at this moment is Marie Antoinette.
Doña Catalina de Alencastre *(Angel Guerra)* adopts a more
extensive web of correlatives. The flux of her imagination
sweeps aside all geographical and chronological obstacles. At
one time or another she claims to be a descendant of the Reyes
Católicos, the English Royal House of Lancaster, and the
Byzantine emperors. Although her aberration is more extreme
than Isidora's, both women share a similar mechanism of
compensation. La de Alencastre, like Isidora, tries to escape
vulgarity and poverty. When under an emotional strain she
flaunts her imagined ancestry and vents a paroxysmal scorn on
her plebian husband. The mere mention of palaces and castles
unsettles her. Galdós aptly describes one of her outbursts as
an "escena tragicómica" *(5,* 1356).

Doña Catalina's lucid moments counterbalance her spiraling
imagination—she is never totally mad. Her imagination, however, is what makes her interesting. Galdós was perhaps aware
that she and the rest of her family were too unique, too eccentric
for most readers, but he was not unduly concerned about this.
It is a sign of the romantic realist's approach to fiction that
what is normal has little to do with what is real or true. When
Galdós first introduces the Babel family, he asks the reader to
accept its members at face value, even if they seem unbeliev-
able: "los Babeles . . . son de todo punto inverosímiles, lo cual
no quita que sean verdaderos" *(5,* 1216). No student of Galdós'
realism can afford to overlook this remark.

The historical correlatives which Isidora Rufete and doña

Catalina de Alencastre invent when they feel oppressed by
reality are specific figures from the past. By and large, however,
Galdós' characters do not assume any specific historical role.
Instead, they float off into a vaguely chivalrous, vaguely heroic
golden age. Such is the case with José de Relimpio *(La desheredada)*. The stimulus to Relimpio's dreams of glory is
alcohol. When drunk, he imagines himself Isidora's protector,
"el noble, enamorado y valiente caballero, defensor y amparo
de la hurí" *(4,* 1162). Rosalía Bringas needs no artificial stimulus to draw her away from the pedestrian life she leads, unless
don Manuel Pez can be qualified as such. Pez represents the
chivalric ideal, the gallant savior of ladies in distress. By comparison with the insipid Bringas, he is practically a symbol of
knightly love. Note how the author registers Pez's appeal to
Rosalía's sensibilities: "¡Y qué finura y distinción de modales,
qué generosidad caballeresca! . . . Seguramente, si ella se veía
en cualquier ahogo, acudiría Pez a auxiliarla con aquella deli-
cadeza galante que Bringas no conocía ni había mostrado
jamás" *(4,* 1627). Rosalía considers herself worthy of Pez; she
believes they were meant for each other. Therefore she too, in
her imagination, is an exile from that uncertain period of history when all men were caballeros and all women damas.

Maxi Rubín *(Fortunata y Jacinta)* evades reality—the most
painful aspect of which is his own timidity and rickety physique—by taking refuge in a fantasy life of heroism and adventure. He imagines himself a soldier, in martial attitudes; in his
pipe dreams he corrects his thinning hair, misshapened nose,
and crooked legs; and when he walks down the street he pretends to be "pursuing adventures" *(5,* 161–63). His great
dream is to be loved by an honorable woman, so when he
meets and falls in love with Fortunata he transforms her
according to the demands of his imagination. It is not surprising, moreover, that Maxi should dream of "lavaduras de manchas" or that Galdós should refer to him as a "generoso galán,"
for he seems to have fled the year 1874 for some age more
propitious to romance. But Maxi (unlike Ido del Sagrario, for
example) does not limit his historical correlatives to the baroque or romantic periods. When he sees Fortunata in various

stages of dress and undress he is reminded of amazons and of biblical beauties like Rebecca, Bathsheba, and the Samaritan woman *(5,* 179).

Rafael del Aguila (the *Torquemada* series) presents a more pathetic case of escapism. Blind and helpless, he listens enthralled whenever an old veteran relates his military adventures in North Africa. Rafael's mechanism of compensation is not really a product of his imagination, but rather a vicarious enjoyment of another's exploits. These tales of former valor are his only sanctuary against the materialism of contemporary society and his own sedentary life:

> Para Rafael, en el aislamiento que le imponía su ceguera, incapaz de desempeñar en el mundo ningún papel airoso conforme a los impulsos de su corazón hidalgo y de su temple caballeresco, era un consuelo y un solaz irreemplazables oír relatar aventuras heroicas, empeños sublimes de nuestro Ejército, batallas sangrientas en que las vidas se inmolaban por el honor. *(5,* 990)

Although these adventures are recent—the veteran had served under General Prim—they satisfy that "nostalgia for heroism" which surges through Rafael and so many other characters in the Novelas contemporáneas.[12]

For Rafael, as for Isidora Rufete, José Relimpio, Rosalía Bringas, and Maxi Rubín, history has the glamour of romance. This is not unusual. The great majority of readers would probably agree that the past has its enticements. Even today, the historical novel has a great mass appeal, being vaguely within the category of "escapist fare." It is easy to empathize with those characters of fiction who withdraw into the past. The humorous effect of such withdrawals is often accompanied by a sting of compassionate recognition on the part of the reader.

One of the most common metaphorical procedures in the Novelas contemporáneas is the use of historical names and nicknames. In *La de Bringas* Galdós frequently calls don Francisco "Thiers," omitting his true name altogether *(4,*

12. Gullón, p. 146.

1639). The same thing happens in *El amigo Manso,* where doña Cándida's nickname, Calígula, is as likely to appear in the text as her true name (see *4,* 1190–91, where Calígula crops up four times). With Torquemada, the procedure is carried one step farther. This character's name is the same as that of an actual historical figure, an infamous inquisitor. By dubbing his fictitious moneylender thus, Galdós indicates the unrelenting tenacity with which he squeezes his victims. But because Galdós' Torquemada is himself a victim (the reader perceives this very quickly), the name loses its unpalatable historical associations and becomes instead a sort of comic tribute to the moneylender's professional zeal. When one reads, on the first page of *Torquemada en la hoguera,* that certain contemporary historians call him "Torquemada el Peor," even his capacity to do much harm is thrown into doubt. Comic hyperbole clips his ferocity. In this way, the name Torquemada joins the list of epithets which, in Rabelaisian profusion, Galdós scatters throughout the novel on its hero's behalf: "inhumano," "fiero sayón," "implacable fogonero de vidas y haciendas," "feroz hormiga," "animal," "tacaño," "verdugo," and so on. This exaggerated terminology is like one of those sulfurous representations of the devil, in which pitchfork, horns, tail, and other garish accessories combine to create an utterly harmless image.

Literary metaphor functions in much the same way as historical metaphor. The two are closely related. Isidora Rufete, for example, would never have invented her particular correlative—Marie Antoinette—if she had not been addicted to reading historical potboilers. Maxi Rubín compares Fortunata to certain biblical heroines because he has read an illustrated edition of the Bible *(5,* 179). Naming a character after a literary figure—Milagros, in *Miau,* has the nickname "la pudorosa Ofelia"—is as much a question of literary history as of literature per se. And in a larger sense, the use of archaic language and the chronicle device and any attempt at parody or burlesque invariably harken back to a specific literary model (as *Don Quixote)* or formula (as invoking the Muse).

The two literary correlatives which occur most frequently in the Novelas contemporáneas are pulp fiction (the novela por entregas) and Cervantes' *Don Quixote*. In Chapter 2 it was shown how *Tormento* and *La desheredada* satirize the novela por entregas. *La desheredada* is worth further analysis because of all the novels it is the best example of how destructive realism and romantic realism coexist. I have said repeatedly that satire and irony help to expose and correct distortion, but (and again I repeat), in order to expose distorted values, the author must depict these values in their original state. He must create, isolate, select, and even exaggerate them. Distortion is a necessary adjunct to criticism. One may compare the process to the sport of bowling: the object is to level the pins at the end of the alley, but the pins first have to be set up before anyone can knock them down. Rarely does the novelist make a strike. In *La desheredada,* for example, Galdós takes healthy aim at his "pins"—false values, the legacy of bad literature, and so on—but some of them remain standing. They have entered the reader's consciousness. They are part of the text.

The whole problem of metaphor hinges on this point. With this in mind, here again is a passage from *La desheredada* in which Isidora visualizes herself as a fictitious heroine just about to come to life. This passage was previously chosen as an example of satire; it is now presented as an example of metaphor. Isidora's correlative could be the heroine of any typical romance:

Los libros están llenos de casos semejantes. ¡Yo he leído mi propia historia tantas veces . . . ! Y ¿qué cosa hay, más linda que cuando nos pintan una joven pobrecita, muy pobrecita, que vive en una guardilla y trabaja para mantenerse; y esa joven, que es bonita como los ángeles, llora mucho y padece porque unos pícaros la quieren infamar; y luego, en cierto día, se para una gran carretela en la puerta y sube una señora marquesa muy guapa, y va a la joven, y hablan y se explican, y lloran mucho las dos, viniendo a resultar que la muchacha es hija de la marquesa, que la tuvo de un cierto conde calavera? Por

lo cual, de repente cambia de posición la niña, y habita
palacios, y se casa con un joven que ya, en los tiempos de
su pobreza, la pretendía y ella le amaba. *(4,* 1011)

During this brief daydream, the reader's horizon expands with
Isidora's. The devotee of fiction is usually willing to play along
with anything resembling a story. In this case his "inner eye"
sees exactly what Isidora sees—girl, garret, rogues, coach,
marquise, happy ending—and just as vividly. But he knows
the author's true intentions. Cerebral warnings foil the seduction and restore the reader to the safety of a derisive attitude.

This interlude has the fascination of all plays within plays.
It makes Isidora an eccentric, a person one would not meet
in the course of daily routine. It adds humor and zest to the
narrative, and all this is entirely due to metaphor.

Part I of *La desheredada* ends with a letter which Isidora's
uncle (?) writes to her from El Tomelloso, a town in La Mancha
(4, 1061–63). The letter, with its archaic, moralizing flavor
and its mixture of good sense and disparate, is an adaptation
of don Quixote's advice to Sancho Panza before Sancho goes
off to govern his island. Cervantes' novel, then, is Galdós'
correlative in this section of *La desheredada.* So unmistakable
is the connection that a reader might wonder at Galdós' audac-
ity in edging so close to the original. Aside from having a
debt to Cervantes that he was proud to acknowledge, Galdós
modeled the pseudo-canon's letter after *Don Quixote* for
definite reasons. The most important was to emphasize, by
analogy, how thoroughly literature had been a part of Isidora's
upbringing. Quijano-Quijada spent a lot of time reading
novels and undoubtedly drummed every notion he ever read
into Isidora's head. With this letter, the source of her falsification becomes clear.

Galdós, by transcribing the canon's advice in Cervantine
style, shows the old uncle to be completely daffy. Despite the
fact that his participation in the action is tangential, he is
characterized in such a way that he sticks in the reader's memory. It was necessary to say something of Isidora's background;
what better way to furnish biographical material than by

means of a vivid, humorous document instead of a matter-of-fact, potentially dull flashback?

Quijano-Quijada's letter is entirely humorous from salutation—"Mi querida sobrina (o cosa tal)"—to farewell—"tu amantísimo tío (o cosa tal)." He counsels Isidora on the proper deportment of an aristocrat, not for a moment doubting that she really is one. The sententious gravity of his depositions amuses the reader, who already knows that Isidora is of humble birth. It is this chasm between very dignified rules of morality, breeding, and decorum and a person destined not to benefit by them that strikes the note of comedy in the canon's letter. When these rules bear on the most unlikely situations, the effect is wildly ludicrous: "Usa siempre las mejores formas," says Quijano-Quijada, "y hasta cuando quieres ofender, hazlo con palabras graciosas y suaves. Si tienes que dar una bofetada, dala con mano de algodón perfumado, que así duele más" *(4,* 1062).

This letter is only one of countless Cervantine echoes heard throughout Galdós' works. In Chapter 3 I spoke of the chronicle or fictitious authorship device in *Nazarín* and pointed out that it was unquestionably a hand-me-down from *Don Quixote.* The ironic detachment which the device produces is at variance with *Nazarín's* lofty subject matter. Were the hero merely an itinerant adventurer instead of a Christ figure, this would not be the case. *Nazarín* is an aesthetic failure because *Don Quixote* is its correlative. The reader, from beginning to end, is so conscious that Cervantes' novel lurks behind the scenes that he tends to compare Nazarín with Quixote instead of with Christ. Thus Nazarín becomes an object of comic irony, not of veneration. Because the structural correlative *(Don Quixote)* and the thematic correlative (Christ) are at odds with one another, the use of literary metaphor is self-defeating. Had Galdós confined himself to religious metaphor here—Nazarín as a modern Christ—he would have accomplished what he set out to do: ennobled the hero, reinforced his status as a character, and made him larger than life.[13]

13. Alejandro Miquis of *El doctor Centeno* is another hybrid Christ-Quixote.

Literary metaphor is more successful when the author's intentions are comic. It is one of a host of techniques by which Galdós makes doña Cándida (Calígula) a memorable comic personage. Since Cándida is habitually seized by a "numen hiperbólico" *(4,* 1191), Galdós has Manso, the narrator of the novel, describe her behavior in mock-epic terms. A Homeric phrase foretells Cándida's descent upon the unsuspecting family of indianos:

> Como el buitre desde el escueto picacho arroja la mirada
> a increíble distancia y distingue la res muerta en el fondo
> del valle, así doña Cándida, desde su eminente pobreza,
> vió el provechoso esquilmo de la casa de mi hermano y
> carne riquísima donde clavar el pico y la garra. (4, 1190)

The "sanguinario Calígula" succeeds in ingratiating herself and entertains her newly adopted family with a lengthy account of her ailments: "Sus dolencias eran lastimosa epopeya, digna de que Homero se volviera Hipócrates para cantarlas" *(4,* 1191). Cándida's correlative in these passages is epic literature. Her list of woes must have been as monumentally boring as the catalog of ships from the *Odyssey,* but no matter; her characterization is not run-of-the-mill. Literary metaphor, along with several techniques of caricature, bloat her to an abnormal size. She easily shoves the more normal characters—Peña and Irene, for instance—out of her way and onto a secondary plane.

Galdós makes similar use of epical associations as he recounts the financial straits of the Babel family. Here metaphor is a kind of stylization which wipes out all compassion for the people involved. Like the violence of an animated cartoon, the problems of the Babels cannot touch the reader, except to make him laugh:

> Ofrecía la casa un cuadro de miseria y desastre, cuyas
> tintas siniestras y accidentes luctuosas traían a la memoria
> las ruinas de ciudades, las pestes y hambres épicas can-
> tadas por la musa antigua, sin que faltaran, en medio de

tan lúgubres episodios, rasgos cómicos de esos que hacen
llorar. *(5, 1219)*

Galdós did not write about misery in an objective or naturalistic way, except in *Misericordia,* nor did he depict it melodra-
matically like the humanitarian novelists. Through a strange
fusion of metaphor and irony, he stylized its grinding monotony
and desperation. The "rasgos cómicos" which he mentions in
reference to the Babels may conceivably produce tears of
hilarity, but not, as a lover of paradox might be led to imagine,
tears of compassion.

When Maxi Rubín breaks open his piggy bank *(Fortunata y
Jacinta)* it is symbolic of his break with the past. Most novelists
would have summarized the act in a sentence or two, but
Galdós, with his urge to inflate the details of daily life, lingers
over the event. He enters Maxi's mind, which during this
episode is like a thief's and an assassin's. Maxi constructs his
own correlative: although not explicitly stated, it is a sen-
sational newspaper account of a crime. Newspapers are hardly
belles-lettres, but they are literature, and literature of a special
metaphorical cast. A newspaper isolates the news and in so
doing enshrines and often distorts it. What one reads in the
press is over and above ordinary reality; it is a distillation of
everything meant to excite curiosity. When Galdós transforms
a simple act into a lurid "item," he guarantees the reader's
attention. As in the previous example of the Babels, the technique here is metaphorical, even if the aftereffect is ironic.

Maxi takes pity on his "victim," who is an "old and loyal
friend," but this does not restrain him. The "assassin" hammers
away at the "groaning" artifact, first "wounding," then "killing"
it. Afterward he gathers up the "gold, silver and copper inners"
and the shattered remains of the corpse: "Los cascos esparcidos
semejaban pedazos de un cráneo y el polvillo rojo del barro
cocido que ensuciaba la colcha blanca parecióle al criminal
manchas de sangre." Maxi tries to obliterate every trace of the
crime, terrified lest his aunt find him out. He confronts doña
Lupe, sure that she suspects something. This not being the
case, he flees: "se embozó bien en la capa y apagó la luz de su

cuarto para coger los restos de la víctima y sacarlos oculta-
mente" *(5,* 170–72).

All this seems a bit infantile, which is just the impression
Galdós wants to convey. Maxi is twenty-five years old but
looks much younger. Sickly, shy, and tongue-tied in company,
pained by his physical unattractiveness, he has always lived in
a fantasy world. He has never made love to a woman and never
asserted his independence from the imperious doña Lupe. Then
he meets and falls in love with Fortunata. Determined to make
an honest woman of her, he must find some money to enable
her to live respectably. Destruction of the piggy bank is the
first defiant act of his life. By associating it with a grisly crime—
the piggy bank takes on an autonomous life of its own—Maxi
reveals his nervousnesss and guilty fear, his lack of maturity
and childlike subservience to doña Lupe. One reacts with a
mixture of sympathy and ironic superiority, a reaction that is
a direct result of metaphor. Because one sees Maxi distort an
inconsequential deed into something traumatic, one understands him in all his pathetic impotence. This one episode tells
more about him than any amount of straight narrative could
possibly have.[14]

Religious metaphor is sustained throughout the entire length
of *Miau.* The novel is about Villaamil's quest for a position in
the Administración. The luckless aspirant tends more and
more to consider his need in quasi-religious terms. The gift of
a job would be (to emulate Villaamil's own thought processes)
manna from Heaven. He is in the position of a suppliant, for
whom every day without colocarse is, in the context of the
book, a martyrdom. His torture is written all over his face:
"Tenía la expresión sublime de un apóstol en el momento en
que lo están martirizando por la fe, algo de San Bartolomé de
Ribera cuando le suspenden del árbol y le descueran aquellos
tunantes de gentiles" *(5,* 555). The very bed he sleeps in,
with its lumpy mattress and broken springs, contributes to

14. For a discussion of literary metaphor in *El doctor Centeno,* see
Chap. 1, pp. 24–25, above.

the hell of his existence: "la cama habría podido figurar dig-
namente en las mazmorras de la Inquisición para escarmiento
de herejes" *(5, 566).*

But Villaamil is a heretic by Administración standards. His
long bureaucratic career was marked by an honest discharge
of duty. He never robbed a penny. His behavior toward the
state, his employer, was of an unheard-of saintly nature. Even
doña Pura, Villaamil's wife, complains of his being too faithful
a votary of "San Escrúpulo bendito" *(5, 561).* In spite of all
this, he is summarily let go just two months before he can
retire with a small pension.

Having worked for the Administración for so many years,
Villaamil is now like a man without a home. One might say
that he has ceased to live. To be a cesante is to be expelled
from paradise. He hounds the ministries "como sirviente
despedido que ronda la morada de donde le expulsaron,
soñando en volver a ella" *(5, 610).* Naturally he is bitter about
the injustice done him and the subsequent refusal of anyone to
give him work for a few months: "bienaventurados los brutos,
porque de ellos es el reino . . . de la Administración" *(5, 563).*[15]
He is convinced that someone is out to get him and develops
a persecution complex.

Despite his anger at the rank cruelty of the Administración,
Villaamil identifies that entity with God. It has always been
his sustenance. It has given him his daily bread, most of his
friends, his topics of conversation, and his spiritual nourish-
ment. He has worked incessantly for its greater glory and even
devised a formula for its rehabilitation. This formula is the title
of the novel—*Miau.* The letters m, i, a, and u stand for "morali-
dad," "income tax," "aduanas" (protective tariffs), and "unifi-
cación de la deuda." Villaamil goes about trying to convert
his former associates in the ministry to this cult.

Since he associates the Administración with God, Villaamil's

15. Compare this to the exchange by two other malcontents within
the Administración.

> Bienaventurados los brutos . . .
> —Porque de ellos es la nómina de los cielos. *(5, 616–17)*

prayers are, as Galdós says, an "absurd mixture of piety and bureaucracy" *(5,* 640). As before, biblical phrases transform the context of the novel: "Si es verdad que a todos nos das el pan de cada día, ¿por qué a mí me lo niegas? Y digo más: si el Estado debe favorecer a todos por igual, ¿por qué a mí me abandona?" *(5,* 640).[16]

Villaamil's great mistake is to believe that God has anything whatsoever to do with the Administración. Luisito's conversations with the Almighty, show that His influence does not extend into such murky depths. The bureaucratic world is the devil's demesne, and the devil in *Miau* is Villaamil's brother-in-law, Víctor Cadalso.

Cadalso is a nonbeliever: "No creo en Dios . . . ; a Dios se le ve soñando, y ya hace tiempo que desperté" *(5,* 581; see also p. 633). Galdós and his characters often allude to his diabolism. His entrance into the peaceable Villaamil household is likened to that of Hell itself *(5,* 580); Abelarda compares the apparition to Mephistopheles *(5,* 581); he brandishes a "diabolical little laugh" *(5,* 610); after possessing Abelarda's soul ("le había absorbido el alma"), "a stroke of infernal inspiration" impels him to suggest that they run away together *(5,* 643, 644); before jilting her, he commends himself to his "guardian demon" and leaves his castaway's presence "like a soul that Satan carries off" *(5,* 646, 647); when he decides to remove Luisito from his grandparents' house—they have nursed, raised, and loved the boy—he becomes "an apocalyptic beast," the blackest soul God ever let loose on the earth *(5,* 667).[17]

Cadalso is a bureaucratic success, however. Amoral, wanton in his allegiances, and dishonest with public funds, he receives a promotion. For Villaamil the injustice is too much to bear. He begins to lose faith. He has been worshipping a false idol

16. This type of comic travesty of religious motif is a tradition in Spanish literature. See, for example, *El libro de buen amor* and Cervantes' *Rinconete y Cortadillo.*

17. Aside from his diabolism, Cadalso could almost be a blood brother to Juanito Santa Cruz *(Fortunata y Jacinta).* Like Juanito, he is physically attractive, fluent, adept at worming his way out of a tight spot. He is also a wonderful parody of the Byronic hero.

and has been in the grips of a false religion. The Administración, which he persisted in believing to be fair, moral, and Godlike, has let him down. His end is nihilism and suicide:

> De veras que siento ganas de acabar con todo lo que vive, en castigo de lo mal que se han portado conmigo la Humanidad, y la Naturaleza, y Dios . . . . Todos me han abandonado, y por eso adopto el lema que anoche inventé y que dice literalmente: Muerte . . . Infamante . . . Al . . . Universo. *(5,* 679)

Even prior to this final metamorphosis, the letters m, i, a, and u are used a number of times to express Villaamil's growing despair and bitterness. They become a religious metaphor at the end of Chapter 25, when some employees of the Administración, having ridiculed the "morality, income tax" program, dub its progenitor "Miau." Villaamil overhears the mocking reference and accepts the tag. It is like the I.N.R.I. of the Cross, he says. "Ya que me han crucificado entre ladrones, para que todo sea completo, pónganme sobre la cabeza esas cuatro letras en que se hace mofa y escarnio de mi gran misión" *(5,* 657).

During the course of the novel, Villaamil comes to renounce everyone and everything, with the exception of his grandson Luisito. Luisito is his one link to the authentic God (as opposed to the diabolical providence in which he had placed his trust). The little boy has spasms or seizures, during which he envisions himself speaking to God. Galdós believed that children were better able to communicate with the Almighty and understand His purposes than adults. At one point he refers to "esos rasgos de sabiduría que de la mente divina pueden descender a la de los seres cuyo estado de gracia les comunica directamente con aquélla" *(5,* 621). The idea is not uncommon. As it turns out, Luisito is truly clairvoyant. In his final conversation with God, he learns that his grandfather will never be given a job. God instructs the boy to communicate this information to Villaamil: "El estupor de Villaamil fué inmenso. Eran las palabras de su nieto como revelación divina, de irrefragable autenticidad"

(5, 675). The old man's hesitation about doing away with himself disappears.

Thus there are two main threads running through *Miau,* each exerting a certain leverage on the other. To begin with, Villaamil's fate depends on an abstract force within the Administración. As it becomes clear that he will not be placed, this force grows more and more evil. The result is that Villaamil suffers from a persecution complex and thinks himself a martyr and a Christ (this would not be so bad if he did not also believe that he was excommunicate). However, at the same time there is a countermovement embodied in Luisito. Luisito convinces Villaamil that God, instead of refusing him, *wants* him. It is a movement away from rejection and toward acceptance. For Villaamil, therefore, suicide is not so much an escape as a liberation.

Miau resembles certain of Balzac's tales of martyrdom *(César Birotteau* and *Père Goriot)* but stands apart from them in its religious configuration for comic effect. Nowhere is the comedy more apparent than in the word "miau" itself, which is a combined religious-animal correlative (Villaamil's wife, daughter, and sister-in-law all look like cats).[18] Without the many religious correlatives in *Miau,* the novel would lose much of its intensity. It would be ponderous, humorless, and uniformly gray. Certain details—Cadalso's arbitrarily wicked treatment of Abelarda, for instance—would make no sense. (Since Cadalso represents the devil, the reader does not need an explanation for his perverse behavior.) And Luisito's role as the messenger of God, in which capacity he settles once and for all the denouement of the novel, would quite literally be a deus ex machina with little or no relation to the novel as a whole.

The rich description of Pedro Polo's school in *El doctor Centeno* is another example of religious metaphor used to vitalize a context. From his students' point of view, Polo's pedagogical methods are nightmarish. Galdós wants to describe them as a child might see (and feel) them and thus

18. See Chap. 1, p. 26, above.

chooses the correlative of a martyrdom. Classroom routine, says the author,

> era una rueda de tormento, máquina crudelísima, en la cual los bárbaros artífices arrancaban con tenazas una idea del cerebro, sujeto con mil tornillos, y metían otra a martillazos, y estiraban conceptos e incrustaban reglas, todo con vehemencia, con golpe, espasmo y relinchar de dientes por una y otra parte. *(4,* 1311)

This is an allusion to the martyrdom of St. Catherine. Further illustrations of Polo's pedagogical maxim—"Siembra coscorrones y recogerás sabios"—evoke something on the order of the "slaughter of the innocents." The correlative of martyrdom gives a perfect idea of how grotesque Polo's methods are and how much the children suffer from them. In addition, it complements other distortive techniques which Galdós employs in this passage, namely, the personification of inanimate objects and the awarding of autonomy to parts of the body. The combination of these techniques and religious metaphor gives a cartoon-like air to the whole. Because of this, Polo's brutality makes the reader laugh, not wince. Like Torquemada, he is harmless, though for different reasons.[19]

There are few descriptions of nature in the *Novelas contemporáneas,* except in *El caballero encantado, Nazarín,* and *Halma.* The landscape for the most part is strictly urban. Flats, streets, and shops tend to blot out the earth and sky. If landscape description does appear in a text, it is usually in the form of a brief topographical survey devoid of lyric rapture. Galdós was equally unromantic insofar as the connection between nature and human psychology is concerned. There are no storms to orchestrate emotional crises, or autumn leaves to fall with the spirit, or "romantic fallacies" to make the irony

---

19. The *Novelas contemporáneas* abound in religious metaphor. For examples other than those given here, the reader should consult Gustavo Correa's *El simbolismo religioso en las novelas de Pérez Galdós* (Madrid, 1962).

hit home. In fact, these are the very things Galdós satirizes in *Tormento*. Recall how he describes Amparo, the orphan-heroine, waiting for the sweetheart who never shows up:

> la fúnebre soledad de la humilde casa no se interrumpió en aquel tristísimo día. Para que fuera más triste, ni un momento dejó de llover. Amparo creía que el sol se había nublado para siempre, y en la mortaja líquida que envolvía la Naturaleza, veía como una ampliación de la misma lobreguez de su alma. *(4, 1551)*

Later, her abortive suicide attempt takes place within earshot of the happy chirping of mechanical birds—a nice dig at the romantic fallacy *(4, 1555–56)*. Details such as these show how cleverly Galdós incorporated the standard features of romantic pulp fiction into *Tormento*.

When Galdós uses nature (in the sense of climate, land-scape, natural disaster, cosmic phenomena, and so on) as a metaphor, he does so with a comic purpose. He portrays a character who, in a fitful mood, craves upheaval, or he describes some cosmic fireworks that herald an auspicious event on earth. Milagros, in *La de Bringas,* hopes that some natural disaster will occur to prevent her creditors from pounding at her door: "A veces digo: '¿No habrá un cataclismo, un ter-remoto o cosa así antes del día diez?'" *(4, 1629)*. In lieu of a natural catastrophe, she would settle for a man-made one—a revolution, for example,[20] The comedy here arises from the transfer of petty domestic crises onto a plane of cyclopean proportions. Like so many of Galdós' characters who fail to see their problems in proper perspective, Milagros is overwhelmingly self-centered. In her choice of such outrageous correlatives as an earthquake and a revolution (the implication being that these convulsions are the only ones awesome enough to counteract her own problems), she reveals herself as an incurable romantic. The reader, of course, reacts ironically. As

20. For the connection between this kind of metaphorical distortion and the irony of reference, see Chap. 1, pp. 18–20, above.

in so many previous examples, an initial distortion of reality is brought back into focus by the corrective lens of irony.

While Milagros appeals to the forces of nature for help, Dulce, in *Angel Guerra,* appeals to them for revenge. Furious at Angel for having followed Leré to Toledo, Dulce would like to see the whole city destroyed: "¡Que no reventara en Toledo un grandísimo volcán, y les hiciera polvo a todas!" *(5,* 1306). She confines her volcanic wrath to Toledo only because she attributes Angel's waywardness to the intrigues of clerics and Jesuits *(5,* 1306).

Villaamil, wandering through the outskirts of Madrid, associates a few denizens of the countryside—the birds and young trees—with his unhappy married life and his wretched treatment at the hands of the state. At first he seems content. He admires the landscape: "Paréceme que lo veo todo por primera vez en mi vida, o que en este momento se acaban de crear esta sierra, estos árboles y este cielo" *(5,* 675). He joyfully feeds a band of sparrows. But his anger surges forth as the sparrows begin to fly away. He curses them for abandoning him just as everyone else has done: "Pillos, granujas, que después de haberos comido mi pan pasáis sin darme tan siquiera las buenas tardes" *(5,* 679). Before this, he walks near some trees recently planted by the city; as foster children of the municipality they are hateful and can be uprooted in good conscience: "El Municipio . . . es hijo de la Diputación Provincial y nieto del muy gorrino del Estado, y bien se puede, sin escrúpulo de la conciencia, hacer daño a toda la parentela maldita" *(5,* 679). Just as Abelarda, in a destructive rage, had attacked the innocent Luisito, so Villaamil vents his anger on these innocent plants. Nature has joined the conspiracy against him.

In his first novel, *La Fontana de Oro,* Galdós jokingly described the welcome that the cosmos gave to Elías (Coletilla) at his birth. Why Galdós saw fit to garnish his narrative with such a gratuitous stab at humor is anyone's guess. Perhaps— and this is only conjecture—he wanted to suggest the superstitions and ignorance of mid-eighteenth-century Spain (Elías was born in 1762). One can almost imagine Torres Villarroel, in one of his artful and enlightened moods, relating that, although born like everyone else,

> no por eso dejaron de verificarse al exterior algunos prodigios. Observóse en el cielo de Ateca la conjunción nunca vista de las siete Cabrillas con Mercurio; la luna apareció en figura de anillo, y, al fin, salió por el horizonte un cometa que se paseó por la bóveda del cielo como Pedro por su casa.[21]

In spite of its tenuous link with the rest of the novel, this little passage has a nice extravagance. It is reminiscent of those baroque paintings in which some royal entry takes place amid the trumpeting of putti and the applause of tritons.

Years later, when Galdós narrates one of Torquemada's rare bursts of generosity, he again uses the images of a universe gone haywire. In *Torquemada en la hoguera,* the moneylender's son falls ill and the father blames himself. The boy's illness is an expression of the Almighty's ire; the father (so he believes) has sinned against "Dios-Humanidad"—that strange deity palmed off on him by his friend Bailón. Torquemada tries to make amends. When he goes to collect his rents one Sunday, he is uncommonly kind to the tenants who cannot pay and tries to mollify those who complain of landlord neglect. A tenant sums up the stupefaction which Torquemada's newfound concern for "la Humanidad" causes everywhere: "Ahí tenéis por qué está saliendo todas las noches en el cielo esa estrella con rabo. Es que el mundo se va a acabar" *(5,* 918).

A third and final example of nature metaphor, where the correlative is again a prodigious eruption of natural phenomena, occurs at the beginning of *Torquemada en la cruz*. The narrator notes that doña Lupe is dead and that "comets, cyclones and earthquakes" had announced the catastrophe *(5,* 937).

Thus far in this study Galdós' last novel, *La razón de la sinrazón* (1915), has been mentioned only in passing. As it

21. *La Fontana de Oro,* p. 54.

happens, this theatrical fable is full of nature metaphor. It is an allegory, a genre usually defined as prolonged metaphor.[22] Periodically throughout the work the "espíritus burlones" of nature make an appearance. These invisible spirits are symptoms of sinrazón, which, in turn, is what is wrong with Spain: official corruption, opportunism, hollow oratory, and national discord. In the final pages of *La razón de la sinrazón,* the diabolical spirits and the evils they represent are banished during an eclipse of the sun. Harmony is triumphant. There is a return to the land, a purification of the positivist ideal of hard work, and a new emphasis on education.

The most basic kind of animal metaphor involves nothing more than a simple physical comparison: for example, the Miaus look like cats; their physiognomy is permanently feline.[23] A slight variation occurs when, in a fit of anger, a character suddenly undergoes a metamorphosis. This happens to Ido del Sagrario: "Las carúnculas del cuello se le inyectaban de tal modo, que casi eclipsaban el rojo de la corbata. Parecía un pavo cuando la excitación de la pelea con otro pavo le convierte en animal feroz" *(Fortunata y Jacinta, 5,* 92). A more elaborate metamorphosis, couched in classical, full-bodied

22. The Peces, described in Chap. 2, are also allegorical in that they represent a prolonged animal metaphor.

23. It is interesting to trace the ramifications of the word "miau," since they go far beyond the confines of animal metaphor (and religious metaphor as well). At the beginning of the novel, "miau" refers only to the physical appearance of three women, characterizing them from the outside. As the work progresses, "miau" comes to symbolize several inner realities. Every bit of self-analysis on the part of Luisito, Abelarda, and Villaamil is rooted in the word. For Luisito, it signifies the injury done to his amour propre: an insult which haunts him even after the insulter—"Posturitas"—dies. For Abelarda, "miau" is the best description of herself, her family, and the futile life they all lead: it is more or less the equivalent of pobre cursi. And for Villaamil, "miau" is everything that wrecks his happiness. This includes not only the Administración, but the spendthrift Pura, the useless Milagros, and the stupid, gullible Abelarda. As was said before the word "miau" gives to this novel an extraordinary unity of tone.

simile, makes Abelarda's attempted infanticide even more gruesome than it would seem otherwise:

> Como las fieras enjauladas y entumecidas recobran, al primer rasguño que hacen al domador, toda su ferocidad, y con la vista y el olor de la primera sangre pierden la apatía perezosa del cautiverio, así Abelarda, en cuanto derribó y clavó las uñas a Luisito, ya no fué mujer, sino el ser monstruoso creado en un tris por la insana perversión de la naturaleza feminina. *(Miau, 5, 664)*

Galdós compares Abelarda to a wild beast and then goes one step farther: she is a monster. Animal metaphor often concludes as something monstrous or grotesque. This adds another dimension to what first appears to be a method of characterization lacking nuance.

Monstrousness implies physical deformity, and the Novelas contemporáneas are full of deformed individuals. Few are as violently compromised by their appearance as Mendizábal *(Miau)*. He is a kind of missing link—a zoological hybrid, an ape-man, a vindication of Darwin *(5, 587)*. His apelike features, however, are not the result of an arbitrary whim on Galdós' part. Mendizábal is a sullen reactionary whose bugaboos—materialism, rationalism, and religious freedom—would disappear only with a Carlist victory and a new Inquisition. But if Mendizábal's appearance is symbolic of his political views, it does not reflect upon his character. He is a decent man and sensitive to a degree. Like Villaamil, he is outwardly ferocious and inwardly kind.

Children are not exempt from physical deformity. Isidora Rufete gives birth to a macrocephalic infant whose huge head is perhaps symbolic of his mother's "delirante ambición y . . . vicio mental" *(4, 1064)*. Valentinico, Torquemada's child by Fidela del Aguila, is macrocephalic and worse: he grunts, is destructive, bad-intentioned, and mentally retarded *(Torquemada y San Pedro, 5, 1136)*. Galdós describes him as one would describe an animal—sniffing the air, wiping his snout, and barking at people. All this is borrowed from the descriptive techniques of naturalism.

Valentinico, the supposed reincarnation of Torquemada's first child, is a complete antithesis of the latter: he is a brute and an idiot, whereas the original Valentín is an angel and a genius. Valentinico is meant to symbolize a social desbarajuste. The monstrous child is the offspring of parents who have nothing in common: the newly rich Torquemada, clinging stubbornly to his niggardly ways, and the aristocratic Fidela, forced by the ruin of her class to marry a boorish parvenu.

The original Valentín has too large a head and a slightly deformed skull, but this just adds to his charm. He is perfect—a supernatural being, a mathematical genius whom Torquemada (himself no slouch at figures) consults "no pocas veces." Religious metaphor lifts him above the rest of mankind: he is "angelito," "Anticristo," and "Cristo niño entre los doctores" *(Torquemada en la hoguera, 5,* 911–12). His father proudly presents him as "el monstruo de la edad presente" *(5,* 911). Here "monster" is synonymous with "prodigy." Of all the thousands of characters that Galdós created, there is no better example of romantic-realistic characterization than Valentín. Galdós does not contradict reality—child prodigies *do* exist. Instead he raises the real to its highest common denominator, to its *ne plus ultra* level of intensity.

The two main aspects of monstrousness—physical deformity and prodigious ability—reach bizarre proportions in *Angel Guerra.* Leré, the heroine of the novel, tells of the child-monsters born to her mother. A pair of these have survived. One, without the intelligence of a dog or cat, can barely qualify to the order of primates. His polyp-like appearance is the most hideous thing in the Novelas contemporáneas *(5,* 1258–59, 1318). There is little artistic justification for his inclusion in *Angel Guerra,* except perhaps as a foil to the psychologically grotesque (but very handsome) Babels.[24] If this is the case,

24. The constrast between the grotesque (the Babels, Leré's animal-like brother) and the sublime (Leré, the spiritual ambience of Toledo) recalls some of Victor Hugo's theoretical pronouncements on romanticism. See Wolfgang Kayser, *The Grotesque in Art and Literature* (Bloomington, 1957), pp. 56–59. Valentín and Valentinico offer a similar contrast.

an element of symmetry might be seen to emerge from this haphazardly constructed novel. Leré's other brother is a musical prodigy, a second Mozart *(5,* 1259). Not only is he a great pianist, but he can also imitate the multiple sounds of an organ by some weird manual and vocal dexterity: "Metiéndose los dedos en la boca y poniendo los labios no sé cómo, imitaba el registro flauteado, los bajoncillos, dulzainas y qué sé yo, con tanta perfección que parecía que estaba usted oyendo el órgano de la catedral" *(5,* 1260). Again I am at a loss to explain how all this is relevant to the plot or theme of *Angel Guerra.* If Galdós wanted to show that his heroine came from unusual stock, he need not have gone to such extremes.[25]

Whether or not one agrees on the merits of *Angel Guerra* as a work of art, it must be said that Galdós, here and elsewhere, had a propensity for the grotesque. In this respect he stands apart from most of his immediate contemporaries in Spain—Alarcón, Pereda, Palacio Valdés, Valera—and joins a particular current of Spanish artistic expression which defies any strict chronological frontier. This current flows from *El libro de buen amor* through *El buscón,* Goya, and, to choose a very recent example, Buñuel's film *Viridiana.* The Arcipreste's *pastoras,* Quevedo's dómine Cabra, Goya's *Proverbios* and *Caprichos,* and Buñuel's beggars (not too far removed from the beggars who crowd the portals of the church of San Sebastián in *Misericordia)* all abound in grotesque physical deformities. Spanish painting, especially, has never shirked from physical grotesqueness. Velázquez' dwarfs and Ribera's *Clubfoot* (Louvre) face the spectator man to man and eye to eye.[26]

The Spaniard not only confronts the artistic representation

25. Her monster background is very nearly the only interesting thing about Leré. She is supposed to be unique and extraordinary. Most readers, however, would not find a personality shaped by religious vocation and/or frigidity very unusual at all.

26. There are two dwarfs in the *Novelas contemporáneas:* Sor Marcela *(Fortunata y Jacinta),* with "ojos . . . como los de algunas bestias cuadrúmanas" *(5,* 238), and Ujo *(Nazarín),* a "pobre monstruo" *(5,* 1741–43).

of deformity but savors it. This suggests the medieval-baroque orientation of his culture. Sometimes one can find an odd association of physical deformity and the medieval-baroque theme of vanitas: the decay and death of beauty, the vanity of all worldly goods. A striking example of this association takes place in *Lo prohibido,* where the narrator's clinical tone gives to the example in question an air of grand-guignolesque, post-romantic decadence. As in certain works of Valle-Inclán, this tone is merely the icing on a very Spanish cake.

The narrator of *Lo prohibido,* José María de Guzmán, has had a tempestuous affair with his cousin, the very beautiful Eloísa. The latter suffers from a strange malady which at one point mars her features to a repugnant degree.[27] José María visits her sickbed and unknowingly provides a final and, in its macabre delectation, most castizo sample of animal metaphor:

> causóme indecible terror la certidumbre de que aquella monstruosidad era la cara que conocí en la plenitud de la gracia y la hermosura. Parecióme enorme calabaza, cuya parte superior era lo único que declaraba parentesco con la fisonomía humana. Mas en la inferior la deformidad era tal, que había que recurrir a las especies zoológicas más feas para encontrarle semejanza. ¡Pobre Eloísa!
> *(4,* 1829)

Physiological metaphor refers to the physical expression of emotion. Perhaps this sounds a bit more complicated than necessary: one has only to think of a tear, a sigh, or a blush to realize how elemental the whole idea behind physiological metaphor really is. Of course the symptoms just mentioned are normal occurrences. Of interest here are the more peculiar physiological reactions to emotion—the tics and tricks which draw Galdós' characters away from normalcy.

Physical tics afford an easy means of identification, especially if the same tic is repeated consistently whenever its owner is distraught or excited. It is a quick and vivid way to sketch a

27. Eloísa's disease is correlative to her immorality and greed.

character and is a standard feature of comic technique. Consider once more the case of Eloísa in *Lo prohibido*. She has a horror of feathers, at certain times experiencing the cruel sensation that a feather is stuck in her throat. This sensation comes upon her whenever she sees some bibelot or objet d'art she wants to possess:

> Hay aquí una cosa que . . . la semana pasada me produjo dos noches de fiebre, con escalofríos, amargor de boca, calambres, cefalalgia y cuantos males nerviosos te puedes figurar. No era pluma lo que yo tenía en mi garganta, sino un palomar entero y verdadero. *(4,* 1708)

What begins as an obsessive emotional need ends in disease, a disease that always recurs on schedule.

Galdós had such an ample supply of physiological quirks in his portfolio that he did not have to use the same one consistently, even with a single personage. It is possible, however, to group most of the physiological disorders which afflict his characters into a single correlative: neuropathic-epileptoid disease. Epilepsy, of course, is a disease of the nerves; the correlative is in duplicate only because Galdós frequently and unscientifically employs "epileptic" as a synonym for "nervous," and vice versa. For example, Abelarda's first attempt on Luisito's life is said to be due to "una de esas auras epileptiformes que subvierten los sentimientos primarios en el alma de la mujer" *(Miau, 5,* 648). Yet a few days prior to this near-infanticide, Abelarda feels a sudden urge to kill her father. Her "malignidad parricida" is not caused by an epileptoid attack but by a nervous disorder: "Algo hubo en ella de ese estado cerebral (relacionado con desórdenes nerviosos, familiares al organismo femenil), que sugiere los actos de infanticidio" *(5,* 642).

Galdós believed that women were more prone to nervous afflictions than men. The quote above indicates this, as does a remark made by the Condesa de Laín in *El abuelo.* A neuropath herself—whether by choice or inheritance nobody knows—she says that "arrechuchos nerviosos" are "la epidemia

de las señoras" *(6,* 101). Galdós usually took a jaundiced view
of these "arrechuchos nerviosos." Indeed, they spark a moment or two of slapstick humor in the Novelas contemporáneas.
Fainting spells and swoons have always been among the joys
of slapstick, and Galdós was not one to miss a chance to
tease his women on their facile and somewhat theatrical
genius for mental evaporation. Milagros *(La de Bringas)* caps
a long tale of woe with an operatic plea for money and an
opportune fade-out: "le entró una congoja y una convul-
sioncilla de estas que las mujeres llaman ataque de nervios, por
llamarlo de alguna manera, seguida de un espasmo de los que
reciben el bonito nombre de síncope" *(4,* 1616). Verbal irony
flicks aside this dramatic display of nerves. Milagros was an
early adept at method acting.

Physiological metaphor is effective in the creation of relatively minor characters because it requires no development.
Sometimes, though, it can be used in conjunction with other
types of metaphor to vary and facet a characterization. Doña
Catalina de Alencastre, already burdened with a historical
pedigree dating back hundreds of years, must also endure a
daily siege of epileptic vibrations brought on by family problems *(Angel Guerra, 5,* 1216).[28] Physiological metaphor may
also serve to complement one of the mainstays of caricature,
the ruling passion. Galdós writes that Felisita, a minor personage in *Angel Guerra,* has two preoccupations in life: one
is with the Toledo Cathedral, and the other with keeping her
house meticulously clean. He goes on to say that a hitch in
either case would cause Felisita to suffer some kind of physiological malaise. From here on, the matter is very simple.
Galdós has only to mention any occurrence (the more trifling
the better for comic purposes) having an adverse effect on
Felisita and report her physiological reaction. When she learns,
for example, that a group of nuns is poverty-stricken, she
experiences "grandísima pena . . . con bolo histérico, pirosis
y titulación del párpado derecho" *(5,* 1438).

Nervous disorders that strike children are unfit for comic

28. There is also a reference to her "risa epiléptica" *(5,* 1517).

treatment.[29] A novelist would alienate his public immediately if he presumed otherwise. Galdós skirts this danger by emphasizing the dreams and visions of neuropathic children rather than the outward symptoms of their distress. He thus averts the reader's sorrow and even extracts a bit of humor without offending anyone's sensibilities. Isabelita Bringas is a delicate little girl with "predisposiciones epilépticas" *(4,* 1586). These are aroused by the slightest flurry of emotion and aggravated by any difficulty she might have in digesting her food. Instead of depicting her as a spastic child, Galdós dwells upon her phantasmagoric dreams. In these dreams the everyday events of the Royal Palace transform themselves into a strange and prophetic puppet show. Isabelita's malady is stylized, and her physical anguish becomes submerged in her subconscious.

Luisito's visions *(Miau)* are brought on by an ailment resembling a mild form of epilepsy, but it is not clear whether this ailment can properly be discussed in terms of metaphor. It is not correlative to anything, seeming to occur independently of any emotional or psychological shock on Luisito's part. His spells are preceded by a spasm, a chill in the spine, and a sudden trance-like drowsiness. He falls asleep and sees God, with whom he speaks and quickly familiarizes himself. These conversations are expertly contrived, especially in view of the Scylla-Charybdis nature of the two interlocutors. Galdós foregoes any pathetic account of Luisito's malady. He whisks the reader almost immediately into the child's fanciful and amusing dreamworld. Luisito considers the visitations a very special treat; therefore Galdós can maintain a humorous tone in describing them. The reader looks forward to them as much as the child does, forgetful of the illness that brings them on. Stylization here, much more than in Isabelita's case, seems to immunize both character and reader against the pain of physiological disorder.

29. I do not mean to imply that, otherwise, Galdós always makes comic hay out of nervous disorders; I have merely chosen comic examples. For a perfectly deadpan description of a like malady, see Galdós' account of one of Maxi Rubín's jaquecas *(5,* 212).

Metaphor skirts so close to caricature that at times the two coincide. Doña Catalina de Alencastre is included in this chapter to show how several kinds of metaphor may overlap. But since her physiological quirk is as constant as her genealogical one, and neither of these vary or evolve in any appreciable way, she easily qualifies as a caricature. So does Felisita. Isidora Rufete has an *idée fixe* (or ruling passion) which places her well within the domain of caricature.

Technicalities must not be allowed to obstruct the larger view of things. Metaphor and caricature are not mutually exclusive. They are mechanisms which share the same gear and charge the same engine. Both help spark and move the Novelas contemporáneas.

Chapter 5: CARICATURE AND TYPE

It is an easy matter to relate satire and irony to realism. Both cling to what is life-sized; both preserve human scale and delight in pulling human beings down a peg. They strip man of his custom-tailored clothes and stuff him into some less flattering garment which shows how gawky and imperfect he really is. What stands exposed—vanity and delusion—are the familiar embarrassments of humanity. It is logical that they should also be among the stays of fiction.

As readers we should be acquainted with much of the folly a novelist exhumes. We are therefore inclined to believe that satire and irony, the tools of excavation, are realistic. They confirm our own experience, which we blithely assume to be representative of some universal human condition.

Every reader interprets literary realism on the basis of personal experience. But however useful this may be in appraising an author's diagnosis of individual case histories, it may hamper an appraisal of his artistic purpose. In order to reconcile metaphor and caricature to realism, the term "realism" must be shorn of its approbatory halo, by which the reader's personal experience—the sum total of his knowledge of the world—glows with self-sufficiency. To say that a work of art is realistic is, in normal usage, to adopt a utilitarian standard: it is a sop to the false notion that we have seen it all and know it all. It is solace of a kind—appeasement based on recognition. A few critics have set restrictions on literary realism by confining it to the narrow berth of normalcy. This is comforting but wrong, because it implies that realism is only a verification of what one knows to be true.

To accept the premise that realism in literature includes only that which is normal or verifiable one would have to discuss metaphor and caricature in an appendix to this study. Their

presence in the Novelas contemporáneas would be thought
jarring, their comic contribution whimsical and without purpose. Such is not the case, however. For one thing, metaphor
is often the accomplice of irony, and satire is inconceivable
without caricature-like distortions. In other words, metaphor
and caricature are affixed to the most basic props of fiction.
Infinitely more important is the fact that art is an interpretation,
and not merely a reproduction, of life. Metaphor, for example,
seems to shun reality in a quest for absurd and uncommon
relationships, but these relationships have a self-contained
logic all their own. Like an audiovisual aid of sorts, they
animate the author's ideas and make his characters more
solid and concrete.

Of all the major novelists, Dickens has been most severely
taken to task for being a caricaturist. One critic rather scorn-
fully says that his caricatures are "of an obvious, farcical
kind, irresistible but cheap."[1] Even if one were to admit the
"realism as experience as normalcy" criterion, it would not
be totally inaccurate to reply that people seem obvious and
farcical as often as they seem subtle and complex. The trouble
is that readers are in the habit of diverting their attention from
appearance to motivation. They fear oversimplification and
accept symbolism only if it is sufficiently abstruse. They no
longer enjoy sharp distinctions of right and wrong and tremble
at the word "melodrama."

Mario Praz, the critic who belittles Dickens' caricatures,
fails to say what kind of caricature he would prefer instead.
From the general tenor of his remarks it is clear that he dis-
approves of the technique altogether on the grounds that it
violates realism. True realism, according to Praz, "does not
shrink from wretched human details." Dickens "is debarred
from true realism partly by his tendency towards theatricalism
. . . [and] partly by his Victorian repugnance for everything
that is crude and offensive to delicacy."[2] There are several
holes in this argument. Praz extols Trollope's realism, and

1. Praz, *The Hero in Eclipse*, p. 173.
2. Ibid., p. 149.

Trollope is as Victorian as Dickens. Furthermore, what could be more offensive than evil, which Dickens describes again and again? The critic would like to believe that Dickens was constitutionally allergic to realism. This is the kind of criticism that blames El Greco's elongated figures on some supposed astigmatism.

For every critic who disparages Dickens' methods there are ten who do them justice. The best defense is an essay by George Orwell which gets to the heart of the problem:

> His [Dickens'] characters are even more distorted and simplified than Smollett's. But there are no rules in novel-writing, and for any work of art there is only one test worth bothering about—survival. By this test Dickens' characters have succeeded, even if the people who remember them hardly think of them as human beings. They are monsters, but at any rate they *exist*.[3]

This is certainly not hero worship; it is equitable criticism and, as such, is typical of the entire essay. Throughout, Orwell avoids any single criterion, as Praz's "true realism," and instead tries to explain why Dickens wrote the way he did. He states that Dickens was a moralist with an uncompromising sense of good and evil, that he regarded progress not in terms of mass action or social welfare, but as individual enlightenment and conversion. Given this background, one can understand why Dickens was a caricaturist. He dealt in absolutes. These, along with an almost religious belief in redemption, were part of his world view. To spurn his art as unrealistic because it reflects this world view and not one's own is like saying the Ten Commandments are unrealistic because one does not live by them. Of course, one may question Dickens' original assumptions about humanity, but this is a different matter entirely.[4]

3. George Orwell, *Critical Essays* (London, 1946), p. 51.
4. For a factual rather than critical account of Dickens' techniques of caricature, see Earle R. Davis, "Dickens and the Evolution of Caricature," *PMLA, 55* (1940), 231–40. For a general defense of literary

Of all Galdós' novels, *Doña Perfecta* is the most like those of Dickens. It leans heavily on caricature. One of the author's best books, it has always disturbed certain critics because of its distortions. Who ever met anyone like doña Perfecta or don Inocencio? No one perhaps (although the warped kind of thinking they represent exists, in other forms, to this day). But these caricatures are not a defect of the book; they are its greatest asset. Whether or not the reader has had dealings with a Perfecta or an Inocencio is totally beside the point; Galdós wanted to write a polemic and he did. Judged as such, *Doña Perfecta* is a powerful work.

In *Doña Perfecta,* Galdós uses the techniques of caricature for symbolic purposes. His people are the embodiments of good and evil, progress and reaction, ignorance and enlightenment, and so on. This is what readers and critics find so disconcerting, especially if they know Galdós through the Novelas contemporáneas. In these later novels, the techniques of caricature are more modestly applied. Only rarely—as in the case of doña Juana Samaniego *(Casandra),* the reincarnation of doña Perfecta—does caricature go so far as to create a figure of transcendent goodness or evil. Because the Novelas contemporáneas are for the most part nonideological, the caricatures which abound therein arouse no partisan passions in the reader. They cannot offend his conception of political reality, for instance. On the other hand, the caricatures in *Doña Perfecta* may seem unreal to him because they challenge some of his convictions regarding Spanish orthodoxy, traditionalism, and the like. The book then becomes a misrepresentation of truth.

It is unfortunate, but unavoidable, that one should have to justify caricature by reference to realism. Ever since the Renaissance, the idea that art should aim at an exact reproduction of reality has had a huge appeal. Even the first known apologist of caricature, the Italian painter Annibale Carracci,

---

caricature, see Lucien Refort, *La caricature littéraire* (Paris, 1932), pp. 4–11.

felt obliged to make assurances to the effect that distortions do not really distort. His theories have been interpreted as follows:

> similarity is not essential to likeness. The deliberate distortion of single features is not incompatible with a striking likeness in the whole. True caricature in this sense is not content with drawing a long nose just a little longer, or a broad chin just a bit broader. Such partial distortions are characteristic only of superficial or immature work. The real aim of the true caricaturist is to transform the whole man into a completely new and ridiculous figure which nevertheless resembles the original in a striking and surprising way.[5]

Although this theory is centuries old, it is remarkably well suited to the subject at hand. It recalls Galdós' warning about the Babel family quoted in Chapter 4: "son de todo punto inverosímiles, lo cual no quita que sean verdaderos" *(Angel Guerra, 5,* 1216). In other words, the Babels may be distorted, but they are true or real nevertheless. The difficulty here arises from the fact that pictorial caricature—a Daumier cartoon, for example—is frequently based on an actual figure or group of figures known to the public on sight. Literary caricature offers no such crutch.

Aside from his remark about the Babels, there are further indications that, for Galdós, distortions of reality are perfectly compatible with literary realism. At least this holds true for Spanish realism, which he thought the most authentic kind. In his prologue to *La Regenta,* Galdós asserts that Quevedo is a realist. He would not have made the assertion had he believed caricature out of bounds to realism. But Galdós does more than tolerate caricature. He feels that Spanish realism is superior *because* it is seriocomic.[6] Caricature, one must therefore assume, is just one of many comic techniques that sustain it.

---

5. E. H. Gombrich and E. Kris, *Caricature* (Middlesex, 1940), p. 12.
6. Prologue to *La Regenta,* p. xi.

A Spanish critic has written the best summary of Galdós' attitude toward realism and caricature:

> para Galdós cabe un arte descriptivo, muy hispánico, en el que realismo y deformación caricaturesca se amalgaman perfectamente, y en el que la exactitud y veracidad en el retrato no sólo no sufren merma por la presencia del toque o toques caricaturescos, sino que, al revés, quedan por ellos reforzadas en una dimensión más importante que la estrictamente fotográfica, al servirse del arte interpretativo y al dar al lector algo más que el dato escueto.[7]

This harkens back to the idea that art is an interpretation, not a mere reproduction, of reality. Galdós' conscious subjectivity, which Baquero Goyanes points out in the passage just cited, shows to what extent his approach to literature differed from that of certain of his theorizing contemporaries.

Without once referring to realism, the French philosopher Bergson, in his essay *Du rire,* wrote what is still the best introduction to literary caricature. He had no such specific aim in mind, of course, and for this reason there is nothing in his essay which quite explains why caricatures can be so terrifying. Much of what Bergson says, however, is so pertinent that it is tempting to bask in the clarity of his ideas for a moment. The following, for instance, is a goodly portion of caricature in a nutshell: "The comic is that side of a person which reveals his likeness to a thing, that aspect of human events which, through its peculiar inelasticity, conveys the impression of pure mechanism, of automatism, of movement without life."[8] Bergson even finds a slot for that aspect of the comic (and an aspect of caricature as well) that mobilizes inanimate objects and anthropomorphizes animals.[9] His only omission has to do with the comic in narrative prose fiction. He virtually ignores the novel in favor of drama and thus concentrates on verbal and situation comedy.

7. Baquero Goyanes, *Perspectivismo y contraste,* p. 46.
8. Henri Bergson, "Laughter," in *Comedy* (New York, 1956), p. 117.
9. Ibid., pp. 62–63.

Since the various elements of caricature are closely inter-related, any treatment of the subject must try to avoid moats and fences. Repetition (speech mannerisms, the ruling passion), mechanization (autonomy of parts of the body, children mimicking adults), elevation of the nonhuman (objects and animals), and certain kinds of physical description frequently reside on each other's property. It should be mentioned that in the Novelas contemporáneas Galdós uses caricature in conjunction with a variety of other techniques. His pure caricatures tend to be minor figures.

Life, says Bergson, is flux, change, and renewal. It is not in its nature to ever repeat itself. Therefore, any mental or physical trait or gesture, any situation, if repeated to the point where it becomes predictable and imitable, will kindle laughter in the spectator. This bond between comedy and repetition was discovered long before Bergson. Ben Jonson's theory of the "humor," which rests on the concept of "ritual bondage," found its literary expression in repetition.[10] Basically, the English playwright and the French philosopher saw laughter as a conditioned reflex.[11] Imagine a steeplechase: suppose all the horses in a race clear the first hurdle except one, who returns to the starting gate over and over again, only to balk at the same hurdle repeatedly. Eventually the public will howl in mere anticipation of its balking. The approach, the sudden halt, the slow trot back to the gate all become so frozen in routine and repetition that one feels capable of imitating the animal's behavior. This can easily be transferred to a human context.

Repetition is fine for comedy but may be fatal to tragedy. It must be handled with the greatest restraint.[12] When grief is piled upon grief with unrelenting insistence, the seed of bathos is ready to sprout. And bathos may tickle as well as cloy. Goriot's prolonged mistreatment by his daughters—will they come to his deathbed or not?—is one step away from comedy.

10. Frye, *Anatomy of Criticism,* p. 168.
11. Ibid. Frye interprets Ben Jonson's theory thus.
12. Ibid.

Here is an example of a tragic motif that is closer to comedy than a traditionally comic device like the verbal refrain. Old Goriot's pleas for company are less impressive than Grandet's harping on "la fête d'Eugénie." Goriot's dilemma exasperates, whereas Grandet's "innocent" phrase is used sparingly, just often enough to sound ominous and terrible.

Speech mannerisms—the repetition of a verbal identification tag, a speech defect, a habitual mispronunciation, or something on this order—are common ingredients in caricature. One such mannerism, called in Spanish a muletilla, consists of a favorite word or phrase that is the trademark of a specific individual. Muletillas are frequent throughout the Novelas contemporáneas, just as they are in everyday life: consider the number of people who carry their "really's" and "you know's" around with them like a verbal annex.[13] Galdós probably acquired his taste for the muletilla from Dickens.[14] Certainly it is an easy way to add sparkle to a characterization. Doña Cándida *(El amigo Manso)* owes much of her genius for scene-stealing to the refrain "una cosa atroz," with which she evaluates every impression or shred of information that enters her mind. So ingrained is the expression that at one point Irene, Cándida's niece, calls her "doña Cosa Atroz" *(4,* 1261–62). Personification of a muletilla also occurs in *Lo prohibido,* where Barragán's wife is dubbed "No Cabe Más," this being her customary preamble to enthusiasm.[15] Her husband relies on the stock phrase "partiendo del principio," which, on one occasion,

13. Those familiar with George Eliot's *Middlemarch* will recall how often Mr. Brooke drops a "you know" every time he opens his mouth. And George Eliot is usually not associated with "cheap" caricature.

14. Vernon A. Chamberlin, "The Muletilla: An Important Facet of Galdós' Characterization Technique," *Hispanic Review, 29* (1961), 296–309.

15. Thackeray, who like George Eliot is thought to have escaped the taint of "cheap" caricature, is not above using a similar kind of personification. Blanche Amory, in *Pendennis,* is the authoress of a weepy book of verse called *Mes Larmes,* to which Thackeray makes frequent allusions. At one point in the narrative he says that "Mrs. Bonner and Mes Larmes came to the door."

he is said to repeat fifty times in fifteen minutes *(4,* 1814). Barragán's use of journalese is nothing compared to Torquemada's, whose speech habits will be examined later in this chapter, for they contribute to his status as a type.[16]

With regard to forms of comic speech other than the muletilla, the influence of Dickens on Galdós is harder to trace. There is nothing in the *Novelas contemporáneas* at all comparable to Mr. Jingle's elliptic staccato *(Pickwick Papers)* or to Mr. Sleary's lisp *(Hard Times).* But there are mispronunciations and malentendus galore, for which members of the lower classes and the newly rich middle class are chiefly responsible. José Izquierdo *(Fortunata y Jacinta)* is much concerned about his "dinidá y sinificancia," and the mayor of Jerusa *(El abuelo)* thinks that "monástica" and "numismática" are synonyms for "onomástica." However, these peculiarities of speech do not recur in any set pattern and are less automatic and predictable than in Dickens. The reader knows that Izquierdo is going to maul his words, but he does not know when or where he is going to strike. There are many other characters in the *Novelas contemporáneas* whose mispronunciations resemble those of Izquierdo and whose misuse of vocabulary resembles that of Monedero's: Fortunata and Torquemada come to mind immediately. The only unique case of mispronunciation in these novels is Almudena's broken Spanish in *Misericordia.* Ironically, it is the sole example of noncomic use of a speech mannerism. Had little Felipe Centeno *(El doctor Centeno)* retained his attachment to the prefix "des," there might have been two examples of consistent mispronunciation. Unfortunately, Galdós nips this bit of linguistic inventiveness in the bud. It is a shame, for the reader grows fond of "desequipaje," "desartillería," "desalumbrado," and other daring flights into the world of antimatter *(4,* 1300).

What the muletilla is to the physical presence of a character, the ruling passion is to his inner life. It might even be thought

16. A distinction should perhaps be drawn between Torquemada's homegrown muletillas—"¡cuidado!" and "¡ñales!"—and his acquired accretions of urbanity.

of as a psychological muletilla, for it changes either very little or not at all. A ruling passion sums up a character in much the same way that "una cosa atroz" sums up doña Cándida.

The concept of the ruling passion has been called a fallacy, but a fallacy that a novelist has every right to exploit.[17] It is a formula that Galdós used in his earliest novels—*La Fontana de Oro* and *La sombra*—and continued to use throughout his career. The term, though, is misleading. "Passion" (aside from its erotic connotations) implies an energetic, dynamic, perhaps even ruthless pursuit of an objective. Galdós' characters, with rare exceptions, are not energetic, dynamic, or ruthless. This is where they differ radically from their counterparts in Dickens and Balzac. Furthermore, the characters chosen here as embodiments of a ruling passion are frustrated whenever they try to control the course of events or impose their will on anyone else. It is better therefore to speak of their manias and obsessions than of their ruling passions.

A mania or obsession can make a minor figure spring to life. Tristana's mother *(Tristana)* appears only in a flashback covering some two pages of text in the Aguilar edition of Galdós' works. Nevertheless, through selection and simplification, Galdós saves her from oblivion. He gives her a strong silhouette, if not a profound psychology: "Dos manías, entre otras mil, principalmente la trastornaban: la manía de mudarse de casa y la del aseo." Here is the framework for a comic characterization. All Galdós has to do is to stretch both manias as far as they will go. He says that doña Josefina changes her domicile at least once a month, and that there is often a smell of camphor wafting up from the meals she serves *(5, 1545)*; that eventually her memory and sanity dissolve to make room for her two manias; and that, finally, one of the two kills her. Doña Josefina's life-span (which for the reader begins with her husband's death) ends on a predictable note: "en uno de los cambios de domicilio, ya fuese por haber caído en casa nueva, cuyas paredes chorreaban de humedad, ya porque Josefina usó zapatos recién sometidos a su sistema de

17. Gullón, *Galdós, novelista moderno,* p. 159.

saneamiento, llegó la hora de rendir a Dios el alma" *(5, 1546).*[18]

Villaamil's obsession with m, i, a, and u (morality, income tax, protective tariffs, and unification of the debt) was discussed at some length in Chapter 4. However, there is another obsession as deeply embedded in his mind. Villaamil wants a job desperately, but he pretends not to expect one in the hope of being pleasantly surprised. This is optimism disguised as pessimism. Villaamil wears his pessimism as some people wear amulets—to attract good fortune:

> Vale más seamos pesimistas, muy pesimistas, para que luego resulte lo contrario de lo que se teme . . . . Sí, Ramón, figúrate que no te dan nada, que no hay para ti esperanza, a ver si creyéndolo así viene la contraria . . . . Porque yo he observado que siempre sale la contraria.
> *(5, 564)*

Whenever anyone asks about his prospects, Villaamil violently insists that all expectation is futile. He claims to have resigned himself to his jobless fate. At the same time, he haunts the ministries hoping for some windfall, scans the newspapers for lists of political appointees, and prays to God for help—but all to no avail. A broken man, he finally decides to buy a gun and do away with himself. After choosing a suitable spot in a field outside Madrid, a terrible thought looms up to embitter his last moments: perhaps the gun will not go off, or (and this possibility is decidedly worse) perhaps he will only wound himself. His wretched life will drag on as before, and he will be more of a laughingstock than ever. At this, Villaamil's obsession takes over in a final act of fidelity. He imagines the worst with all his might so that the opposite will come about: "¿Apostamos a que falla el tiro? ¡Ay! Antipáticas *Miaus,* ¡cómo os vais a reír de mí! . . . Ahora, ahora . . . . ¿A que no sale?" *(5, 683)*. He fires and falls dead.

Villaamil is not a pure caricature—his anguish is caught in

18. The parallel between Josefina and Felisita *(Angel Guerra)* is obvious. Caricature is often indistinguishable from metaphor.

too much detail. Moreover, his predicament is not self-contained or isolated. It reveals itself most clearly when set off against the outside world—family, friends, and, above all, bureaucratic Spain. Social friction dulls the profile of caricature. This is what separates Villaamil and most of Galdós' figures from Dickens' caricatures. As a British critic remarked:

> It is really alien to Dickens' gift that his people should be made to talk to each other. When he attempts this he merely succeeds in making them talk *at* each other; like actors. His natural genius is for human soliloquy not for human intercourse.[19]

It is understandable, then, that Villaamil should be most Dickensian precisely at those moments when he talks *at* people (the m, i, a, u dogma) and when he soliloquizes (the pessimism-as-best-policy reflex).

This reflex repeats itself like any self-imposed affectation, but it is more complex than mere automatism (Bergson). Villaamil's mental habit bespeaks the inner tension and aggressiveness of casuistic argument. Still, the reader will overlook this nuance. He will react to Villaamil's "¿A que no sale?" with laughter—macabre laughter, to be sure. Perhaps the reader will even feel a bit ashamed of himself in retrospect. But there is something inescapably comic about a man who clings to the idiosyncrasies of a lifetime in the midst of disintegration and ruin.

A down-at-the-heels ex-bureaucrat has a vague professional contour—one does not know the man just because one knows his line of work. But a sea captain, especially an ex-sea-captain, is another story. As soon as Galdós states what don Pito's *(Angel Guerra)* profession has been, one can almost predict what the character will be like. This is because seamen, particularly in nineteenth-century fiction, often conform to a professional type (not to be confused with a socioeconomic type). Don Pito conforms so thoroughly that he emerges as a costumbrista figure. This is not meant to be derogatory: Galdós

19. V. S. Pritchett, *The Living Novel* (London, 1946), p. 77.

could take certain stock figures like the poet and the wet nurse
and paint them with considerable dash. With other stock figures
—the misanthrope, the señorito, and the cesante—Galdós
cleared a new path for himself. It is unfair to compare don
Pito with Villaamil, because the latter is a major character,
but he can be compared with Moreno-Isla *(Fortunata y Jacinta)*
and Frasquito Ponte *(Misericordia)*. He suffers by comparison
with them, however, not because he is a caricature, but because
he is *déjà vu*. Fiction has stylized and stereotyped very few
professions as completely as it has don Pito's. Even a clever
variation on the ex-seaman theme, as in Cheever's recent
The Wapshot Chronicle, returns to the same motif: obsession
with the sea.

Don Pito is an exile on land. He has a stinging nostalgia for
the sea. But Madrid and Toledo, where the events of *Angel
Guerra* take place, are landlocked cities. When sober, Pito is
painfully aware that he is far from his native habitat, and he
wanders about in a manic-depressive state. Luckily, he can
usually get his hands on a bottle. Alcohol stokes his furnace
and enables him to navigate rather buoyantly through urban
bays and canals. His greeting becomes "¡ah de a bordo!" and
his favorite expression "avante toda." As in the case of doña
Josefina, Galdós stretches Pito's mania as far as it will go.
The ex-sea-captain stops a passerby and asks, "¿No es usted el
pasajerito de Glasgow?" *(5,* 1303). He goes from Havana to
Le Havre in a matter of seconds and still has the energy to
warn a wagoner about high tides and an approaching squall
(5, 1303).

Pito passes the first test of seaworthiness—a healthy thirst—
with flying colors. Galdós obligingly has him pass the second
as well: "La afición al mujerío . . . fue la debilidad capital de
su vida y ocasión de sus quebrantos" *(5,* 1426). Pito dutifully
meets the demands of his profession by wooing the servant-girl
Jusepa.[20] His obsession with the sea has all the right trappings
—nautical vocabulary, alcohol, "mujerío." Whenever he floats

20. The scenes between Pito and Jusepa are farcical. She is muscular,
he is a weakling, and the drubbings go in one direction only. Recall the
farcical beating of José María by Camila in *Lo prohibido.*

into the reader's ken, they trail behind. His characterization is based wholly on the repetition of a single motif and its usual by-products. This literary type belongs to the folklore of fiction.

Speech mannerisms and psychological obsessions stress the mechanical side of human nature. As Bergson points out, this mechanization of life seems comical to the spectator. How often one laughs at a person whose habits are as regular as clockwork and who gets upset by any change in routine. The fussy bachelor, the tea-at-home dowager, and the slave to the weather forecast all obey this comic principle.

As regards the subject of children behaving like grownups, there is a shift in emphasis from the mechanical repetition to the mechanical imitation of life. It is amusing to watch children imitating their elders. At whom does one laugh, the model or the imitator? The answer is that one laughs at both. A child takes on the configuration of a robot, of a thing, when he repeats words and ideas that he does not understand. At the same time, these words and ideas lose all their dignity and importance when a child bandies them about. They are reduced to the level of a toy or a game, again a thing. Two processes of degradation are at work simultaneously.[21] When, in *El doctor Centeno,* Felipe and Juanito del Socorro discuss "la Deuda" and "la Hacienda," amusement is derived from the children themselves and from the reductio ad absurdum of erstwhile weighty matters. Even a straightforward report of adult conversation has this dual effect: Juanito says, "—Hiji . . . , hiji . . . , ¿no sabes? *Esto se va* . . . . Vamos al decir, que viene revolución. Los señores lo dicen. Ya está la tropa apalabrada. Se arma, se arma." Felipe, not to be outdone, adds, "Pues algo va a pasar . . . , porque ayer don Pedro, en la mesa, dijo que esto se pone feo . . . , ¿oyes?, y habló del Gobierno, de la Tropa, del *Porsupuesto*" (4, 1323).

21. For the idea of the comic as degradation, see Sigmund Freud, *Wit and Its Relation to the Unconscious,* trans. A. A. Brill (New York, 1916), pp. 337–38 and passim. See also Casares, *El humorismo y otros ensayos,* p. 36.

One of the funniest moments in *Tormento* is when Joaqui-nito Pez, barely into his teens and already a budding orator, harangues an imaginary audience with "Señores, volvamos los ojos a Roma; volvamos a Roma los ojos, señores, ¿y qué veremos? Veremos consagrados por primera vez la propiedad y las libertades personales" *(4, 1472)*. Besides capturing the machinelike accuracy of a precocious mind, this is good satire of Spanish parliamentarianism. By placing such rhetoric in the mouth of a youngster, Galdós indicates that in Cortes more time was spent in airing forensic formulas than in debating urgent issues.

Freud talks about certain remarks which children make in all innocence but which sound clever or obscene coming from adults. He calls such remarks "naïve-comic."[22] Even a prude might find it impossible to stifle a laugh when, in *Fortunata y Jacinta,* the Pituso, thought to be Santa Cruz's illegitimate son, addresses Jacinta as "Putona" *(5, 118)*. This is a good example of how the effect of a word is checked by the naïveté of the person who employs it. Outrage at such language in a child is caused only by a secret fear the child has been taught or trained to speak that way.

A child's mimicry of adult behavior or speech reduces what once was alive (in its implications or consequences) to the level of a thing. This mechanization of life is carried to its most extreme form in literature whenever an author bestows semi- or complete autonomy upon parts of the human body. It is something that would occur only to a writer with a penchant for caricature. In Spanish literature, Quevedo set a precedent for the use of this technique in his classic *El buscón*. Everyone remembers Cabra—the emaciated schoolmaster whose whiskers were afraid of being eaten by his mouth and whose Adam's apple was liable to go hunting for food on its own. Galdós believed that Quevedo was a comic genius, and the Novelas contemporáneas bow in his direction more than once.[23] But

22. Freud, pp. 361–62.
23. Quevedo is "el hombre más gracioso que ha existido en el mundo" *(El doctor Centeno, 4, 1396)*.

the acrobatics found in Quevedo's description of Cabra are rare in these novels. Galdós was restrained both by subject matter and temperament from ever converting a human being into a pincushion for puns. This holds true with regard to his general technique of characterization and the specific descriptive technique now under discussion.[24]

Galdós' restraint in mechanizing parts of the human anatomy is seen in his portrait of Juan Bou *(La desheredada)*. The following is mild by comparison with Quevedo's dehumanization of Cabra: "Su cara, enfundada en copiosa barba negra y revuelta, mostraba por entre tanto áspero pelo dos ojos iguales: el uno vivísimo, dotado de un ligero movimiento rotatorio; el otro fijo y sin brillo" *(4,* 1078). Whenever Bou coughs, "el ojo rotatorio se le echaba fuera, mientras el apagado se escondía en lo más hondo de la órbita" *(4,* 1078). Galdós makes no attempt to overplay Bou's defect, whereas Quevedo would probably have lingered over it voluptuously.[25] In this instance Galdós is closer to Dickens than he is to Quevedo. The same is true for another aspect of caricature, the mechanical display of emotion.

Doña Cándida *(El amigo Manso)* is an opportunist without money or scruples. She relieves the first of these problems by a bold plan of action which dramatizes her second deficiency: she tries to sell her niece to a rich indiano. The scheme is foiled, but Cándida denies any wrongdoing and fights her accuser with the most formidable weapon in her arsenal, mechanical tears: "pugnaba Calígula por traer a su defensa un destacamento de lágrimas, que al fin, tras grandes esfuerzos, asomaron a sus ojos." She summons and swells these tears at will. At the same time, her double chin, which contains an impatient swarm of lies and hoaxes, throbs in seeming independence of the rest of her body *(4,* 1252). Compare this to a brief

24. Baquero Goyanes explains the difference between Quevedo's hyperbole and Galdós'. See *Perspectivismo y contraste,* pp. 53, 76.

25. For another instance of Galdós' relative restraint on this score, see his descriptions of Maxi Rubín's double-jointed body in *Fortunata y Jacinta, 5,* 161, 471.

passage in Dickens' *Hard Times:* Mrs. Sparsit, a more sinister version of doña Cándida, "occasionally sat back in her chair and silently wept; at which periods a tear of large dimensions, like a crystal earring, might be observed (or rather, must be, for it insisted on public notice) sliding down her Roman nose."[26] Details may vary, but the guiding spirit behind these two passages is very similar.

Dickens and Sterne are masters of the technique of personifying inanimate objects and animals and deployed it with great zest. Galdós is more staid. He seldom personifies inanimate objects or animals except when viewing reality through the eyes of a child. Even the piggy bank sequence in *Fortunata y Jacinta* is meant to show how immature and childlike Maxi still is. Of all the Novelas contemporáneas, *El doctor Centeno* contains the greatest amount of personification.

In the first scene of *El doctor Centeno,* Felipe is eating a modest picnic lunch on the outskirts of Madrid. After eating, he lights a cigar. Arduous enough for an adult, this requires a siege-like persistence in a boy. Metaphor and caricature together record his efforts. A battle takes place (metaphor), "desperate, horrible, titanic." The enemy is a monster, perhaps a dragon, that tries to defend itself from the flames but whose members twist and crack and finally give way (personification). What happens shortly thereafter is easy to guess: the boy gets sick to his stomach, and the monster, victor at last, falls from his hands *(4,* 1296–97). Later in the novel Galdós personifies a few inanimate objects in Pedro Polo's classroom in order to suggest how everything in that purgatory is rigged against the pupils: "Las negras carpetas, al abrirse, bostezaban, y los tinteros, ávidos de manchar hacían todo lo posible por encontrar ocasión de volcarse" *(4,* 1311).

Animals occasionally undergo a similar humanization. Canelo, the porter's dog in *Miau,* is bored by window-shopping

26. Charles Dickens, *Hard Times* (London, Oxford University Press, 1955), p. 186. Note that Mrs. Sparsit's "Coriolanian nose," "Roman features," and "Roman nose" suggest something of the Calígula quality of doña Cándida.

(5, 556) and has the good sense to abandon a funeral pro-
cession in favor of some more lively street adventure:

> en cuanto entendió que se trataba de enterrar, cosa poca
> divertida y que siempre sugiere cosas misantrópicas, dió
> media vuelta y tomó otra dirección, pensando que le tenía
> más cuenta ver si se parecía alguna perra elegante y sen-
> sible por aquellos barrios. *(5, 635–36)*

Canelo is Luisito Cadalso's friend. Galdós personifies him as
part of an attempt, frequent throughout *Miau,* to see reality
through a child's eyes. There is a delightful moment when
Luisito, just after his first vision of God, is struck by Canelo's
pensive air. Only too happy to attribute this to the dog's having
seen God as well, Luisito regrets that Canelo cannot talk and
corroborate the great event *(5, 560).*

Most people take the word "caricature" to mean exaggeration. This is a correct definition, sanctioned by the dictionary.
However, in speaking of literature, to equate caricature with
exaggeration is to court the danger of removing a term from
its original context (in this case the pictorial arts) and failing
to adapt it to a new context. Problems arising from the transfer
of the term "baroque" are yet to be ironed out to everyone's
satisfaction. To avoid confusion, I have grouped several kinds
of exaggerative techniques normally associated with caricature
beneath the heading "metaphor"—hence the removal of physiological and animal correlatives and the grotesque to Chapter
4. Despite this precaution, however, there remains a kind of
exaggeration of a purely descriptive or pictorial nature which
could not be relegated to the preceding chapter. This will be
called "hyperbole."[27]

Some of Galdós' descriptions, in their notation of human
ugliness, are as comical as Fielding's. The fact that beauty
never quite unleashed a comparable flood of hyperbole in

27. It is the term that Baquero Goyanes prefers in *Perspectivismo y
contraste.*

Galdós may be attributed to his distaste for pulp fiction.[28] One need not worry about any saccharine pulp effect when reading about Jusepa, don Pito's inamorata in *Angel Guerra* *(5,* 1426). As Galdós explains, she is one of nature's "antidotes against love." Her body, though lithesome enough, cannot offset the unfortunate impression caused by the head it supports: "una patata por nariz, ojos de pulga, boca de serón, color de barro crudo, cabellos ralos, desiguales y no muy blancos dientes." This cornucopia makes starvation seem almost pleasant, but Pito cannot resist. He idealizes Jusepa's appearance just as don Quixote idealizes Aldonza Lorenzo's. She becomes his goddess, the elusive object of his passion. Jusepa's ugliness, then, is comical not only because it is so definitive, but because it inspires a constancy wholly unwarranted by the normal laws of infatuation.

Less reminiscent of Cervantes but much more impressive is Galdós' hyperbolic description of Tía Roma in *Torquemada en la hoguera.* This singular character is so old and ugly that she fully merits the title "madre de las telarañas" *(5,* 933). The author captures Tía Roma's musty mass to perfection:

> era tan vieja, tan vieja y tan fea, que su cara parecía un puñado de telarañas revueltas con la ceniza; su nariz de corcho ya no tenía forma; su boca redonda y sin dientes menguaba y crecía, según la distensión de las arrugas que la formaba. Más arriba, entre aquel revoltijo de piel polvorosa, lucían los ojos de pescado, dentro de un cerco de pimentón húmedo. Lo demás de la persona desaparecía bajo un envoltorio de trapos y dentro de la remendada falda, en la cual había restos de un traje de la madre de doña Silvia, cuando era polla. *(5,* 922)

This is one of the most vivid descriptions in all of Galdós. The reader can picture the ancient parasite in her heap of rags as clearly as if she were standing in front of him. The author's

28. It is interesting to note that in the *Novelas contemporáneas* his beautiful women are full-bodied, strong, and sometimes earthy. Galdós abandons, in these novels, the pale, sylphlike beauty of a Clara *(La Fontana de Oro)* or a Rosario *(Doña Perfecta).*

graphic skill always seems to surpass itself whenever he portrays such relics of humanity. Even in *La Fontana de Oro,*
the sketch of Salomé, one of "Las Tres Ruinas," stands out
from its companion sketches in bold relief.

Tía Roma is more than a caricature, however. Neither her
physical appearance nor her first exchange with Torquemada
(5, 922–23) gives any hint that she does other than fawn in
ragpicker fashion before her benefactor. The reader is entirely
unprepared when she refuses Torquemada's gift of a mattress.
This is a marvelous scene. Tía Roma refuses the mattress
because Torquemada has slept on it for years. She believes
it has absorbed, as if by osmosis, all his sins, his niggardly
ideas, and his numerical calculations and machinations. The
superstitious old crone is certain that Torquemada's avarice
has crept into the mattress like vermin. If she were to sleep
on it, toads, slimy snakes, and devils with bats' ears would
carry her off to Hell in the hour of her death. She follows
these horrors with an account of Torquemada's squalid, pinch-
penny past. Here, in this savage exposé, is the prehistory of
one of Galdós' most successful creations, the usurer Torquemada. In this character, Galdós employs the techniques of
caricature with greater sophistication than anywhere else. At
the same time, he synthesizes in Torquemada the historical
evolution of Spain's middle class.

The typical usurer of nineteenth-century fiction is a caricature. He is racked by a single obsession—monetary gain. Like
a sailor's obsession with the sea, this lust for money carries
with it certain traditional overtones, namely, sangfroid and
miserliness. If one were to accept Tía Roma's account of
Torquemada's past life, one might be led to believe that his
usury was all of one piece, in accord with expectations. But
Tía Roma's truculent attack appears just two chapters from
the end of *Torquemada en la hoguera.* Galdós, meanwhile,
has made it clear that his usurer is not one of those "metaphysical" usurers who live only to watch their funds multiply.
Instead, says Galdós, Torquemada has always been the usurer-
positivist, willing to transact with the spirit of the age. How-

ever mean and tightfisted this paterfamilias might have been early in his career (1851–68), he loosens up considerably during his prosperity (1870–81). He is not averse to certain refinements of diet and dress and even brings a carpet and spring mattresses into his home. His wife startles the neighborhood by wearing a fur coat. By the mid-1870s, Torquemada and family become full-fledged members of the middle class.

Even though Galdós, with characteristic irony, says that Torquemada spared no expense "of doctor and drugstore" to save his wife's life (as if this were a unique display of magnanimity), it is clear that miserliness, one of the traditional overtones of usury, is relaxed in Torquemada's case. There is certainly no comparison between him and Balzac's Gobseck, who lives in cheap lodgings, never gives a care to the creature comforts (except for an occasional good meal), and wants only to accumulate more and more gold for the power it gives him. Nor can one compare him with that king of misers, Grandet. Grandet's avarice is absolute, his domestic habits show no outward evolution, and even his dress remains the same. To compare Torquemada with Scrooge is totally out of the question. Torquemada evidently does not conform to any model the reader may have drawn for himself.

What of sangfroid, the other companion of usury? Once again, Torquemada surprises the reader. The very first sentence of *Torquemada en la hoguera* indicates that he will lose his self-possession and will suffer: "Voy a contar cómo fué al quemadero el inhumano que tantas vidas infelices consumió en llamas" *(5,* 906). In the same paragraph, the reader learns that his is a "caso patético." His son falls ill, and Torquemada writhes in anguish. As the boy sinks lower and lower, Torquemada grows more and more desperate. His mental distress is acute. He dashes through the streets in search of charity cases, trying to assuage God's anger by giving to the poor. He paces about the house, sleeps and eats fitfully, lashes out at the doctor, even bangs his head against the wall. When Valentín dies, his father, who for days has been living at fever pitch, gets hysterical and finally collapses.

This emotionalism is at odds with the cold, calculating

image of avarice that Balzac presents in the forms of Gobseck and Grandet. If anything, it brings Shylock to mind. Gobseck is impenetrable and impassive. The only concession he ever makes to family allegiance is to bequeath a sum of money to a distant relative who for years has been a streetwalker. Otherwise, "il économisait le mouvement vital, et concentrait tous les sentiments humains dans le *moi*."[29] Grandet is even more impassive. The only emotion he allows himself is a sardonic joy, and this only when business warrants it. Personal matters, even his wife's death, never melt his glacial attention to *les affaires*. Torquemada is very different. He can barely control his emotion.

Another way in which Torquemada departs from stereotype involves his ingenuousness. Always a nonbeliever, it suddenly occurs to him that God might really exist and that Valentín's life is the price he (Torquemada) must pay for sins past and present. He imagines the boy to be God's weapon of revenge. So completely does this idea take hold that for the first time Torquemada shows an interest in religion. He begins to listen carefully to his friend Bailón's religious doctrines, which include a belief in reincarnation. Claiming to have been a priest in ancient Egypt, Bailón relates how he seduced a lovely priestess and incurred the wrath of Isis and Apis; for these misdemeanors he was buried alive. This doctrine of reincarnation blooms in Torquemada's mind only after a long incubation period; it does not appear again until *Torquemada en la cruz*. But Bailón's other doctrine, to the effect that "God is Humanity," bears early fruit. To help humanity, in Torquemada's rather free interpretation, is to placate God (if God exists). And, by extension, to buy humanity is to buy God. This explains why Torquemada becomes so kind to his tenants, why he offers a no-interest loan to a debt-ridden nobleman, and why he tries to give his mattress to Tía Roma.

Torquemada is so ingenuous that he inspires pity in the reader. Professionally odious, he is nevertheless the victim of his own ignorance in this private crisis. Faced with his son's

29. Honoré de Balzac, *Gobseck,* in *La Comédie humaine, 2,* 636.

illness, Torquemada is a lost soul. The reader overlooks his guilt.

There is a final difference between Torquemada and the typical moneylender of fiction: he can do no harm. From the outset, there is nothing menacing about Torquemada or his surroundings. The reader is never made to enter any somber alleyway or dismal inner sanctum. Torquemada never walks in stealth, never counts his gold or leers diabolically. On the contrary, he is a Halloween figure. The opening paragraphs of the novel, with their synthesis of verbal irony, comic religious metaphor and hyperbole, and their promise of a "caso patético," immediately tell the reader that he need not be afraid of Torquemada.

In spite of his concessions to material comfort, his emotionalism, his relative innocence, and his harmlessness, Torquemada does not totally contradict the preconceived mental image of a usurer. He sees life as a transaction. He values nothing on earth or in Heaven, be it person, thing or idea, for its own sake, on its own terms. Everything is reduced to a question of profit, loss, barter, bribe, interest, down payment, purchase, or swindle. Nothing is esteemed, everything appraised. The intrusion of this bookkeeper ethic upon every situation and emotion is constant. It is a reflex that functions like clockwork, always there, always predictable. To a far greater extent than Villaamil's pessimism reflex, Torquemada's obsession with business represents the whole man, overshadowing everything else in his personality. As it repeats itself over and over again, the element of caricature in Torquemada emerges more and more clearly. Even at the end, after Valentín's death, there is no conversion of the heart, no remorse, no spiritual progress of any kind. Torquemada feels cheated because he did not get his money's worth from God. And if the child was carried off as compensation for the father's sins, then everything is now squared away between Heaven and earth. Torquemada owes nothing to the powers on high, and he returns to his usury with a vengeance.

One might object that Torquemada truly adores his son and that this sentiment is untainted by base motives. It is true

that he loves the child; the question is, what is there about him
that he loves the most, and how does he express this love?
Recall Torquemada's reaction to his wife's death. Doña
Silvia was another person he loved, and his sorrow at her
passing was deep and genuine. But what does Galdós choose
to relate about doña Silvia? Only that after forty years of
marriage she was just like her husband—usurious and hard-
working *(5,* 907). Torquemada loved her because she was a
faithful reflection of himself. Egoism certainly lies very near
the heart of many relationships; the trick is to discover what
quality the ego finds most attractive. In Torquemada's case,
it is business acumen.[30]

Valentín, Torquemada's son, is a mathematical wizard.
His genius is such that even Torquemada consults him on a
few occasions. When brought before a group of elderly mathematicians, Valentín leaves them gasping. They see in this
freak of nature another Newton. The father is beside himself
with joy. When Valentín gets sick, Torquemada's first thought
is that God is envious and wants to expropriate the boy—that
is, the immense fortune that Valentín will make some day:
"Porque su hijo, si viviese, había de ganar muchísimo dinero,
pero muchísimo, y de aquí la celestial intriga" *(5,* 919).

However, Torquemada is willing to renounce whatever
pecuniary advantages might accrue from his possession of the
boy provided Valentín gets well. This "sacrifice" proves how
deeply ingrained Torquemada's obsession with money is. Here
is a clue to the humor of the novel: Torquemada's greed,
avarice, and cruelty are not emphasized, as with Scrooge,
Grandet, and Gobseck. What is emphasized is the single
point of reference to which he always returns as to a magnet.
There is one episode in the book which is a particularly good
example of this "comic return." Torquemada visits an artist
who is dying of tuberculosis and cannot afford to buy medicine.
For once, one expects the usurer to be altruistic. And so he is
at first: the reader is thrown completely off the track. Torque-

30. Torquemada's affection for doña Lupe *(Torquemada en la cruz)* is
another case in point.

mada tears up the artist's promissory note and insists that his financial aid is a gift, not a loan. Just before leaving the studio, however, he decides to take a few paintings with him as souvenirs. The reader suddenly realizes that for Torquemada the paintings are not souvenirs, but collateral. Moreover, they are collateral which, according to his estimate, might someday be worth as much as his gift of money: the artist's death is imminent, and the value of his paintings will increase thereafter.

Torquemada's soul is contractive, not expansive. In true positivist fashion, it latches onto the specific within the general instead of the other way around. The usurer lives in a shrunken world. This becomes clear in the episode where Torquemada goes out into the night to sprinkle alms among the beggars. At one point he looks up at the sky. For the first time in his life, he contemplates its beauty. He is especially taken with the stars, which are so lovely they remind him of coins: "Las había chicas, medianas, y grandes; algo así como pesetas, medios duros y duros" *(5,* 921). He is also impressed by their numbers and decides to have Valentín, when he recovers, solve the following problem: "si acuñáramos todas las estrellas del cielo, ¿cuánto producirían al cinco por ciento de interés compuesto en los siglos que van desde que todo eso existe?" *(5,* 921). There is nothing mysterious or overpowering about the universe. Sums of money are its only poetry.

At the very end of the novel, Galdós answers the question posed a moment ago: what does Torquemada love the most about Valentín, and how does he express this love? After burying the child, Torquemada goes home and takes down from the kitchen wall the slate on which Valentín always did his arithmetic. A few problems are still chalked there. Torquemada kisses and embraces it disconsolately, because to him it is the portrait of his son. It is this slate rather than any photograph or other personal effect that Torquemada will treasure as a memento. He orders a gilt frame for it, intending to hang it as an icon in his bedroom.

Torquemada's love for his son is a form of egoism. His feeling toward him is not one of pride but of vanity. Like all those who take delight in their possessions, he assumes that he is envied by everyone. When God "steals" the future potentate, envy is the motive. To attribute such a motive to God is to deny His existence, and Torquemada is a nonbeliever.[31] Whenever he goes through the motions of charity, it is a lie. His charity is a conciliatory bribe to a competitor, not to God. It is also a kind of insurance policy on which Torquemada pays premiums. Like a man who is utterly convinced that his house is fireproof but who buys fire insurance so that no one can accuse him of negligence, Torquemada tries to make himself invulnerable to blame or guilt by helping the needy. Though he seems to be protecting his son, he is really protecting himself. His bribes, or premiums, form the substance of three key scenes in the novel. Repetition is again the source of comedy.

The first scene takes place shortly after Valentín falls ill. Torquemada goes out to collect his rents. Some of his tenants throw themselves on his mercy; others curse his hide; still others ask that he make certain repairs. His son bedridden with a serious disease and the preachings of Bailón fresh in mind, Torquemada meets every complaint, curse, and request with a proclamation of goodwill:

> Yo soy humano; yo compadezco a los desgraciados; yo les ayudo en lo que puedo, porque así nos lo manda la Humanidad; y bien sabéis todas que como faltáis a la Humanidad, lo pagaréis tarde o temprano, y que si sois buenas, tendréis vuestra recompensa. *(5,* 918)

The tenants are incredulous. One of them, as we know, finds a parallel between Torquemada's behavior and the fact that a comet has lately been seen in the sky. But Torquemada has not really changed a bit. He has only insured himself against accusing fingers: "No salgan ahora diciendo que es por mis maldades, pues de todo hay" *(5,* 918). He is happy because he expects Valentín to recover.

31. Bailón's idea that "God is Humanity" is a further spur to non-belief.

Home once more, he finds no change in Valentín's condition. That night, he bombards every beggar he can find with alms. On the following day, the boy gets worse. The bribes have not been big enough. It is time for a larger one. Torquemada visits a destitute nobleman whose application for a loan he had refused some days before. He now offers this client a loan at an unprecedented twelve percent. The client turns it down. He makes it five percent, and no luck. Interest-free, and still the nobleman rejects Torquemada's offer, saying that he no longer needs the money; whereupon Torquemada accuses him of hardheartedness. Here is an obsession carried to its logical extreme. Since Torquemada believes that generosity will insure his son's survival, a refusal to accept this generosity is an act of brutality.

Finally, there is Tía Roma's rejection of Torquemada's mattress—another bribe spurned. This too is brutal, because Tía Roma does not have a cent to her name and Torquemada believes that poverty and Christianity (i.e. "Humanity") are bound together in some sort of reciprocal pact. Earlier, in the initial stage of Valentín's illness, he had asked Tía Roma to pray to God for this very reason: "Reza tú también, reza mucho hasta que se te seque la boca, que tú debes ser allá muy bien mirada, porque en tu vida has tenido una peseta" *(5, 922)*. Now as she declines Torquemada's gift and berates the donor in a scathing tirade, the usurer feels that he has been discredited. But Torquemada feels that Tía Roma has compromised him only because she has *voiced* her opinions; it is quite beyond his imaginative powers to suppose that God might be omniscient in any extrasensory way.

In these three episodes, comedy results from Torquemada's circumscribed view of reality. He thinks and feels in one direction only, however geniune his thoughts and feelings may be. One may compare the structure of *Torquemada en la hoguera* to that of a wheel. The usurer's love for his son makes the novel move. When this happens, the spokes and hub are also set in motion. The spokes are the various episodes of the novel, and the hub is the point at which they converge. Every revolution of the wheel—the father's tenacious love for his son—turns the hub of transaction. After Valentín's death, the rim and spokes of the wheel drop off, and only the hub, automotive, remains.

The convergence of all things into one hub is obsession or mania, a typical feature of caricature. What makes *Torquemada en la hoguera* unique is the way Galdós welds this feature of caricature onto the structure of his novel. Characterization and organization are interlocked, thus creating a masterful sense of unity which is increased by the brevity of the work. It is more properly a novelette than a novel, and its time span covers only about a week. The limits on length and time do wonders for Galdós' style. Terse and pithy, without a word gone to waste, *Torquemada en la hoguera* ranks with *La de Bringas* as the best written of the Novelas contemporáneas. The characters in the novel are among the most dynamic in Galdós' repertory. Torquemada is always in a febrile state, ready to burst at the seams at any moment. Tía Roma, in the mattress episode, spits out the bile of a lifetime. Valentín is like a celestial flame, burning himself out amid shrieks and convulsions. Bailón, for all his religious twaddle, is primitive and lusty. Even the painter Martín and his mistress (already known to the reader as Isidora Rufete) live with a strange intensity: he is half-crazed with disease, and she darts about as if every minute were his (and her) last on earth.

Of the other three novels in the *Torquemada* series, *Torquemada y San Pedro,* the concluding novel, is the one that most closely resembles *Torquemada en la hoguera.* The book records a later phase in the moneylender's transactions with God. This time it is his own survival that Torquemada wants to guarantee, not his son's. The San Pedro of the title refers to a priest, Gamborena, from whom Torquemada tries to exact some assurance that Heaven's gates will open for him. This, of course, is just another safeguard or premium, just in case God and the saints should happen to exist; Torquemada never abandons his religious skepticism.

Torquemada, who by now has become very rich, and in whom the miser has replaced the usurer, plans to leave a third of his estate to the Church. In exchange, he hopes to retire to a comfortable afterlife and enjoy a fair return on his investment. But he must have a guarantee and badgers Gamborena for one: "Haya por ambas partes lealtad y buena fe, ¡cuidado!, porque, francamente, sería muy triste, señor misionero de mis entretelas, que yo diera mi capital y que luego resultara que no había tales puertas, ni tal gloria ni Cristo que los fundó" *(5,* 1157). This, however, is only part of the story. In the back of Torquemada's mind lurks another idea: his expressed intention to leave part of his fortune to the Church has so predisposed things in his favor (he thinks) that his life on earth will never end. When he gets sick and recovers, he feels that God is a true man of His word; on suffering a relapse, he raves, "Esto es un engaño, una verdadera estafa, sí señor" *(5,* 1190).

Torquemada y San Pedro differs from the first novel in its greater stress on Torquemada's miserliness. It also plays up his egoism more strongly, since his own health and salvation are now his primary concerns. An existential interpretation of the character suggests itself under these conditions. Torquemada's one motive force in life has become the accumulation of wealth. He hoards money, securities, properties, jewelry, and works of art because this is his raison d'être. If he forsakes all this, he will cease to exist as Torquemada—hence his religious skepticism. In order to believe in an extraterrestrial existence, one must scuttle mentally one's goods and chattels. This is impossible for Torquemada. He must take them with him because they are him.

The humor in *Torquemada y San Pedro* is derived from Torquemada's constant return to a single point of reference. Basically, it is the same comic return observed in *Torquemada en la hoguera.* The old alliance between comedy and repetition still holds firm. In *Torquemada en la cruz* and *Torquemada en el purgatorio* repetition is again a stimulus to laughter.

In the first of these two, one laughs at Torquemada's ungainly strides toward self-improvement. A friend tells him that wealth demands a degree of social flair and polish. Torquemada is gradually convinced of this and begins to refine himself accordingly. The process is mainly verbal: he acquires new words as quickly as he acquires new money. But whenever he forgets himself, loses his temper, or drinks too much, the old Torquemada breaks through the veneer of good breeding in all his primordial loutishness. This is what Galdós calls "la grosería que informaba su ser efectivo, anterior y superior a los postizos de su artificiosa metamorfosis" *(5,* 973). These retrogressions occur often enough to be predictable.

As regards comic technique, *Torquemada en el purgatorio* is a continuation of the preceding novel. It describes Torquemada's growing affluence and respectability. The high point of the book is a banquet given in his honor, after which he delivers a speech that is a hash of platitudes and clichés. It is a thorough recapitulation of everything Torquemada has assimilated in the way of refinement. With great expertise he scatters bits of science, philosophy, mythology, Shakespeare, economic theory, and statecraft to the captive minds of the banquet hall, most of whom are vastly impressed by it all. They applaud wildly, either because they are ignorant and lacking in taste or because they too worship "the golden calf." Torquemada's speech, every assimilated word and phrase of which appears in italics in the text, is Galdós' greatest triumph in the realm of verbal comedy.

The other major source of humor in *Torquemada en el purgatorio* stems from the clash of temperaments between Torquemada and his sister-in-law, Cruz del Aguila (Torquemada has remarried). Each step of their relationship is marked by a confrontation and a defeat for the miser. Cruz forces him to hire a French chef, purchase a title, maintain a palatial home, and entertain lavishly. Repeatedly Torquemada's bravado and invective wilt before a stronger will than his own. He does himself such violence by bowing to the dictator's commands that his only consolation lies in the forthcoming reincarnation of Valentín (Torquemada's second wife is pregnant). The baby will signal a rebirth of his own intrinsic being, for the original Valentín, with his genius for figures, was the quintessential Torquemada. Here is another example of the comic return.

One must take note of a subtle difference between *Torque-*

mada en la cruz and *Torquemada en el purgatorio.* In the former, the miser is almost a clown. He trips all over himself, committing a number of social and linguistic blunders. There is much of the cursi about him. In *Torquemada en el purgatorio,* however, he begins to criticize the society in which he moves. More and more he becomes Galdós' mouthpiece. He is honest and perceptive. He knows himself and is true to himself. The reader respects his opinions. When, after his speech, Torquemada admits to having uttered reams of nonsense, one realizes that he has no delusions. More important, he has taken the measure of those whom he was able to impress so easily—they are fools. Torquemada is not deceived with regard to the contemporary Establishment. If he can dupe them, he is their intellectual equal, perhaps their superior. The reader may draw his own conclusions about the business and professional elite of Spain in the 1890s.

The gist of what has been said thus far may be summarized very briefly. Galdós chose one of the standard techniques of caricature, the obsession (or ruling passion), as a foundation upon which to construct Torquemada's personality. In *Torquemada en la hoguera* he shook this foundation, so to speak, by making Torquemada a prey to emotions which, in nineteenth-century fiction, were not usually associated with the obsession in question (avarice). In the other three novels, he shook the foundation even more strongly by charting Torquemada's outer metamorphosis and rise in the world. In short, emotion and evolution set Torquemada apart from caricature.

In the second half of the nineteenth century, the urban population of Spain showed an ever-increasing social mobility. Although this trend began in the first half of the century with the desamortización, or sale of church property, it only gained momentum decades later. As usual, Spain lagged behind the rest of western Europe. It is also worth noting that social mobility there was a stunted replica of what had taken place elsewhere. The rural population, which consisted of the majority of Spaniards, was virtually excluded from it. Indeed, the infallible harbinger of social change on a national scale—mass emigration to the city—has only lately appeared on the Spanish horizon.[32]

When Galdós addressed the Real Academia Española in 1897, he used the word "nivelación" ("leveling") to describe what was happening to the structure of contemporary Spanish society. He saw the breakdown of monolithic classes, such as pueblo and aristocracy, and their gradual reabsorption into an amorphous middle class of blurred frontiers.[33] This hybrid class was becoming more and more tightly knit. Its members resembled each other in dress, speech, even physiognomy. Galdós therefore suggested that novelists abandon the generic types of bygone years and write instead about individuals as yet unmolded by "el convencionalismo de las costumbres."

Torquemada en la hoguera, though written eight years before Galdós' speech, is a practical application of the author's ideas. What he did was to recreate one of his own generic types, a type molded by "el convencionalismo de las costumbres." The Torquemada who pops up now and again in *El doctor Centeno, La de Bringas,* and *Fortunata y Jacinta*—sweaty palms, dirty clothes, honeyed courtesy, inflexibility—has a very professional air; his words, dress, gestures, and physique practically announce his trade. These details, though still present, are shunted aside in *Torquemada en la hoguera.* Torquemada is no longer a professional type, but a man who suffers. The emphasis is no longer on what he does, but on what he is and what he endures.

Galdós' purpose in writing *Torquemada en la hoguera* was to paint a full-length portrait of what had been, until then, a generic type. He had done the same thing a year before in *Miau* with the cesante. But Galdós could not forget Torque-

32. Cataluña has always been an exception.
33. Galdós expressed the concept of nivelación at greater length in *Torquemada en el purgatorio:* "Reconozcamos que en nuestra época de uniformidades y de nivelación física y moral se han desgastado los tipos genéricos y que van desapareciendo, en el lento ocaso del mundo antiguo, aquellos caracteres que representaban porciones grandísimas de la familia humana, clases, grupos, categorías morales" (*5,* 1040). The passage continues in this vein.

mada. Apparently he felt that it was not enough to have caught him in a private, domestic crisis as a man rather than a moneylender. Thus in 1893 he resurrected his protagonist of four years before and began once again to recreate him. This is something of an overstatement. What he really did was to enlarge upon the first two chapters of *Torquemada en la hoguera,* where he had sketched, in broad strokes, the moneylender's absorption into the middle class. Galdós transplanted these chapters into new soil and allowed them to root and flourish there through the length of three additional volumes. The great irony is that Torquemada again emerges as a socially representative type (which is why the remarks of 1897 to the Real Academia seem amusing and contradictory in retrospect). Galdós ran the whole process of nivelación through a sieve, and Torquemada was the result. In brief, Torquemada had been a generic type in the Novelas contemporáneas prior to 1889; in *Torquemada en la hoguera,* written in that year, he became a sharply defined individual; and in the succeeding volumes, he becomes, with no loss of individuality, a type in the Marxist sense. He reflects the social mobility that arose from capitalism, the foremost social determinant of the nineteenth century.[34] One might even regard the last three *Torquemada* novels as a single, sweeping historical metaphor. Torquemada would be the subject, and socioeconomic change in nineteenth-century Spain his correlative. Clearly Torquemada is literally larger than life. Just as clear is his comic appeal: Galdós himself must have laughed aloud when he got the idea of making a miser the transcendent symbol of laissez-faire economics and Comtian philosophy.

Society is never static in the Novelas contemporáneas; it is always evolving. There are constant reminders that people, like nations, rise and fall. They buy or liquidate, are on the rise or on the skids. This is also true of social classes. In the last three *Torquemada* novels, Galdós describes what had been happening in Europe since the 1820s: the old aristocracy was selling

34. The only determinism in which Galdós believed was historical determinism. He is closer to Taine and Marx than to Darwin.

out, and a new bootstrap class was taking over. This is what Galdós calls "la ley del siglo, por la cual la riqueza inmueble de las familias históricas va pasando a una segunda aristocracia, cuyos pergaminos se pierden en la obscuridad de una tienda, o en los repliegues de la industria usuraria" *(5,* 1123).

In the last decades of the century nivelación had become a commonplace. The average citizen did not have to be told what was going on; he could see for himself. Even the idea that the old aristocracy needed an infusion of new blood had been popularized long ago. There is a good illustration of this in *Torquemada en la cruz.* Torquemada first berates himself for seeing so much of the Aguilas, a family of impoverished aristocrats. But then he changes his mind. Why should he not hobnob with the Old Guard? He reflects as follows:

La aristocracia, árbol viejo y sin savia, no podía ya vivir si no lo *abonaba* (en el sentido de *estercolar)* el pueblo enriquecido. ¡Y que no había hecho flojos milagros el sudor del pueblo en aquel tercio del siglo! ¿No andaban por Madrid arrastrados en carretelas muchos a quienes él y todo el mundo conocieron vendiendo alubias y bacalao, o prestando a rédito? ¿No eran ya senadores vitalicios y consejeros del banco muchos que allá en su niñez andaban con los codos rotos, o que pasaron hambres para juntar para unas alpargatas? Pues bien: a ese *elemento* pertenecía él, y era un nuevo ejemplo del *sudor de pueblo fecundando* . . . . No sabía concluir la frase. *(5,* 972)

Torquemada is not the first character in Galdós to symbolize the process of nivelación. Cristóbal Medina *(Lo prohibido)* is of low birth but inherits enough money to start lending it out at interest to members of the aristocracy, holding mortgages on their homes as collateral. As their fortunes decline, his rise. One of Medina's friends says, "Las mermas de aquellas casas son los crecimientos de ésta" *(4,* 1812). He has the reputation of being a skinflint and of charging usurious rates of interest. Despite his wealth, his manners are coarse, and he prides himself on this. Another character in *Lo prohibido* who prefigures

Torquemada is don Isidro Barragán. A peddler in the Plaza Mayor in the 1860s, he is now (1883) one of the richest men in Madrid. He too has become rich by lending money. His one figure of speech, "partiendo del principio," is a blight on the language. He is a "golden ass" as Torquemada is a "golden calf": "las coces de aquel burro de oro eran el providencial castigo de la sociedad por el crimen de haberle erigido" *(4, 1814).*

Pepet, in the dialogue novel *La loca de la casa* (1892), prefigures Torquemada's social evolution even more closely. Pepet is raised on a large estate where his father is employed as a laborer. The owner of the estate is a Barcelona merchant with ties to the local aristocracy. Pepet goes to America and makes a fortune. On his return to Spain, he finds the merchant on the verge of bankruptcy. Pepet bails him out by marrying into the family.

La loca de la casa is the first of Galdós' novels to have economic nivelación as its central theme. It precedes *Torquemada en la cruz* by a year. Both works demonstrate nivelación through marriage. In both the male protagonist is something of a boor—a surly, self-made man—and there is a conflict between idealism and positivism. Artistically, though, they are worlds apart. In *La loca de la casa* the main characters are so patently symbolic they lose all individuality. Pepet and his bride symbolize, respectively, positivism and idealism.[35] Their union conciliates these two extremes, Pepet becoming more supple and generous, and Victoria more businesslike and practical. Another difference is the fact that *La loca de la casa* is abstract, while the *Torquemada* novels are concrete. The former is smothered by its thesis, the latter enriched by it. One would enjoy the *Torquemada* novels without being aware of their typic content; one can enjoy *La loca de la casa* only as a period piece.

Torquemada marries into the Aguila family and saves them from starvation. His wife, Fidela, is a rather anemic personage, and one need not be concerned about her. But Cruz (his sister-

35. Note that one of the characters refers to positivism as the "mal de la época" *(5, 1656).*

in-law) and Rafael (his brother-in-law) are as deeply enmeshed in contemporary social reality as Torquemada himself. Cruz's voice is one of expediency. Aristocratic but penniless, she bows to necessity. She as head of the family arranges the marriage between Fidela and Torquemada. A firm believer in noblesse oblige, she wheedles, humiliates, and threatens Torquemada into financing that belief. She might be compared to a free-spending constitutional monarch with lavish tastes and a passion for reform. Torquemada, her subject, remains stubbornly republican and budget conscious. They rarely see eye-to-eye.

Rafael is the conservative. In his view, his sister's marriage to Torquemada contaminates the Aguila family and all it has ever stood for.

> Desde el día de la boda, . . . desde muchos días antes, se trabó entre mi hermana Cruz y yo una batalla formidable; yo defendía la dignidad de la familia, el lustre de nuestro nombre, la tradición, el ideal; ella defendía la existencia positiva, el comer después de tantas hambres, lo tangible, lo material, lo transitorio. *(5,* 1108)

Galdós made Rafael blind, not because Rafael fails to see how society has evolved, but because he refuses to admit that its evolution is irrepressible. Even after Fidela's marriage, he continues to believe that she will leave her husband. He cannot imagine that a bond could be forged between them. When her child Valentinico is born, Rafael is again set back. He cannot think about the child without feeling an urge to destroy him. But of course he never does destroy this product of nivelación. Finally, when the most prominent men of Madrid deify Torquemada at the banquet given in his honor, Rafael knows he is beaten. Society not only hosts and applauds Torquemada, it *is* Torquemada. Rafael realizes that his brother-in-law not only is immune to the virtues of the Old World but would hardly even acknowledge them as such.

Rafael becomes more and more convinced of his own uselessness. He is an anachronism. He is no longer the center of his sisters' attention as he was before Fidela's marriage; Valentinico has taken his place. The crossbreed has usurped the privileged position of the pure aristocrat. The child points to the future, Rafael to the past. When Torquemada buys (as an investment) an old ducal palace and its unique collection of paintings, books, and armor, Rafael says, "es preferible la muerte al desconsuelo de ver lo más bello que en el mundo existe en manos de Torquemada" *(5,* 1110). Shortly thereafter, he commits suicide.

The moneylender has come a long way. He has put his foot in the middle class, consolidated his position there, and then gone on to join the new aristocracy. The Marquis of San Eloy (the title Cruz made him buy) is no longer a usurer, but a promoter. His verbal refinements, filched from Cortes and the press, conceal the fact that his father was a castrater of pigs. He is respectable and a Philistine. He believes in science and progress. Religious skepticism is the crowning glory of this "hijo del siglo."[36]

Galdós ended the *Torquemada* series by reverting to the central motif of *Torquemada en la hoguera,* the protagonist's transactions with God. Now, however, these transactions are more than a succession of episodes involving a single individual; they are, in the author's view, pockmarks on the face of a society that has allowed money, business, common sense, and the pursuit of progress to stifle all idealism. Galdós was certainly not opposed to practical religion in the humanitarian sense; he always preferred active charity to mysticism and reclusion. But the idea that materialism should become a secular dogma, like socialism and nationalism, with its own cult and ritual repelled him.[37] Says Torquemada:

Ahí tiene usted a los militares, cuyo oficio es matar gente, y nos hablan del *Dios de las batallas.* Pues ¿por qué, ¡por vida de los ñales!, no hemos de tener también el *Dios de las haciendas,* el *Dios de los presupuestos, de los negocios* o del *tanto más cuanto? (5,* 1188)

36. Torquemada describes himself as such *(5,* 1101).
37. For a discussion of secular dogmas in the latter half of the nineteenth century, see Robert C. Binkley, *Realism and Nationalism* (New York and London, 1935), pp. 70–71.

For all their humor, the last three *Torquemada* novels contain a bitter critique of positivism.[38] Galdós felt it had gone too
far, the same conclusion Dickens had come to forty years
earlier in *Hard Times*. The passage that follows is prophetic of
what Galdós would see happening to Spanish society in the
1890s:

> It was a fundamental principle of the Gradgrind philos-
> ophy that everything was to be paid for. Nobody was ever
> on any account to give anybody anything, or render any-
> body help without purchase. Gratitude was to be abol-
> ished, and the virtues springing from it were not to be.
> Every inch of the existence of mankind, from birth to
> death, was to be a bargain across a counter. And if we
> didn't get to Heaven that way, it was not a politico-
> economical place, and we had no business there.[39]

Balzac's Gobseck conveys the same message more succinctly:
"L'or est le spiritualisme de vos sociétés actuelles."[40] Galdós'
disenchantment with positivism is further seen in *Halma*
(1895), *Misericordia* (1897), and *El abuelo* (1897). The
Marquis of Feramor, don Carlos Moreno Trujillo, and Senén
are titans of fiscal responsibility but are totally lacking in
spiritual largess.

But these are bit players, foils to other characters. They
resemble generic types, since the historical process which
molded them seems to have run its course by the time they
appear on the scene. Torquemada, by contrast, is part of a
historical process. Its reality is his reality. Just as one speaks of
the Spain of Galdós, one might also speak of the Spain of
Torquemada. Unamuno did—"¡Pero la España de Torquemada!"—and unwittingly paid tribute to Torquemada's status
as a fictional character representative of Spanish history in
the latter half of the nineteenth century.[41]

38. One should remember that Galdós used the term "positivism" as
a synonym for "materialism."

39. Dickens, *Hard Times*, pp. 288–89.

40. *Gobseck*, p. 27.

41. Unamuno, *Autodiálogos*, p. 106.

Chapter 6

THE HUMOR OF FAMILIARITY

It is said that during World War I the novels of Trollope enjoyed a vogue among British readers, especially among soldiers sent to the front. The war made people crave some reassurance that British society was as it used to be: traditional, stable, and timeless. As Spanish society reaches the point where it contracts more and more twentieth-century neuroses, readers will flock back to the Novelas contemporáneas in ever-increasing numbers. For in Galdós, the family unit remains intact and closely knit, no matter what else may change; his people, with a single exception, are never lonely; his city is a rather cozy place which bears no dehumanizing grudge against its tenants; and his style is at times so informal that it makes communication between human beings seem easy.

Galdós the moralist employs satire and irony. Galdós the romantic realist is steeped in metaphor, caricature, and type. What kinks or contradictions the literary personality of Galdós might have vanish in the author's familiarity of style and subject matter.

One might argue that any judgment of an author's works based on the degree of familiarity between text and reader is akin to that "realism as experience as normalcy" criterion so painstakingly snubbed in Chapter 5. However, the low-key type of realism so often associated with Galdós is no better than those less evasive varieties mentioned so far. Familiarity per se is not a criterion for judging Galdós. Nor is humor derived from familiarity necessarily better than humor derived from satire, irony, metaphor, caricature, or type. Like beauty, humor is in the eye of the beholder.

The novel that best exemplifies familiarity of style is *Tor-*

quemada en la hoguera. It is written with a breezy informality
rare even for Galdós. The novel begins with the words, "Voy
a contar." This direct first-person approach, with "you" understood (Voy a contar*le),* invites the reader to make himself comfortable, to "gather round," as it were. The second paragraph
begins as follows: "Mis amigos conocen ya, por lo que se me
antojó referirles, a don Francisco Torquemada." Galdós assumes that the reader already knows Torquemada. His show
of confidence has a pleasant democratizing effect: everyone is
equal here; everyone understands each other; there is no need
to beat around the bush. But the "se me antojó" puts Galdós
clearly in charge. He is a professional weaver of tales and has
this situation well in hand. It is a comfort to know that one's
guide is experienced.

Galdós then draws the reader into the tale he is narrating. He
becomes a potential character in the story about to be told:

> ¡Ay de mis buenos lectores si conocen al implacable
> fogonero de vidas y haciendas por tratos de otra clase,
> no tan sin malicia, no tan desinteresados como estas
> inocentes relaciones entre narrador y lector! Porque si
> han tenido algo que ver con él en cosa de más cuenta;
> si le han ido a pedir socorro en las pataletas de la agonía
> pecuniaria, más les valiera encomendarse a Dios y dejarse
> morir. *(5,* 906)

This compassion for the reader is delightful. The reader knows
that Galdós had his tongue in his cheek when he wrote this
passage; he knows that Galdós invented Torquemada; and
yet he cannot help being charmed by Galdós' fatherly concern
for his welfare and his Olympian view of society. The implication is that if he were to get mixed up with Torquemada,
Galdós would surely find out about it.

The same thing happens a bit further on. The author says
that doña Silvia, Torquemada's wife, is dead. He apologizes for
breaking the news so suddenly: "Perdónenme mis lectores si les
doy la noticia sin la preparación conveniente, pues sé que
apreciaban a doña Silvia, como la apreciaban todos los que

tuvimos el honor de tratarla y conocíamos sus excelentes prendas y circunstancias" *(5,* 907). This of course is sarcastic: doña Silvia was her husband's cohort in usury. But it is sarcasm which does not hurt anyone. One has the impression that Galdós was really fond of doña Silvia, if for no other reason than having created her. She was part of his circle of acquaintances. Galdós treats the reader as if he were part of that circle also. This points to an aspect of familiarity having more to do with subject matter than with style: the more of the *Novelas contemporáneas* one reads, the more one likes them. It is as hard to know Galdós after reading just one of these novels as it is to know a city by strolling through a single street. One must settle there for a while and explore. To be fair to the author of the *Novelas contemporáneas,* one should swallow the series whole. The same is true for other writers whose characters and settings reappear constantly—Balzac, Trollope, Faulkner, Anthony Powell, and the rest. If one takes the plunge and reads long and hard enough, even their faults will become likable in the end. They too will have become familiar.

Enjoyment of any one of the *Novelas contemporáneas* increases with a thorough knowledge of them all. The following information, for example, would mean nothing to a stranger: Galdós says that Torquemada "vivía en la misma casa de la calle de Tudescos donde le conocimos cuando fué a verle la de Bringas para pedirle no recuerdo qué favor, allá por el 68" *(5,* 912). Without having read *La de Bringas,* one would scarcely know what the author was talking about. On the other hand, the habitué of these novels fleetingly recalls a whole group of people he once knew quite well. They come back in a flash. Even if the recollection is vague, the sensation of having been there before is very sharp.

Galdós strengthens the familiar tone of *Torquemada en la hoguera* with such expressions as "Pues digo," "Vamos a otra cosa," "Pues señor," "En lo que digo," and "Digo yo ahora" *(5,* 908–912). Others dot the text. The effect of these intrusions is to make writing seem as easy as speaking or breathing. The author is completely relaxed. He is not the least bit self-conscious. He does not pretend to be a litterateur.

Those critics who reproach Galdós for narrative unkemptness
should reexamine some of the Novelas contemporáneas, starting with *Torquemada en la hoguera.* It takes tremendous skill
to write with such confidence. Everyone has seen acrobats
and musicians who "make it look easy." Much of the pleasure
derived from their performance is due to one's absolute trust
in their abilities. Many critics fail to notice how reliable
Galdós' narrative technique is, perhaps because it does not
smack of the ivory tower. Except for his misuse of the
chronicle device and his sad experiments with dialogue novels,
he usually pulls off any effect he wants. In *Torquemada en la
hoguera* he holds the reader in the palm of his hand because
he does not patronize. His familiarity is unforced. He does not
try to ingratiate himself with the reader but assumes instead
that the reader is already a friend.

Apart from his amiable sallies in the first person, Galdós
makes the rest of his narrative chatty to an extreme. One critic
speaks of the author's "oral style" in *Fortunata y Jacinta,* but
Torquemada en la hoguera is unsurpassed in this respect.[1]
A snatch of colloquial speech pops up in every other sentence.
To list each example would take hours, even though the
novelette covers only twenty pages in the Aguilar edition. Here
is a sampling from the first few chapters: "Total"; "Todo iba
como una seda"; "Claro que"; "por más señas"; "criatura más
mona"; "revienta doña Silvia" (for "muere"); "parecía cosa del
otro jueves"; "Los tíos aquellos" (the eminent mathematicians
who interview Valentín); "la viuda aquella cascó" (for
"murió"); "con mucho aquel"; "verbigracia"; and "Todo esto
le parecía de perlas" *(5,* 906–13).

In *Torquemada en la hoguera* the narration is every bit as
colloquial as the dialogue. If the novelette were read aloud,
a listener would find it almost impossible to say exactly where
the narration stops and the dialogue begins. Although *Torquemada en la hoguera* is unique in this respect, many of the
Novelas contemporáneas show the same peculiarity at given
moments. It is an oversimplification, therefore, merely to

---

1. Gilman, "La palabra hablada y *Fortunata y Jacinta,*" p. 549.

include Galdós among those novelists who have a fine ear for dialogue. In the works of these authors the reader is usually aware of attempts to reproduce popular, rustic, or slang-ridden speech. Whenever one pays tribute to an author's skill along these lines, one is unconsciously expressing amazement that a writer could so successfully counterfeit speech *so unlike his own*. One rarely has this feeling with Galdós. Since informality is the hallmark of his narrative style, the transition from narration to dialogue in his novels often escapes notice.

Spaniards have a very sane attitude toward their spoken language: they treat it with a certain irreverence. Often they prefer color to clarity. Furthermore, their speech cuts across class barriers. There is no snob appeal based exclusively upon pronunciation or choice of vocabulary (except as regards South-American Spanish). Verbal remilgos are as suspect there as certain Briticisms are in the United States. All this is symptomatic of what many people, including Galdós, have frequently observed—namely, that Spanish society is inherently one of the most democratic in the world. This helps explain why a genuine comedy of manners has rarely appeared in Spanish literature. In a comedy of manners, one's defenses are never down. One never shows one's hand. What is left unsaid is often as important as what is said aloud. Talk is insinuating and follows certain conventions. Speech is determined by class—it is one of the proprieties. Wit and esprit are associated with the upper classes or the intellectual elite. Lower-class characters are usually excluded. In Spain, however, socarronería is at everyone's disposal.

Galdós never wrote a comedy of manners in the drawing room sense. Indeed, like Dickens, he has been accused of not knowing how to portray an aristocrat. How could he, when the Spanish aristocracy as a class lacked a unique linguistic contour? Even the monarchs, from Isabel II to Alfonso XIII, were most admired for what they had in common with the pueblo—castizo speech and democratic manners.

A passage in *Lo prohibido* describes how unsuited the Spanish language is for sophisticated repartee. At Eloísa's fashionable dinner parties, the frank and hearty flavor of

Castilian always thwarts the efforts of French syntax to refine it:

> Allí se podía observar, con respecto a lenguaje, los es-
> fuerzos de un idioma que, careciendo de propiedades para
> la conversación escogida, se atormenta por buscarlas,
> exprime y retuerce las delicadas fórmulas de la cortesía
> francesa, y no adelantando mucho por este lado, se refugia
> en los elementos castizos de la confianza castellana,
> limándoles, en lo posible, las asperezas que le dan
> carácter. *(4,* 1724)

The populacho invents expressions which the upper classes later prune of crudities. These expressions, however, never lose their original "gracia" *(4,* 1724).

In the Novelas contemporáneas, members of the middle and upper classes rival the populacho in pungency of speech.[2] A good example is Guillermina Pacheco *(Fortunata y Jacinta).* Very near the top of the social ladder, Guillermina is by birth and reputation an "ilustre señora" and "insigne dama" *(5,* 75–76). Some of her friends belong to the nobility *(5,* 76). Nevertheless, she easily holds her own against the verbal broadsides of José Izquierdo. She counterattacks with such earthy terms as "holgazanote," "bruto," "infelizote," "vende-humos," and "Bobalicón" *(5,* 122–25). Doña Lupe *la de los pavos,* from the same novel, is strictly middle class, but her speech is often colorfully plebeian. Like Guillermina, her forte is the use of diminutives and superlatives for pejorative effect. Maxi is a "señoritingo" *(5,* 198) and Fortunata a "tiota chabasca" *(5,* 194). Lupe also peppers her speech with proverbs and vulgarisms, for example, when she scoffs at Fortunata's pledge to turn over a new leaf: "Vaya, hija, no madrugues tanto. Tú no te acuerdas de Santa Bárbara sino cuando truena. ¿Qué sacaría yo de consolarte ahora y corre-

2. A recent article shows that in *Fortunata y Jacinta* doña Lupe, Feijoo, Guillermina Pacheco, and Juanito make more extensive use of familiar language than do the lower-class characters of the book. See Graciela Andrade Alfieri and J. J. Alfieri, "El lenguaje familiar de Pérez Galdós," p. 30.

girte, si el mejor día volvías a las andadas?" A moment later she adds: "Quien no te conoce, que te compre . . . . Al extremo a que han llegado las cosas, me parece que no debo intervenir ya, ni tomar vela en este entierro" *(5, 468)*.

Doña Lupe, along with the great majority of Galdós' characters, speaks a rich vernacular. Her dialogue is racy, with its wealth of comic invective, plain talk, and proverbs. These are precisely the elements that Galdós failed to utilize in his dialogue novels. In these, dialogue had to be expository, and the inner thoughts of the characters could be revealed only by asides and soliloquies, both of which are rhetorical. Galdós was obviously unable to adjust vernacular speech to the rules of rhetoric. He thus adopted the artificial stage language of the day. This was still the language of Ayala and Echegaray. The following snip of dialogue from *Casandra* (written in 1905) shows how lamentable the results were on occasion:

> *Clementina*
> La carta de Insúa ennegrece más la sombra que me persigue desde esta mañana y la acerca más a mí . . . . ¡Siento frío . . . , terror . . . !
>
> *Alfonso*
> ¿De qué?
>
> *Clementina*
> De mayores dislates de doña Juana, de acciones vesánicas que puedan afectarnos . . . . (consternada) Esto no es vivir. *(6, 144)*

In all the dialogue novels—*Realidad, La loca de la casa, El abuelo, Casandra,* and *La razón de la sinrazón*—the language is flat and stilted. Perhaps this defect could have been avoided if the contemporary theater had not been so grandiloquent. The fact that Galdós chose the dialogue novel to express abstract theses did not help either. This is not wrong in principle: the trouble is that Galdós works from the abstract to the particular, instead of the other way around. His characters are afterthoughts. Their speech does not characterize them; it merely tells why the author created them.

A familiar style is based on something other than ideas—an unaffected use of the vernacular. Galdós excelled at this. Although any author can go slumming now and then for a few picturesque phrases, Galdós did not find this necessary. His style is a true portrait of the man and his society.

A concert hall is only as good as its acoustics: either it reproduces the sound of the music faithfully, or it distorts the sound. Similarly, prose is most successful when attuned to subject matter. Many a book suffers from a style too complex, high-flown, or unimaginative for the subject at hand. The informal style of the *Novelas contemporáneas* is ideal. It underscores what the reader of these novels remembers long after the intricacies of plot are forgotten: the warmth of family life in Spain and the frequent contact and ease of communication between Spaniards of all classes.

In *Fortunata y Jacinta,* Galdós extols a society at once familial and homogeneous. All Madrid is like one family that takes care of its own. Charity aids even the most abject of creatures; a patriarch has his family retainer join him at meals; illegitimate children quickly reenter the fold; a prostitute is apotheosized. Individuals may be unjust, but society is benign.

The plot of *Fortunata y Jacinta* is straightforward. Juanito Santa Cruz, the only son of well-to-do parents, Baldomero and Barbarita Santa Cruz, seduces Fortunata, a girl of the people. He abandons her and later marries his cousin Jacinta. A few years pass and the married couple remains childless. Galdós makes it clear that Jacinta is sterile. Although very much in love with his wife, Juanito takes up again with Fortunata. In the intervening period, she is kept by a number of men but ends by marrying Maxi Rubín, a young man of the middle class. Because Maxi is impotent, the marriage is never consummated. Fortunata, however, only sought in marriage an escape from shame and revilement. She considers Santa Cruz her true husband and goes to him whenever he beckons. Their illicit relationship is seasonable, according to Santa Cruz's urge for novelty and adventure.

Fortunata always thinks of Jacinta, Santa Cruz's wife, as

her rival. Since she believes that a childless marriage is no marriage at all, she feels superior to her. There is no doubt about her own fertility.

The heart of the novel traces Fortunata's change in attitude toward Jacinta. The mistress, aware of Jacinta's reputation as an angelic creature, tries to become her equal. But her progress toward middle-class decorum and respectability is checked by her unbridled pueblo instincts. The only way she can match the woman she has grown to admire is to bear a child to Santa Cruz. Her real triumph, however, comes when she bequeaths the child to Jacinta. This is her great "idea." It compels the Santa Cruz family to esteem her. In the final chapters, Fortunata gives her newborn son to her "amiga" and thus joins the Santa Cruz family by proxy.

The novel ends with the dissolution of the two marriages. Fortunata dies shortly after giving birth, and Maxi is taken to an institution. Jacinta loses all respect for her husband, a stranger in his own household. The Santa Cruz name survives in the person of Fortunata's son.

From this brief outline, one might imagine *Fortunata y Jacinta* to be full of depravity. It is certainly hard to see how sterility, impotence, prostitution, adultery, and insanity could leave much room for humor. Yet this novel, more than any other by Galdós, leaves the impression that people are sane, healthy, honest, and good. The author plays down the salacious and abnormal. Juanito's lust is never described as such. It is an accelerated seven-year itch that does not weaken his love for Jacinta, whom he continues to adore. As for Fortunata's prostitution, the reader is told only that she made the rounds after Santa Cruz abandoned her. Galdós emphasizes her fidelity to her first lover and the pity she feels for Maxi. There is nothing mercenary about her. The author reveals the organic defects of Jacinta and Maxi with great tact, avoiding clinical details and naturalistic case histories. Maxi's breakdown seems less tragic than it is, because in context it often leads to out-and-out farce. The outspoken doña Lupe (Maxi's aunt) and Papitos (the family maid) are usually on hand to give comic relief. Moreover, Maxi willingly enters an institution after

Fortunata's death. By this time, he is at peace with himself.

To understand why *Fortunata y Jacinta* leaves a wholesome impression on the reader, and why Galdós was not amiss in injecting a good deal of humor into its plot and characterizations, one must grasp the sociological implications of the novel. I mentioned earlier that Spanish society, for Galdós, is one of the most democratic in the world. He explains this in Part I of *Fortunata y Jacinta:*

> Es curioso observar cómo nuestra edad, por otros conceptos infeliz, nos presenta una dichosa confusión de todas las clases, mejor dicho, la concordia y reconciliación de todas ellas. En esto aventaja nuestro país a otros, donde están pendientes de sentencia los graves pleitos históricos de la igualdad. Aquí se ha resuelto el problema sencilla y pacíficamente, gracias al temple democrático de los españoles y a la escasa vehemencia de las preocupaciones nobiliarias. Un gran defecto nacional, la empleomanía, tiene también su parte en esta gran conquista. Las oficinas han sido el tronco en que se han injertado las ramas históricas, y de ellas han salido amigos el noble tronado y el plebeyo ensorberbecido por un título universitario; y de amigos, pronto han pasado a parientes *(5, 65)* [3]

3. Galdós was no prophet if he thought class harmony a permanent fact of life in Spain. It is hard to understand how an author, well traveled and well versed in contemporary French literature, could believe that a melting-pot bureaucracy might ease the birth pangs of industrialization. Even when he wrote *Fortunata y Jacinta,* what was true of Madrid could not have been true of Barcelona. Galdós' idyllic view of Spanish society was partly due to his having lived in a commercial and bureaucratic city (as opposed to an industrial one) for most of his adult life. This helps explain why he never became a social reformer like Zola. It also helps explain why, in his portrait of Juan Bou, the hard-working Catalán of *La desheredada,* he ridicules Bou's blasts at class privilege.

Antonio Regalado effectively shatters the myth, nurtured and promoted by a great many critics, that Galdós portrays "toda la realidad española" in the Novelas contemporáneas. See *Benito Pérez Galdós y la novela histórica española,* pp. 194–200 and passim.

The rest of the passage goes on to say that Spaniards are immune to class struggle because a mild socialism runs in their blood; that birth is no longer a factor in class affiliation; and that wealth alone is a determinant in this respect. Finally, Galdós repeats his idea that economic nivelación through marriage has reenforced the democratic spirit of the Spanish people. Anticipating one of the major themes of the *Torquemada* novels, he refers to "la desigualdad de ciertos matrimonios, a los cuales, en rigor de verdad, se debe la formación del terreno democrático sobre que se asienta la sociedad española" *(5, 65–66).*

In an early chapter of *Fortunata y Jacinta,* this democratic terrain brings forth an immense family tree, whose network of roots and branches seems to cover very nearly the entire population of Madrid. Madrid is a microcosm of Spain. By drawing the genealogical table of one family, the Santa Cruzes, Galdós tries to show how members of the aristocracy and middle classes are interrelated. Only the pueblo is missing from this cross section of society. In the course of the novel that class too will graft itself onto the main trunk of the family tree.[4]

The author admits that he would not have been able to draw this genealogical tree without the help of Estupiñá, family retainer to the Santa Cruzes. His presence in this novel adds to its inbred quality and even hints that *Fortunata y Jacinta* may be a roman à clef, for Estupiñá is an affectionate, if cleverly disguised, portrait of Mesonero Romanos, whom Galdós considered the historian laureate of nineteenth-century Madrid.[5] Not only was Estupiñá born on the same day as Mesonero—July 19, 1803—but he also looks like him. His face, with its picaresque eyes and mocking good looks, is a replica of Rossini's. In his early "Crónica de Madrid," Galdós

---

4. Galdós also uses the tree metaphor to denote democratization of the social structure in the Episodio *O'Donnell (3,* 132). See Regalado, pp. 378–79.

5. Ernestina Manuel de Villena served as a model for Guillermina Pacheco, and in my opinion don Evaristo Feijoo is in part a self-portrait of Galdós.

set down the appearance of Mesonero Romanos: "Algo de la bondadosa y al par burlona sonrisa de Rossini hay en la fisionomía del *Curioso Parlante" (6,* 1551). The connection is clear. Perhaps Mesonero's pseudonym led Galdós to characterize Estupiñá as a great conversationalist.

Though unrelated by blood to the Santa Cruzes, Estupiñá has served the family in various capacities for over half a century. He took Barbarita Santa Cruz to school and later performed the same duty for her son, Juanito. He is everyone's confidant. His encyclopedic knowledge of Madrid makes him a canny shopper. Familiar with every stall in the marketplace and friendly with every clerk, he accompanies Barbarita on her daily round of purchases, telling her where and what to buy. No other character in the Novelas contemporáneas can better qualify as the archetypal Madrilenian than Estupiñá. One is reminded of something a British writer said about the inhabitants of Madrid and the special feeling they have for their city:

> They know their city. They regard it with that homely affection all Spaniards feel for their home towns. They feel about it domestically, as they feel for their family and their friends. They never boast about it. They neglect it with love. They have nothing of the civic pride of a Parisian, a Londoner, or a New Yorker. Madrid is a familiar place, entirely personal, without loneliness. It must be the only city without loneliness in the world.[6]

Completely good-hearted and devoted to his protectors, Estupiñá is one of several angelic characters who give to *Fortunata y Jacinta* a fairy-tale air. Others are Guillermina Pacheco, Jacinta, and the elder Santa Cruzes.

The Santa Cruzes repay Estupiñá's devotion in kind. On one occasion, when don Baldomero wins the lottery, he has Estupiñá share in the winnings though the latter had not joined the lottery pool: "Don Baldomero II se sonrió con aquella

---

6. V. S. Pritchett, *The Offensive Traveller* (New York, 1964), pp. 158–59.

bondad patriarcal tan suya, y sacando otra vez lista y lápiz, dijo en alta voz:—Rossini, diez reales: le tocan mil doscientos cincuenta" *(5,* 127). This little episode, with its Dickensian joviality and bounty, is typical of the first part of the novel. Don Baldomero's domestic kindness is repeated on a larger scale by Jacinta and Guillermina, who visit the slums of Madrid and distribute food, money, and clothes among the needy.

The elder Santa Cruzes are idealized (not sentimentalized). Their one questionable trait is a purblind pride in their son, but this no more flaws their character than Benina's habit of filching flaws hers *(Misericordia)*. Galdós calls the Santa Cruzes "el matrimonio más admirable del presente siglo" *(5,* 26). Even physically they make an exemplary couple. He is sixty yet looks like forty. She is fifty-two but could pass for thirty-two. Their love for each other strengthens with the years.

The Santa Cruzes are rich, a fact that adds considerably to their being a model couple. Galdós invented the perfect source of wealth for them—piece goods. The pages in which the author, in minute detail, traces the evolution of the textile trade from the turn of the century to the recent past are superb studies in costumbrismo. They enable him to trace the evolution of fashion, which is history on an intimate, familiar scale. Madrid's progress from backwater town to European capital is seen in the way its inhabitants dress. So are its political upheavals and the rise to power of its middle class.

In no other of the Novelas contemporáneas does history have the charm of a family album. The commercial saga of the Santa Cruzes and Arnáizes (Barbarita's family) gives a homely touch to the entire period between 1800 and 1860. Galdós speaks of the founding of Singapore and its adverse effect on Spanish trade with the Orient; of how the dry-goods establishments of Madrid had to search for new sources of supply; of the railroad, which opened up the Spanish market to European textiles; and of the taste for somber "northern" colors, which exiled to the lower classes that most picturesque of national garments, the Manila shawl. All this information, though completely factual, has the fragrance of keepsake and sentiment. It is bound up with the fortunes of the Santa Cruzes and is interspersed with their own personal recollections.

In spite of his general statements about Spanish society and his panorama covering half a century of Madrilenian commerce, Galdós always trains his sights on the family unit. One result is an almost total lack of social satire in *Fortunata y Jacinta*. Juanito Santa Cruz is a señorito, yet he is always an individual, not a costumbrista type. Moreno-Isla, the anglicized Spaniard, would have made the perfect ironic commentator. Instead, he is the only study of loneliness in the Novelas contemporáneas. Galdós could easily have satirized the clotheshorse female during his survey of the changing fashions of Madrid, but he spurned the opportunity. His jibes at bureaucracy and romanticism, two of his favorite targets in the past, are playful and ephemeral. It is extraordinary that *Fortunata y Jacinta,* by far the longest of the Novelas contemporáneas, should be less critical of society than any of the others, except for *Tristana* and *Torquemada en la hoguera,* which ironically, are the shortest novels in the series.

The absence of criticism does not imply the absence of a point of view. Although *Fortunata y Jacinta* contains a bright picture of the Spanish social structure—the lack of satire is a sign of this, as is the Santa Cruz beneficence—the novel does more than praise the status quo. If anything, it shows how Spanish society is changing for the better. The pueblo, the one class of society which until that time had not taken part in the process of nivelación, finally enters the mainstream of Spanish life. In so doing, it adds new sap to the family tree.

Though the novel was written in 1886–87, the events of *Fortunata y Jacinta* take place during 1869–74. Galdós links the political climate of that period to the plot and characters of the book: Juanito pivots between anarchy and stability just as Spain did prior to the Restoration. But this does not explain why Galdós, ended his novel with an estrangement instead of a reconciliation.

Fortunata y Jacinta reflects a social ideal more accurately than it does a political reality. The years 1869–74 are the very years in which Torquemada, having finished his "apprenticeship," enters the middle class. Fortunata also enters the middle class, with the difference that in her case nivelación is organic rather than economic. Although her relationship to the Santa Cruzes is illegitimate, her child will bear the family name and will be its legitimate heir. In a way, this infusion of new blood into the Santa Cruzes is comparable to the infusion of new money into the Aguilas. Fortunata's fertility and Torquemada's wealth both permit the survival of families that have reached a dead end. Both characters are pueblo, and both ransom a society that has become overrefined and soft. As Galdós says in *Fortunata y Jacinta,*

> el pueblo, en nuestras sociedades, conserva las ideas y los sentimientos elementales en su tosca plenitud, como la cantera contiene el mármol, materia de la forma. El pueblo posee las verdades grandes y en bloque, y a él acude la civilización conforme se le van gastando las menudas de que vive. *(5,* 407)

Torquemada and Fortunata begin as pueblo. Morally neither is perfect: he dabbles in usury, she in prostitution. The two eventually settle among people of a higher social class: he, with the Aguilas, and she, with the Rubíns, don Evaristo Feijoo, and Juanito Santa Cruz. Torquemada marries above him, and his wife gives birth to a monster; Fortunata "marries" Santa Cruz (this is how she sees it) and gives birth to a normal child. Why? Why is Galdós' point of view so critical of nivelación in the *Torquemada* series and so uncritical in *Fortunata y Jacinta?* There are many possible answers, but the one that makes the most sense is the following: Galdós, who was all in favor of the pueblo being absorbed into the middle class, was fearful lest it monopolize this class. The idea that economic enrichment would allow the pueblo to impose its tastes and standards on the rest of society was odious to him. This is obvious in the *Torquemada* novels, where Galdós is more sympathetic to Rafael del Aguila than to Torquemada. It is even clearer in *La loca de la casa,* for Pepet is one of the most disagreeable characters in the *Novelas contemporáneas.* There is little danger that Fortunata will ever impose her standards on society because she is not a symbol of economic nivelación. Neither is she the product of any historical determinant. Her absorption into the middle class is an accident of history. Nothing could be less revolutionary or smack less of the class struggle than the protective canopy under which Galdós leads Fortunata into the promised land. Like Estupiñá, she is an object of charity, the recipient of kindness from above. The author plays down the poor-girl-wronged-by-rich-man theme and that of the underdog's revenge on society. If anything, Fortunata is the orphan brought in from the storm.

Fortunata y Jacinta reflects the social ideal of universal charity. This ideal is exemplified in the way Fortunata and Estupiñá, the two pueblo representatives who figure most conspicuously in the novel, are treated by nearly everyone else—as part of the family. Recall the comparative ease with which the Rubín family accepts Fortunata. Outside of the Russians, one cannot imagine a nineteenth-century novelist even dealing with a similar situation. True, doña Lupe is struck dumb when she learns of Maxi's plan to marry a soiled article, but curiosity soon softens her intransigence. After the bride-to-be spends a few months in a nunnery (cleansing her soul), no one seriously objects to the forthcoming marriage. Even Nicolás Rubín, Maxi's brother and an ordained priest, takes the event in stride. There is never any talk of scandal, social disgrace, disinheritance, or the like. Friends of the Rubíns are invited to the wedding. It seems quite natural that Fortunata should reside with doña Lupe, thrash things out with her, meet her friends—in short, be adopted.

Fortunata is also "adopted" by don Evaristo Feijoo. Feijoo is an aging bachelor of comfortable means who keeps Fortunata for a few months during which her prospects would otherwise have been very bleak: having left her husband to become Santa Cruz's mistress, she is abandoned by the latter when his ardor cools. She has no money and no place to go. Feijoo takes her in and makes her his mistress. Although passionately in love with Fortunata, Feijoo's position gradually evolves from that of a lover to that of a father. As his health declines, his attitude toward Fortunata becomes more and more paternal:

"Aquel que te quiso como quiere el hombre a la mujer no existe ya . . . . Eres mi hija. Y no es que hagamos un papel aprendido, no; es que tú serás verdaderamente para mí, de aquí en adelante, como una hijita, y yo seré para ti un verdadero papaíto" *(5,* 351–52). In his will, Feijoo leaves a few gifts to the woman he now calls his stepdaughter *(5,* 355) and arranges for her to receive an annuity after his death.

Not only Feijoo's concern for Fortunata's future but also the ideas the two have in common with regard to morality emphasize their father-daughter relationship. Both believe that society's moral code, especially as it applies to marriage, need not be a restraining influence if la Naturaleza wills that it be broken. Feijoo expresses this most clearly when he says, "Lo que llaman infidelidad no es más que el fuego de la Naturaleza, que quiere imponerse contra el despotismo social, y por eso verás que soy tan indulgente con los y las que se pronuncian" *(5,* 339). But whereas Feijoo has always conducted his affairs in the most discreet and decorous manner possible, doing nothing to shock society, Fortunata behaves impetuously, without regard for appearances. Feijoo thus takes it upon himself to teach Fortunata how to manage an extramarital affair in good taste. Since Feijoo is most likely expressing Galdós' own point of view (the author's bachelorhood, his known fondness for women of the pueblo, and the mystery which to this day envelops his sentimental adventures all tend to confirm this), the inbred quality of *Fortunata y Jacinta* once again becomes apparent. It is not surprising that Galdós should want to include himself among the vast number of personages who, in this novel, constitute the family of Madrid.

Basically, Galdós sees Fortunata (the pueblo) as a child. Her wrongdoings are due to ignorance and inexperience. In spite of everything, she has a childlike innocence. When she speaks, her mispronunciations add to this impression. Even her social progress is like that of a child's: she learns from Maxi, from Feijoo, and especially from Jacinta, whom she tries to imitate. Her progress is commensurate with her faith in Jacinta, which she never loses.

No one gives Fortunata up for lost. Galdós' characters

believe in regeneration. Guillermina Pacheco's reputation as a saint is not due only to her charitable works; her saintliness stems mainly from her belief that even the most wretched specimens of humanity, like Mauricia *la dura,* are capable of reform and salvation. The other characters do not articulate this belief or make it a personal creed. Nevertheless, they behave as if charity and a certain amount of indulgence were second nature to them.[7] Their lines of communication with the less fortunate never break down. Collectively they possess an esprit de corps which the reader of *Fortunata y Jacinta* will feel most intensely.

This underlying spirit relieves the novel of all sordidness. *Fortunata y Jacinta* emits optimism and well-being because Galdós presents a favorable picture of the world in which his characters live and die. It is a world where class distinctions are replaced by familial hierarchies. No wonder, then, that in the context of late nineteenth-century fiction, *Fortunata y Jacinta* should take on some of the glow of a fairy tale.

Much of the humor in *Fortunata y Jacinta* emerges from the cyclic pattern of family life: birth, maturation, courtship, marriage, succession, and death. Other sources of humor may be found in certain customs and conventions native to Spain: political attitudes, the tertulia, Spanish Catholicism, and so on. In order to suggest something of its breadth and variety, the humor of *Fortunata y Jacinta* must be examined in context, in relation to the novel as a whole.

Juanito Santa Cruz is an only child, the "adorado nene" of his parents *(5,* 13). They pamper him from birth. Even after marriage, he receives a handsome allowance from his father, who is proud that his son is idle: "no había podido sustraerse a esa preocupación tan española de que los padres trabajan para que los hijos descansen y gocen" *(5,* 85). All parents, if they have come up the hard way, want their children's lives to be an improvement on their own. But the trait Galdós attributes

7. Guillermina's words, "Hay que ser indulgente con la miseria, y otorgarle un poquitín de licencia para el mal" *(5,* 123), are typical of everyone's attitude in this novel. See also Feijoo's "sé que decir *humanidad* es lo mismo que decir debilidad" *(5,* 334).

to don Baldomero is very Hispanic and has bred generations of señoritos—spoiled scions of the upper classes in Spain. An overweening self-love rules their behavior. They are still a part of the Spanish scene, but when Galdós describes Juanito's passage from boyhood to manhood, national boundaries fade away. The author's vignettes of an only child brought up by doting parents have a universal appeal: Barbarita helping her son with his lessons, her awe of his intellect, her concern when he stays out late, and, above all, her fears about his projected trip to Paris. Don Baldomero tries to convince his wife that a trip to "la Babilonia parisiense" will be good for the boy, but she demurs. Their debate on the advantages and disadvantages of exposing a young man to the rigors of French hospitality is beautifully observed *(5,* 17–18).

In the course of their talk, don Baldomero recalls that his own unbringing was so strict he could not even exchange a few pleasantries with a member of the opposite sex. When his parents chose a fiancée for him, he was scarcely able to say a word in her presence. He thus pleads the cause of the new generation and insists that Juanito go to Paris, sow his wild oats, and learn something of the ways of the world.

A comparison of the customs of older and younger generations usually yields a low-key humor, especially when, as in this case, the nostalgic note intrudes just a bit. Galdós was not a sentimentalist with regard to the past, but in these early chapters of *Fortunata y Jacinta* he enjoyed reconstructing it. He provides a roman-fleuve in miniature, in which the quaint customs of those days prepare the reader for a leisurely narrative in the present.

Juanito returns from Paris in better shape than ever, but a few years later he gives his mother something else to fret about. Low-life expressions begin to contaminate his speech, he dresses in torero style, and he drops his old friends for new company. The phase marks his first liaison with Fortunata. Estupiñá is delegated to spy on Juanito, but he never reports anything to the boy's mother. She can only deduce what is going on. After about ten months Juanito becomes his old self again. Nevertheless, Barbarita is set on preventing any recurrence of "sarampión" (measles) in her son and arranges his marriage to Jacinta, his first cousin.

Jacinta's background is similar to Juanito's in that her parents are dry-goods merchants too. But the Arnáiz family is less prosperous because of its size. Jacinta's mother has given birth to seventeen children, eight of whom have died. In telling of this thinning of the ranks, Galdós adopts a slightly ironic, off-hand tone that routs the sadness of death. He makes death seem like such a normal part of life that it almost loses significance. There is nothing tragic or pathetic about the following:

> Al ver la estrecha casa, se daba uno a pensar que la ley de impenetrabilidad de los cuerpos fué el pretexto que tomó la muerte para mermar aquel bíblico rebaño. Si los dieci-siete chiquillos hubieran vivido, habría sido preciso poner-los en los balcones como los tiestos o colgados en jaulas de machos de perdiz. *(5,* 31)

When doña Isabel de Arnáiz dies just a few months before her daughter's wedding, Galdós announces the event with picturesque colloquialisms, thus minimizing its importance: "Su muerte fué de esas que vulgarmente se comparan a la de *un pajarito*. Decían los vecinos y amigos que había *reventado de gusto*" *(5,* 47). This is as if an American or English novelist said that such and such a character "kicked the bucket" or "gave up the ghost." The good-natured acceptance of death, without orations or lamentations, is very typical of Galdós and is constant throughout the Novelas contemporáneas.

The highlight of Part I of *Fortunata y Jacinta* is the section entitled "Viajes de novios," in which Galdós follows Juanito and his bride on their honeymoon. Although the marriage was arranged, it shows every sign of being perfect. Galdós is superb as he recounts Jacinta's nervousness on her wedding night, the flamenco terms of endearment she learns from Juanito, the lovers' language they use to speak to each other, their mutual hilarity at whatever does or does not strike their fancy, and their blissful ignorance of time. There is nothing saccharine about these episodes. On the contrary, Galdós enjoys teasing his characters. Even the dialogue is full of badinage; heartfelt expressions of love and fidelity repel both husband and wife.

Galdós is at his best when he studies the psychology of the young bride: "Fuerte en la conciencia de su triunfo en el presente, Jacinta empezó a sentir el desconsuelo de no someter también el pasado de su marido, haciéndose dueña de cuanto éste había sentido y pensado antes de casarse" *(5,* 48). Jacinta's quest for information about her husband's past eventually leads to his full confession of his seduction of Fortunata. At first the story comes out in bits and pieces and causes little more than a ripple of uneasiness. But the more Jacinta knows, the more she wants to know. One night, toward the end of the honeymoon, Juanito tells everything. Drunk and delirious, he rambles on about Fortunata's beauty, innocence, and amusing pueblo speech. Apparently she had a child, but his efforts to find and help her were in vain. She disappeared without a trace. Remorseful about the way he brought the girl to ruin, Juanito begs Jacinta to exonerate him. This scene, made more dramatic by the blissful episodes that surround it, marks the only time Juanito is ever completely honest with his wife. It is also the sole instance in the Novelas contemporáneas where Galdós communicates the fear and disillusionment that can sometimes spring from intimacy. Jacinta is hurt and sickened by what her husband says and the way he says it.

This is a momentary cloud, however. The two return to Madrid, a few years go by, and all is well except that there are no children. Jacinta's desire to have a child becomes an obsession that reveals itself in touching ways. Walking along a street, she mistakes the whines of a kitten for those of a child and implores the Santa Cruz doorman to go down into a sewer to save the creature; with her friend Guillermina she visits the Madrid slums and tries to adopt a little boy whom she erroneously believes to be Fortunata's; at the opera one night, she dozes off and dreams that a baby is pressing its hand against her breast, whereupon she starts to unbutton her bodice to nurse it. Her maternal instinct is so strong she would willingly trade places with *any* mother, no matter how poor, and she begins to doubt the wisdom of God in allowing her to

remain childless while awarding a yearly prize to her sister,
who is less well off financially.

Jacinta's frustration is one of the more poignant things in the
novel. Galdós combines humor and compassion when talking
about it. A good example is when he describes Jacinta's love
for all children, without regard to class, appearance, or behavior:

> Se le iban los ojos tras de la infancia en cualquier forma
> que se le presentara, ya fuesen los niños ricos, vestidos de
> marineros y conducidos por la institutriz inglesa, ya los
> mocosos pobres, envueltos en bayeta amarilla, sucios, con
> caspa en la cabeza y en la mano un pedazo de pan lamido.
> *(5, 70)*

Even beggars, dandies, rogues, or chulas, as children, captivate
Jacinta. In passages such as this, Galdós' affection for his characters pervades his style. Ostensibly viewing the world through
Jacinta's eyes, his own kindly response to her misfortune is
what the reader feels most palpably.

Whereas Part I of *Fortunata y Jacinta* concentrates on the
elder and younger Santa Cruzes, Part II is devoted to the
Rubíns—a grotesque disfiguration of the Santa Cruzes. Maxi
Rubín and his brothers are said to have been sired by three
different fathers; the family's connections are few and its
origins are obscure; the elder Rubíns are dead, their business
establishment defunct. Doña Lupe *la de los pavos,* who raises
two of the boys after their parents' death, is a despot by comparison with Barbarita Santa Cruz; Papitos, her scampish little
maid, is bullied by her benefactress (compare Estupiñá). Maxi
is as ugly as Juanito is handsome; this señorito receives a small
allowance which he entrusts to a piggy bank and is pampered
only because he is sickly and fragile; his impotence and his
habit of wishful thinking stand in utter contrast to Santa Cruz's
social poise and sexual energy.

As in Part I, Galdós narrates the story of a courtship and
marriage. But whereas the Juanito-Jacinta union is only gradually revealed as a mismatch (at the end Jacinta realizes that

she would have been much happier with Moreno-Isla), the Maxi-Fortunata union is ludicrous from the very beginning. Maxi's platonic goal—to be loved by an honorable woman—and Fortunata's impulsive yearnings for Santa Cruz point the way to a clash of temperaments so profound as to be irreconcilable. The difference in their physiques heralds this clash: Fortunata is a full-grown beauty, healthy and strong, while Maxi, besides being impotent, is puny and ugly and suffers from migraine headaches. Much of the humor and tragedy that arises from this relationship may be traced to a form of irony mentioned previously—the irony of incongruity. As was explained, the irony of incongruity involves a conflict with nature, convention, or the social norm. In the case of Maxi and Fortunata, it is nature, in the organic sense, whose rules are violated most blatantly. Maxi himself understands this finally, as he says to his wife,

> Nos casamos por debilidad tuya y equivocación mía. Yo te adoraba; tú a mí, no. Matrimonio imposible. Tenía que venir el divorcio, y el divorcio ha venido. Yo me volví loco y tú te emancipaste. Los disparates que habíamos hecho los enmendó la Naturaleza. Contra la Naturaleza no se puede protestar. *(5, 507)*[8]

Maxi makes this comment very late in the novel, however. Earlier he does protest against nature, though he is unaware of it. Before marrying, he jumps at his brother Nicolás' suggestion that Fortunata spend a few months in a convent. His enthusiastic acceptance of this plan and his naïve belief that a dose of religion will make an honorable señora out of Fortunata

---

8. See also his remarks to Ballester after Fortunata's death: "No contamos con la Naturaleza, que es la gran madre y maestra que rectifica los errores de sus hijos extraviados. Nosotros hacemos mil disparates, y la Naturaleza nos los corrige. Protestamos contra sus lecciones admirables, que no entendemos, y cuando queremos que nos obedezca, nos coge y nos estrella, como el mar estrella a los que pretenden gobernarlo" *(5, 547)*.

only prove how ignorant Maxi is of the most basic human drives. He seems oblivious to the physical side of marriage. His inability to make love blinds him to the physical needs of his spouse. He idealizes Fortunata, distorting her completely. Fortunata, at this point, is no less naïve than Maxi. She too believes that life in the convent will change her personality: "¡Quién sabe—se dijo—lo que pasará después de estar allí tratando con las monjas, rezando y viendo a todas horas la custodia! De seguro me volveré otra sin sentirlo" *(5,* 220).

Nature rebels against such simplicity. In *Fortunata y Jacinta* nature is not cruel per se, as it generally is in naturalistic fiction. Rather, it is the great ironist which reveals men to themselves. It works not to crush but to enlighten and makes all four major characters wiser and more mellow by the time the novel ends.

Some of the more intimate scenes between Maxi and Fortunata are embarrassing, almost painful to read. This is because the reader sympathizes with both characters. He knows each of them too well to enjoy their mutual incompatibility. On their wedding night, Maxi goes to bed early, having suffered a migraine attack during the day. On the second night, he asks Fortunata to get into bed with him. Overcoming her repugnance, she obeys. With what Galdós calls an "expresión fraternal y consoladora," she cuts short Maxi's verbal lovemaking and persuades him to go to sleep *(5,* 274). Much later, in a different episode, Fortunata cradles Maxi in her arms and lulls him to sleep as if he were a child *(5,* 440). It is entirely to Galdós' credit that he avoids any cheap laughter at the expense of Maxi's disability. He arranges things in such a way as to force the reader's attention to the tricks that life plays on people. Indeed, this is one of the major themes of *Fortunata y Jacinta*. One is constantly reminded throughout the novel of lost opportunities and warped relationships: if only Moreno-Isla were younger and had married Jacinta; if only Feijoo were younger and had taken Fortunata in tow before Santa Cruz got to her; if only the laws of society obeyed the laws of nature; and so on. This longing for what might have been is felt very keenly by Moreno-Isla, Feijoo, Maxi, Fortunata, and especially Jacinta. In a final chapter of the book Jacinta ponders the capriciousness of the world and in her mind rearranges the past according to the dictates of logic and personal experience:

> venía a discurrir sobre lo desarreglado que andan las cosas del mundo. También ella tenía su idea respecto a los vínculos establecidos por la ley, y los rompía con el pensamiento, realizando la imposible obra de volver el tiempo atrás, de mudar y trastrocar las calidades de las personas, poniendo a éste el corazón de aquél, y a tal otro la cabeza del de más allá, haciendo, en fin, unas correcciones tan extravagantes a la obra total del mundo, que se reiría de ellas Dios si las supiera. *(5,* 544)

Logic has little to do with human relationships, and experience often comes too late to be much good. The passage above, in which the human condition rather than some malign, deterministic natural force is held responsible for the harm people inflict on one another, is the best description of what is meant by the irony of incongruity.

Although the Maxi-Fortunata relationship has its crux in the irony of incongruity, the setting in which their relationship unfolds is a domestic one. Doña Lupe, Juan Pablo, Nicolás, and Papitos anchor the reader's attention to the family unit. The household over which doña Lupe presides may not be as harmonious as the Santa Cruzes', but it is no less castizo for all that. For Spanish readers, the Rubíns will seem just as representative of the national mentality as the Santa Cruzes.

Take, for instance, the characterization of Nicolás Rubín, a priest. In his interviews with Fortunata he uses the concrete imagery so typical of Spanish Catholicism. As far as he is concerned, any love other than spiritual love is the work of Satan: "Sostener otra cosa es renegar del catolicismo y volver a la mitología" *(5,* 216). His religious ideas begin and end with Heaven and Hell. When he discovers that Fortunata has been unfaithful to Maxi, he accuses her of "sembrando muertes y exterminios por dondequiera que va" *(5,* 292). He depicts perdition as a black, devouring mouth, uglier than a dragon's, and he assures Fortunata that her sins have doomed her.

An entire chapter could be written about the literal interpretation that Galdós' characters give to their religion. Catholicism is so much a part of everyday life in Spain that God, Christ, the Virgin, and the saints seem more like close relatives than abstract objects of veneration. The Novelas contemporáneas reflect this familial bond. When, during their honeymoon trip, Juanito and Jacinta visit a cathedral and spend their time embracing at the altar and behind the statuary, it is assumed that God will take no offense: "A Jacinta le causaban miedo aquellas profanaciones; pero las consentía y toleraba, poniendo su pensamiento en Dios y confiando en que Este, al verlas, volvería la cabeza con aquella indulgencia del que es fuente de todo amor" *(5,* 48). Since Catholicism is an everyday affair in Spain, a certain amount of irreverence toward it is to be expected. This never leads to sacrilege among the characters of the Novelas contemporáneas; their anticlericalism most often resembles a family spat. Even Moreno-Isla's skepticism and the violent insults which Torquemada and Mauricia *la dura* hurl at God have less of an impact than would be the case in a novel by Dostoevski, for instance. The Novelas contemporáneas portray a culture so thoroughly impregnated with religion and so devoid of any spiritual conflict between orthodoxy and atheism that for a character to deny God is laughable: it is like denying food or air.

Anyone who knows family life in Spain from the inside will find the diverse political views of doña Lupe, Nicolás, and Juan Pablo most evocative. Doña Lupe, in deference to her dead husband, is a confirmed liberal. Authoritarian by temperament, she nevertheless loathes political absolutism. Juan Pablo, on the other hand, is a Carlist. His shadowy activities on behalf of the ultramontane pretender and his oral defense of the movement once brought him into open conflict with doña Lupe: "Desde un día en que, disputando con su sobrino sobre este tema, se amontonaron los dos y por poco se tiran los trastos a la cabeza, no quiso doña Lupe volver a mentar a los *carcundas* delante de Juan Pablo" *(5,* 207). But although a truce has been called between aunt and nephew, fighting erupts between the brothers. Juan Pablo was summarily dismissed by his king, a move he attributes to the machinations of priests (Carlos' court was thick with right-wing ecclesiastics). His brother Nicolás, though apolitical, is a priest and thus a suitable target for Juan Pablo's pent-up fury. There is a wonderful altercation between the two, in which Juan Pablo accuses the "engarza-rosarios" of undermining the Carlist cause: "Por las sotanas se perdió don Carlos Quinto, y al Séptimo no le aprovechó la lección. Allá se las haya. ¿No querías religión? Pues ahí la tienes; atrácate de curas, indigéstate y revienta" *(5, 222)*. Nicolás takes all this personally and fires back. Only doña Lupe's intervention prevents the brothers from coming to blows. When the Carlists are defeated, Juan Pablo is quick to accept a post in the liberal government of King Alfonso. He tries to save face among his fellow tertulianos by feigning self-sacrifice and a loyalty to his old ideals, but this is purely for show.

The tertulia is an institution which, like so much else in Spanish life, gets its proper share of attention in *Fortunata y Jacinta*. It is with Juan Pablo, an inveterate café buff, that one enters that home-away-from-home so dear to the Spanish male. Actually, the tertulia is an extension of the family unit, with its own rules and hierarchies. Rank, however, is determined by fluency, wit, and force of personality. Those who exercise special authority over their co-members in Juan Pablo's tertulia sit in a favored spot at the table, in a booth against the wall. Their subalterns occupy the outer cluster of chairs.

Juan Pablo belongs to a tertulia that meets in a café near the Puerta del Sol. His is only one of many tertulias that convene in the same locale. Seated next to the bureaucrats there is a tableful of priests, and next to them, a gathering of writers, journalists, and dramatists. A group of engineering students meets in an angle of the café. A spirit of comradeship pervades the premises. Sometimes one tertulia will intermingle with another. Less exclusive than a clique or a coterie, the tertulia epitomizes that ease of communication between Spaniards that Galdós repeatedly extols in *Fortunata y Jacinta:*

Allí brillaba espléndidamente esa fraternidad española en cuyo seno se dan mano de amigo el carlista y el republi-

cano, el progresista de cabeza dura y el moderado implacable. Antiguamente, los partidos separados en público, estábanlo también en las relaciones privadas; pero
el progreso de las costumbres trajo primero cierta suavidad en las relaciones personales, y, por fin, la suavidad se
trocó en blandura. *(5, 295)*

All this seems strangely pastoral in the light of twentieth-century Spanish history, with its civil strife and police spies.
Galdós' picture of a society in which friendship between individuals survives the strain of divergent political views is as
optimistic as his picture of class harmony in Spain. Like the
tree of Madrid, the tertulia is nonrestrictive. It tolerates di-
versity.

Due to Juan Pablo's participation in a tertulia, the reader of
Fortunata y Jacinta overhears a number of political discussions.
One must know something about the way information travels
in Spain to fully appreciate these passages. All news of the
government based on anecdote, hearsay, and rumor; the air
rife with predictions; everyone ready with his own solution
for the nation's ills; public officials picked up and discarded
verbally like cards in a game; the "inside tips"; the skepticism—
all this will sound familiar to Spanish readers of today.

The Rubín and Santa Cruz families, thus far examined
separately, converge in the person of Fortunata. Fortunata
is both a mother and a child. Physically, she provides the
Santa Cruzes with an heir; emotionally, she is unruly and
impetuous but, like a child, free of malice and corruption;
socially, she is a foundling whom various other people in the
novel take under their wing. From this fusion of the attributes
of mother and child in the pivotal character there radiates
forth a kind of humor which, as an offshoot of the humor of
familiarity, might be called the "humor of succession." It would
perhaps be more accurate to say that this humor of succession
radiates *around,* as well as *from,* Fortunata: one might recall
how the elder Santa Cruzes spoil their only child, how Jacinta's
longing for a baby is described in several touching and amusing episodes, and the joy of don Baldomero and his wife when

exposed to little Juanín, their supposed grandson. These scenes, which occur prior to Fortunata's emergence as the central figure in the novel, set the tone for much that follows. For instance, Fortunata's pride in her newborn son, whom she calls "el rey de la casa" (5, 532), is prefigured by the Santa Cruzes' pride in Juanito (whom Galdós at one point refers to as "el príncipe de la casa," 5, 84). Jacinta's visits to the slums of Madrid have their counterpart in Fortunata's obsessive "idea." And the delightful reaction of don Baldomero and Barbarita to the news (false, to be sure) that they are grandparents finds its echo much later in the grandmotherly solicitude that Guillermina Pacheco shows toward Fortunata's baby.

Since *Fortunata y Jacinta* depicts society as a huge family or clan, it is reasonable to expect any new member of the clan to receive a tumultuous welcome. In a society so constructed, the question of succession, or the continuity of life, is bound to take priority over all else. Thus it happens that when Fortunata gives birth the event is of transcendental importance to the community. Galdós indicates this by having swarms of people (or so it seems) converge on the flat overlooking the Plaza Mayor where mother and child are resting. In these last chapters, the helter-skelter coming and going of so many characters resembles the final recapitulation of a musical score. Ballester (the druggist), Ido del Sagrario, José Izquierdo, Segunda (Fortunata's aunt), Encarnación (the maid), Estupiñá, Maxi, Guillermina, and Father Nones all hover about the mother and her newborn and do not leave them alone for a moment. Even doña Lupe makes an appearance, although she is more interested in finding Maxi than in having any more to do with her daughter-in-law. When Fortunata dies, Jacinta and Barbarita are on hand, ready to provide a haven for the baby. Of the major characters in *Fortunata y Jacinta,* only don Baldomero, Juanito, and Maxi's brothers fail to turn up in these climactic chapters. (Feijoo, Moreno-Isla, and Mauricia *la dura* are dead by this time.)

All this bustle and commotion, so different from what is normally expected of a deathbed sequence, alleviates some of the sadness one feels at Fortunata's passing. It is as though

Galdós meant to distract the reader's attention from the more somber side of events and shift it to the brighter side—from death to continuity. By surrounding Fortunata with a host of familiar figures, the author seems to banish, in one stroke, the solitude and oblivion associated with death.

As for Fortunata's baby, his future is secure. Just as his mother was "adopted" by Feijoo and Guillermina, so too Juan Evaristo (later "el Delfinito") will never lack for a family. Guillermina assures Fortunata:

> Porque ha de saber usted que Dios me ha hecho tutora
> de este hijo . . . . Sí, buena moza, no se espante ni me
> ponga esos ojazos. Su madre es usted; pero yo tengo sobre
> él una parte de autoridad. Dios me la ha dado. Si su madre
> le faltara, yo me encargo de darle otra, y también abuela.

Addressing the child, she adds: "Hijo mío, has venido al mundo con bendición, porque, suceda lo que suceda, no estarás nunca solo" *(5,* 513).

The same can be said of every character in *Fortunata y Jacinta,* with the sole exception of Moreno-Isla, who resides in London for most of the year. It is significant that this cosmopolite, an exile by choice and a lonely man, is the one person in the novel whose death is compared to the falling of a leaf from a tree *(5,* 461). If this tree is the same tree of Madrid mentioned earlier, one can perhaps understand why *Fortunata y Jacinta* is such a very conservative novel. It is a paean in praise of traditional Spanish values, which derive much of their strength from the solidarity of the family unit. Moreno-Isla is an expatriate who, in rejecting the geographic insularity of Spain, symbolically rejects his family. Thus uprooted, he suffers from and dies of a weak heart.

CONCLUSION

It has been my plan, throughout this study, to examine the humor of the *Novelas contemporáneas* in relation to realism. We have seen how irony and satire are implicit in the novel, the realistic genre par excellence. We have also seen how metaphor, caricature, and type prevail in, though are by no means limited to, the works of certain nineteenth-century novelists known as romantic realists. Finally, in the last chapter, I have tried to describe a kind of humor borne of low-key realism, dependent on colloquial speech and familial relationships. Of these various kinds of realism and their accompanying forms of humor, the last is undoubtedly the most typical of Galdós. Familiarity is the stock-in-trade of the *Novelas contemporáneas*.

The humor of familiarity is, of course, compatible with other, more aristocratic forms of humor. Galdós can be as witty as one wishes, as is proven by *La de Bringas*. Here, in exposing the hypocrisy and deceit which lurk behind a facade of urbane manners, Galdós proves himself a master of subtle verbal irony. *La de Bringas* is as close to being a true comedy of manners as anything Galdós ever wrote. This is because the novel's main character, Rosalía Bringas, is more class-conscious than family-conscious, something very unusual in Galdós. For the most part, however, the humor in the *Novelas contemporáneas* is rarely witty or subtle. The colloquial tone of the narratives, the frequently banal opinions of half-educated people, their *desbarajustes* and mispronunciations, the incongruous and often farcical jostle of different physiques and temperaments—all these cannot be expected to produce "fine" humor. As for Galdós' characters, they do not regale with those brittle bons mots, that deft verbal skirmishing with which certain novelists denote the civilized mind. They live on a comparatively primitive level.

Menéndez y Pelayo's words about *Fortunata y Jacinta,* "To-do es vulgar en aquella fábula menos el sentimiento," hold true for the Novelas contemporáneas as a corpus of fiction. For in the last analysis, every element in these novels must be related to the ineffable warmth of sentiment that lies at the heart of Galdós' literary personality. The author's generosity of spirit prevents the more destructive ingredients of realism—satire and irony—from ever dominating his works. His obvious affection for a society in which there prevails an easy give-and-take among persons of every rank and condition softens the dissatisfaction he feels toward certain aspects of Spanish life.

Galdós' warmth of sentiment is due to his understanding of the instincts and passions that rule the human animal and his willingness to forgive any transgression against the moral code of society caused by these instincts and passions. Galdós saw flesh as its own redeemer and passion as its own justification. In *Fortunata y Jacinta,* his most ambitious and representative novel, he invests the noble passion (Fortunata) with the attributes of the noble soul (Jacinta). Fortunata's bequest of her child to Jacinta is the gift of flesh to spirit. This belief in nature as a bounty and a blessing, so clearly expressed in *Fortunata y Jacinta,* makes the Novelas contemporáneas unique. The harrowing picture of man in naturalistic fiction is replaced here by a faith in the natural order of things. The author's sympathetic response to the most vulgar and trivial lives stems from his idea that nature, the source of life, is also a source of good. This response—indulgent, quizzical, often paternal—is the sum and substance of Galdós' humor.

BIBLIOGRAPHY

Works marked with an asterisk are not cited in the text or footnotes but were found useful to this study.

Alfieri, Graciela Andrade, and Alfieri, J. J., "El lenguaje familiar de Pérez Galdós," *Hispanófila, 8* (Septiembre 1964), 27–73.

Allen, Walter, *The English Novel,* London, Phoenix House, 1954.

Auerbach, Erich, *Mimesis,* trans. Willard R. Trask, Princeton, Princeton University Press, 1953.

Ayala, Francisco, "Sobre el realismo en literatura," *La Torre, 7* (Abril-Junio 1959), 91–121.

Balzac, Honoré de, "Avant-propos," *La Comédie humaine, 1* (11 vols. Paris, Editions de la Pléiade, 1962), 5–16.

——, *Eugénie Grandet,* in *La Comédie humaine, 3,* 478–649.

——, *Gobseck,* in *La Comédie humaine, 2,* 621–71.

——, *Le Père Goriot,* in *La Comédie humaine, 2,* 847–1085.

Baquero Goyanes, Mariano, *Perspectivismo y contraste,* Madrid, Gredos, 1963.

Baroja, Pío, *La caverna del humorismo,* Madrid, R. C. Raggio, 1919.

*Becker, George J., "Realism: An Essay in Definition," *Modern Language Quarterly, 10* (1949), 184–97.

——, ed., *Documents of Literary Realism,* Princeton, Princeton University Press, 1963.

Bergson, Henri, "Laughter," in *Comedy,* New York, Doubleday Anchor Books, 1956.

Berkowitz, H. Chonon, *La biblioteca de Benito Pérez Galdós,* Las Palmas, El Museo Canario, 1951.

*——, "Galdós' Literary Apprenticeship," *Hispanic Review, 3* (1935), 1–22.

*————, *Pérez Galdós, Spanish Liberal Crusader,* Madison, University of Wisconsin Press, 1948.

————, "The Youthful Writings of Pérez Galdós," *Hispanic Review, 1* (1933), 91–121.

Binkley, Robert C., *Realism and Nationalism, 1852–1871,* New York and London, Harper and Brothers, 1935.

Booth, Wayne C., *The Rhetoric of Fiction,* Chicago, University of Chicago Press, 1961.

Brenan, Gerald, *The Literature of the Spanish People,* Cambridge, Cambridge University Press, 1962.

Casalduero, Joaquín, *Vida y obra de Galdós,* Buenos Aires, Losada, 1943.

Casares, Julio, *El humorismo y otros ensayos,* Madrid, Espasa-Calpe, 1961.

*Casona, Alejandro, "Galdós y el romanticismo," *Cursos y Conferencias,* Año XII, *24,* 139–40–41 (1943), 99–111.

*Cassou, Jean, *Panorama de la littérature espagnole contemporaine,* Paris, Kra, 1931.

Chamberlin, Vernon A., "The Muletilla: An Important Facet of Galdós' Characterization Technique," *Hispanic Review, 29* (1961), 296–309.

Chevalier, Haakon M., *The Ironic Temper,* New York, Oxford University Press, 1932.

Correa, Gustavo, *El simbolismo religioso en las novelas de Pérez Galdós,* Madrid, Gredos, 1962.

Dargan, E. P., *Studies in Balzac's Realism,* Chicago, University of Chicago Press, 1932.

Davis, Earle R., "Dickens and the Evolution of Caricature," *PMLA, 55* (1940), 231–40.

Dickens, Charles, *Bleak House,* 2 vols. London, Chapman and Hall, 1911.

————, *Hard Times,* London, Oxford University Press, 1955.

————, *Little Dorrit,* 2 vols. London, Chapman and Hall, 1863.

Durand, Frank, "Two Problems in Galdós' *Tormento,*" *Modern Language Notes, 79* (December 1964), 513–25.

Eoff, Sherman, "Galdós y los impedimentos del realismo," *Hispanófila, 24* (Mayo 1965), 25–34.

————, *The Novels of Pérez Galdós,* St. Louis, Washington University Studies, 1954.

*Flores, Angel, and Benardete, M. J., eds., *Cervantes Across the Centuries,* New York, Dryden Press, 1947.

Forster, E. M., *Aspects of the Novel,* New York, Harcourt, Brace, 1954.

Freud, Sigmund, *Wit and Its Relation to the Unconscious,* trans. A. A. Brill, New York, Moffat, Yard, 1916.

Frye, Northrop, *Anatomy of Criticism,* Princeton, Princeton University Press, 1957.

Gaskell, Mrs., *Cranford,* New York and London, Macmillan, 1894.

Gilman, Stephen, "La palabra hablada y *Fortunata y Jacinta,*" *Nueva Revista de Filología Hispánica, 15* (1961), 542–60.

Giraud, Raymond, *The Unheroic Hero in the Novels of Stendhal, Balzac and Flaubert,* New Brunswick, N.J., Rutgers University Press, 1957.

Gombrich, E. H., and Kris, E., *Caricature,* Middlesex, King Penguin Books, 1940.

Grant, Mary A., *The Ancient Rhetorical Theories of the Laughable,* University of Wisconsin Studies in Language and Literature No. 21, Madison, 1924.

Gullón, Ricardo, *Galdós, novelista moderno,* Madrid, Taurus, 1960.

*Hafter, Monroe Z., *"Le Crime de Sylvestre Bonnard,* A Possible Source for *El Amigo Manso,*" *Symposium, 17* (Summer 1963), 123–29.

*————, "Galdós' Presentation of Isidora in *La Desheredada,*" *Modern Philology, 60* (August 1962), 22–30.

————, "Ironic Reprise in Galdós' Novels," *PMLA, 76* (1961), 233–39.

*Hendrix, W. S., "Notes on Collections of 'Types,' A Form of *Costumbrismo,*" *Hispanic Review, 1* (1933), 208–21.

*Hennessy, C. A. M., *The Federal Republic in Spain 1868–1874,* Oxford, Clarendon Press, 1962.

Highet, Gilbert, *The Anatomy of Satire,* Princeton, Princeton University Press, 1962.

Hinterhäuser, Hans, Los 'Episodios nacionales' de Benito Pérez Galdós, Madrid, Gredos, 1963.

Hutchens, Eleanor N., "Verbal Irony in Tom Jones," PMLA, 77 (1962), 46–50.

Ilie, Paul, "Antonio Machado and the Grotesque," Journal of Aesthetics and Art Criticism, 22 (Winter 1963), 209–16.

James, Henry, The Future of the Novel, ed. Leon Edel, New York, Vintage Books, 1956.

*Johnson, Edgar, ed., A Treasury of Satire, New York, Simon and Schuster, 1945.

Kayser, Wolfgang, The Grotesque in Art and Literature, trans. Ulrich Weisstein, Bloomington, Indiana University Press, 1957.

Kernan, Alvin B., Modern Satire, New York, 1962.

*Kirsner, Robert, "Galdós and Larra," Modern Language Journal, 35 (1951), 210–13.

*Koestler, Arthur, The Act of Creation, London, Hutchinson, 1964.

*Kris, Ernst, Psychoanalytic Explorations of Art, New York, International Universities Press, 1952.

Kronenberger, Louis, ed., Novelists on Novelists, New York, Anchor Books, 1962.

Levin, Harry, The Gates of Horn, New York, Oxford University Press, 1963.

———, "What Is Realism?" Comparative Literature, 3 (1951), 193–99.

*Livingston, Leon, "Interior Duplication and the Problem of Form in the Modern Spanish Novel," PMLA, 73 (1958), 393–406.

Los españoles pintados por sí mismos, Madrid, Gaspar y Roig, 1851.

*Lubbock, Percy, The Craft of Fiction, New York, J. Cape and H. Smith, 1929.

Lukács, George, Studies in European Realism, London, Hillway, 1950.

*Lynch, Bohun, A History of Caricature, London, Faber and Gwyer, 1926.

Menéndez y Pelayo, Marcelino, "Don Benito Pérez Galdós," *Estudios y discursos de crítica histórica y literaria, 5* (Santander, Consejo superior de investigaciones científicas, 1942), 81–103.

Mesonero Romanos, Ramón de (El Curioso Parlante), *Escenas matritenses,* Madrid, 1862.

*Morazé, Charles, *Les bourgeois conquérants,* Paris, A. Colin, 1957.

Netherton, John Phillip, "The *Novelas españolas contemporáneas* of Pérez Galdós: a study of method," University of Chicago, Unpublished doctoral dissertation, 1951.

O'Donovan, Michael (Frank O'Connor), *The Mirror in the Roadway,* New York, A. A. Knopf, 1956.

Onís, Federico de, "El humorismo de Galdós," *Revista Hispánica Moderna, 9* (1943), 293–94.

Ortega y Gasset, José, *El Espectador,* Madrid, Biblioteca Nueva, 1943.

———, *Meditations on Quixote,* trans. Evelyn Rugg and Diego Marín, New York, Norton, 1961.

Orwell, George, *Critical Essays,* London, Secker and Warburg, 1946.

Pattison, Walter T., *Benito Pérez Galdós and the Creative Process,* Minneapolis, University of Minnesota Press, 1954.

*Peckham, Morse, *Beyond the Tragic Vision,* New York, George Braziller, 1962.

Pérez Galdós, Benito, *Crónica de la quincena,* ed. William H. Shoemaker, Princeton, Princeton University Press, 1948.

———, *La Fontana de Oro,* Madrid, José Noguera y Castellano, 1871.

———, *Obras completas,* 6 vols. Madrid, Aguilar, 1951–61.

———, "Observaciones sobre la novela contemporánea en España," *Revista de España, 15* (1870), 162–72.

———, "Prólogo" to Leopoldo Alas, *La Regenta,* 3d ed. Madrid, F. Fé, 1900.

———, "Prólogo" to José María de Pereda, *El sabor de la tierruca,* Madrid, Imprenta y fundición de Tello, 1889.

———, "La sociedad presente como materia novelable," *Discursos leídos ante la Real Academia Española en las recepciones públicas del 7 y 21 de febrero de 1897,* Madrid, 1897.

———, *Trafalgar,* Buenos Aires, Losada, 1956.

Pérez Vidal, José, *Galdós en Canarias (1843–1862),* Las Palmas, El Museo Canario, 1952.

Praz, Mario, *The Hero in Eclipse in Victorian Fiction,* trans. Angus Davidson, London and New York, Oxford University Press, 1956.

Pritchett, V. S., *Books in General,* London, Chatto and Windus, 1953.

———, *The Living Novel,* London, Chatto and Windus, 1946.

———, *The Offensive Traveller,* New York, A. A. Knopf, 1964.

Refort, Lucien, *La caricature littéraire,* Paris, A. Colin, 1932.

Regalado García, Antonio, *Benito Pérez Galdós y la novela histórica española: 1868–1912,* Madrid, Insula, 1966.

Ricard, Robert, *Aspects de Galdós,* Paris, Presses Universitaires de France, 1963.

———, *Galdós et ses romans,* Paris, Centre de Recherches de l'Institut d'Etudes Hispaniques, 1961.

Río, Angel Del, "Notas sobre el tema de América en Galdós," *Nueva Revista de Filología Hispánica, 15* (1961), 279–96.

Robinson, E. Arthur, "Meredith's Literary Theory and Science: Realism Versus the Comic Spirit," *PMLA, 53* (1938), 857–68.

*Romeu, R., "Les divers aspects de l'humour dans le roman espagnol moderne," *Bulletin Hispanique, 48,* No. 2 (1946), 97–146.

Rourke, Constance, *American Humor,* New York, Doubleday Anchor Books, 1953.

Russell, Robert H., *"El Amigo Manso:* Galdós with a Mirror," *Modern Language Notes, 78* (March 1963), 161–68.

Salvan, Albert J., "L'Essence du réalisme français," *Comparative Literature, 3* (1951), 218–33.

Santayana, George, *Essays in Literary Criticism,* ed. Irving Singer, New York, Scribner, 1956.

Shoemaker, William H., "Galdós' Classical Scene in *La de Bringas,*" *Hispanic Review, 27* (1959), 423–34.

————, *Los prólogos de Galdós,* Urbana, University of Illinois Press, and México, Ediciones De Andrea, 1962.

Tierno Galván, Enrique, "Aparición y desarrollo de nuevas perspectivas de valoración social en el siglo XIX: lo cursi," *Revista de Estudios Políticos, 42* (Marzo-Abril 1952), 85–106.

Torre, Guillermo De, "Nueva estimativa de las novelas de Galdós," *Cursos y Conferencias,* Año XII, *24,* 139–40–41 (Buenos Aires, Colegio libre de estudios superiores, 1943), 25–37.

*Torres Bodet, Jaime, *Tres inventores de realidad; Stendhal, Dostoyevski, Pérez Galdós,* México, Imprenta Universitaria, 1955.

Trueblood, Alan S., *"El Castellano viejo* y la *Sátira III* de Boileau," *Nueva Revista de Filología Hispánica, 15* (1961), 529–38.

Ucelay Da Cal, Margerita, *'Los españoles pintados por sí mismos' (Estudio de un género costumbrista),* México, Colegio de México, 1951.

Unamuno, Miguel de, *Autodiálogos,* Madrid, Aguilar, 1959.

*Walton, L. B., *Pérez Galdós and the Spanish Novel of the Nineteenth Century,* London, J. M. Dent, 1927.

*Warshaw, J., "Galdós' Indebtedness to Cervantes," *Hispania, 16* (1933), 127–42.

Watt, Ian, "Realism and the Novel," *Essays in Criticism, 2* (1952), 376–96.

Weber, Robert J., *The Miau Manuscript of Benito Pérez Galdós,* University of California Publications in Modern Philology, 72, Berkeley and Los Angeles, 1964.

Wellek, René, *Concepts of Criticism,* New Haven, Yale University Press, 1963.

Wellek, René, and Warren, Austin, *Theory of Literature,* New York, Harcourt, Brace, 1956.

Worcester, David, *The Art of Satire,* Cambridge, Harvard University Press, 1940.

Yelland, H. L., Jones, S. C., and Easton, K. S. W., *A Handbook of Literary Terms,* New York, Philosophical Library, 1950.

INDEX

(Works by Galdós are listed alphabetically under Pérez Galdós.)

DATE DUE